Preaching from Inside the Story

LLOYD JOHN OGILVIE INSTITUTE OF PREACHING SERIES

SERIES EDITORS:

Mark Labberton

Clayton J. Schmit

The vision of the Lloyd John Ogilvie Institute of Preaching is to proclaim Jesus Christ and to catalyze a movement of empowered, wise preachers who seek justice, love mercy, and walk humbly with God, leading others to join in God's mission in the world. The books in this series are selected to contribute to the development of such wise and humble preachers. The authors represent both scholars of preaching as well as pastors and preachers whose experiences and insights can contribute to passionate and excellent preaching.

OTHER VOLUMES IN THIS SERIES:

Shouting Above the Noisy Crowd: Biblical Wisdom and the Urgency of Preaching: Essays in Honor of Alyce M. McKenzie edited by Charles L. Aaron Jr. and Jaime Clark-Soles

Preaching Gospel: Essays in Honor of Richard Lischer edited by Charles L. Campbell, Clayton J. Schmit, Mary Hinkle Shore, and Jennifer E. Copeland

Stumbling over the Cross: Preaching the Cross and Resurrection Today by Joni S. Sancken

Youthful Preaching: Strengthening the Relationship between Youth, Adults, and Preaching by Richard Voelz

Decolonizing Preaching: The Pulpit as Postcolonial Space by Sarah A. N. Travis

Preaching from Inside the Story

A Fresh Journey into Narrative

BY

Jeffrey W. Frymire

FOREWORD BY *Clayton J. Schmit*

CASCADE *Books* • Eugene, Oregon

PREACHING FROM INSIDE THE STORY
A Fresh Journey into Narrative

Lloyd John Ogilvie Institute of Preaching Series

Copyright © 2022 Jeffrey W. Frymire. All rights reserved. Except for brief quotations in critical publications or reviews, no part of this book may be reproduced in any manner without prior written permission from the publisher. Write: Permissions, Wipf and Stock Publishers, 199 W. 8th Ave., Suite 3, Eugene, OR 97401.

Cascade Books
An Imprint of Wipf and Stock Publishers
199 W. 8th Ave., Suite 3
Eugene, OR 97401

www.wipfandstock.com

PAPERBACK ISBN: 978-1-6667-3277-1
HARDCOVER ISBN: 978-1-6667-2683-1
EBOOK ISBN: 978-1-6667-2684-8

Cataloguing-in-Publication data:

Names: Frymire, Jeffrey W., author | Schmit, Clayton J., foreword.
Title: Preaching from inside the story : a fresh journey into narrative / by Jeffrey W. Frymire; foreword by Clayton J. Schmit.
Description: Eugene, OR: Cascade Books, 2022 | Lloyd John Ogilvie Institute of Preaching Series | Includes bibliographical references.
Identifiers: ISBN 978-1-6667-3277-1 (paperback) | ISBN 978-1-6667-2683-1 (hardcover) | ISBN 978-1-6667-2684-8 (ebook)
Subjects: LCSH: Narrative preaching. | Storytelling. | Hermeneutics.
Classification: BV4235.S76 F79 2022 (print) | BV4235.S76 (ebook)

The Voice Bible Copyright © 2012 Thomas Nelson, Inc. The Voice™ translation © 2012 Ecclesia Bible Society.

Contents

A Dedication: From the Inside vii
Foreword by Clayton J. Schmit xiii
An Introduction xvii

SECTION ONE: *Journeying into Narrative*

Chapter One: My Journey into Narrative: Questions for Storytellers 3

Chapter Two: The Journey Intensifies: Toward a Narrative Hermeneutic 23

Chapter Three: The Journey into the Mind: We Are Wired for Stories 42

Chapter Four: The Journey into Story: A Philosophy of Stories 60

Chapter Five: Narrative Journey, Narrative Sense: Learning to Preach from the Inside 93

SECTION TWO: *Journeys in Narrative Preaching*

An Introduction to the Practice of Narrative Preaching 109

Chapter Six: The Journey into Grief:
  Moses' Mother Mourns (Narrative Sense; Storytelling Lens) 117

Chapter Seven: The Journey Toward Assurance:
  Mary and Joseph Wonder (Neuroscience and Narrative) 127

Chapter Eight: The Journey from Tishbe:
  Elijah, the Man from Nowhere (Narrative Hermeneutics) 146

Chapter Nine: The Journey at the Altar:
  What Was Zechariah Expecting? (Lowry Loop) 158

Chapter Ten: The Journey of a Storytelling Savior:
  Jesus and His Teaching Method (Jesus and Aristotle) 167

Epilogue: The Journey Commences: Storytelling as Interactive Drama 176

Bibliography 181

A Dedication: From the Inside

To Those Who Assisted the Journey

IN A WORK LIKE this, there are so many people to thank that one hesitates to mention any for fear of forgetting some. However, I owe a debt of gratitude I can never repay to Clay Schmit, my friend and mentor, for guiding me through the most impactful four years of life at Fuller Seminary. He and Carol have been more than friends over the years. My respect for Clay knows no boundaries. He has changed my life and I am grateful.

I also want to thank Charles Bartow and James Kay from Princeton Seminary who gave me the opportunity of a lifetime to teach at that esteemed institution. For an old New Jersey boy born and bred, it was a dream I could never have imagined. The first week after I moved to Princeton, my wife and I drove to South Jersey to visit the grave of my parents. I wanted to let them know that their little boy had done OK for himself. I knew my father, who possessed little formal education but believed that education was the key to success, would have been proud to see his son spend two years teaching at Princeton. And I know my mother, from whom I learned to tell stories, would be pleased that her youngest child was still telling them and using them in his profession.

I'm also grateful to President Tim Tennent of Asbury Theological Seminary who hired me after years of searching for the position of Associate Professor of Preaching. His encouragement and support have freed me up to investigate and develop my interest in narrative preaching. The same is true of my teaching colleagues at the Orlando Campus of Asbury. Steve Gober, Brian Russell, Jim Miller, Rick Gray, Daryl Smith, Joseph Okello, Javier Sierra, Tapiwa Mucherera, Angel Santiago-Valdez, Bill Patrick, Zaida Perez, and Danny Roman-Gloro have encouraged and spoken into my life through their friendship and preaching in chapel and in the classroom. I am forever in their debt for having helped me to become a better preacher and a more grounded professor. Their stories have enriched my life.

Similarly, I am indebted to Dawn Smith Salmons for being my partner in planning and sharing worship in chapel. I have learned much from her about worship and how worship is designed to tell a story. In the same way, all those students who have worked with me and worshiped with me in chapel have forged a greater understanding of narrative and narrative preaching. I am grateful for them all.

I remain appreciative of the good folks who make up the National Association of the Church of God (NACOG) for their acceptance of me and appreciation of my preaching and teaching. NACOG has been my spiritual home for nearly two decades now. For a white man to be accepted so lovingly by an African-American association still astounds me. I am a better person because of their love. I will never be able to fully thank Charles and Sheri Myricks for all the friendship they have shown and the doors of cross-cultural ministry they have opened to me.

I also want to thank Nicole Baker, a friend who worked tirelessly to edit and polish this manuscript. My guess is that the reader is as grateful to her as I am. She was a major factor in allowing this project to go forward. Like so many others who have been a help and encouragement, I appreciate her investment in my writing.

I want to express my deep appreciation to Dr. Ahmi Lee and Dr. Jennifer Ackerman and the folks at the Brehm Preaching Center at Fuller Seminary. I am thrilled to be a part of the Ogilvie Series on Preaching and to continue to serve my alma mater in whatever way I can.

I'm thankful for the congregations I served as preacher during my 30+ years as a local pastor. The ministry of Forrest Plants in Hickory, North Carolina, formed me into the preacher I have become. Forrest was a great narrative preacher and a masterful storyteller. The good people of First Church of God in Hickory had the unfortunate task of sitting through my first, fledgling attempts to be a preacher. They encouraged me in it. I will always be grateful because they added to my story.

The congregation of First Church of God in Boyertown, Pennsylvania, gave me my first full-time charge. I preached Sunday mornings and Sunday evenings for more than five years and developed the disciplines necessary to become what James Earl Massey refers to as "a real preacher." Every week I would find some story, some sermon illustration that I thought was good and shoehorn it into whatever I was preaching on that week. When I didn't really understand how storytelling worked, those good folks showed up week in and week out and listened to me work out my theology and philosophy of stories.

To the congregations of Haines Creek (now Silver Lake) Church of God in Leesburg, Florida, and First Church of God in New Albany, Indiana, I am forever appreciative of the opportunity to try out the concepts of narrative as they were being formed in my heart and soul. I'm sure it took some grace to hear those early attempts. I experimented on them my unseasoned understanding of first-person narratives and story based third-person sermons. I don't know if they were any good or not but they heard enough of the storyteller in me to encourage my pursuit of narrative storytelling.

To First Church of God in Fresno and to the Church of the Foothills in Pasadena, California, I am so grateful for your encouragement and support in my journey into the Academy. I could not have survived financially or emotionally during my preparation for and the pursuit of my PhD work if it had not been for individuals like Demos and Carolyn Gallender, Harold and Conni Hinkle, and Bill and Marjory Norris. They were friends in ways I cannot fully measure. Whenever I tell my story of how God has directed my life, I always think of how they influenced my story.

In addition, I have served three churches since I resigned from full-time pastoring: Life Abundant Church of God in Trenton, New Jersey, as a layperson; Solid Rock Community Church in Kissimmee, Florida, as an Associate Pastor; and Oak Grove Church of God (now Altar), Tampa, Florida, as their Interim Pastor. Each of these churches allowed me to explore the craft of preaching while learning new understandings of narrative approaches. I'm grateful for the ministry of Leon and Lois Alexander at Life Abundant, Whitfield and Jo-Ann Blenman as well as Matt and Rhesa Quainoo at Solid Rock, and the folks at Oak Grove/Altar for their support of me and my preaching. Because of these churches and their leaders, I am a better storyteller than I used to be.

I am the father of three sons (Doug, Jonathan, and Joel) who have all been called to pastoral ministry in the Church of God. I cannot begin to describe the joy and pride I feel as I watch them lead, hear them preach and teach, and see them fulfilling their calling in Jesus Christ. They have heard me preach more times than they can count (and more times than anyone should have to) and yet still call upon their old dad to come and preach for them from time to time in their own pulpits. It humbles me to think they still want to listen to me one more time. I am a blessed father and minister. When my final story is told, it will be these three amazing men, their wives and children that will be the best part of the story of my life.

My father-in-law Rev. John Williams, has been the guardrails of my journey. Dad was a seasoned pastor when I was grafted into the Williams clan and he became my model and advisor in ministry. He remains today the finest pastor I have ever known. When Joanie's mother died years ago, I grieved because she was my greatest fan and most ardent encourager. Mom was an elementary teacher and a curriculum writer. She was one of the most creative people I have ever known. Seeing her work watered the desire within me to understand how creativity works. It was such a powerful example that I did my dissertation on creativity, novelty, and originality in preaching. While I was doing the research, I thought about her often. She was the inspiration for much of my desire to know what creativity is and to be creative in my writing and ministry. If you see any of that here, it is because of her.

Most of all, for more than four decades my wife Joanie, an outstanding minister, preacher, and student in her own right, has been my rock and my encouragement. She has stuck with me through thick and thin and has never wavered in her appreciation and support of my preaching, even when it was not deserved. We have been on this journey together and I cannot imagine doing it without her. I would be willing to do it all over again as long as I could do it with her. She has sat through the same sermon being preached in two or three different services and never complained, even affirming that each one had its own dynamic and quality. If life is, in some way, a play being acted out in real life, Joanie has been the main character of my living. She has traversed every plot twist and turn with me so much so that it is no longer "my story" but "our story."

Finally, I began this project while Dr. James Earl Massey, my friend and lifelong mentor, was battling cancer. He is the one who encouraged me to pursue this line of narrative inquiry. He read my first book and told me to continue to write about this. Through his own writing concerning expository preaching, he called for more work to be done on the kind of narrative inquiry I have taken. In my college days, he sparked my interest in preaching. He taught me how much narrative and storytelling are integral to African American preaching and how to make narrative and stories subservient to a biblical text. I learned how to preach sitting under his leadership for more than ten years when he was the chief clinician at the National Preaching Conference in Dayton, Ohio. I was young, in my twenties, when I learned at his feet. I was older, in my sixth decade, when I attended his funeral in Detroit and heard from preacher after preacher the stories of his life that made Dr. Massey the influencer he was and remains.

One time during a phone call when I was at Fuller Seminary working on my PhD, he told me we were colleagues now and I could call him Jim. I smiled and thanked him for that . . . but I never called him Jim. Not out of lack of friendship, familiarity, or intimacy but out of the respect one has for his teacher. He was and will always be Dr. Massey to me. The best compliment I can give Dr. Massey is that, thirty years after he taught me about preaching in those days in Dayton, when I entered the academy to pursue my doctorate, I never had to unlearn anything he taught me. He was a master preacher and teacher, the epitome of character and class, and the best teacher I ever had. When his battle with cancer ended, those of us who knew him and loved him joined with the heavenly chorus to say, "Well done, thou good and faithful servant." As far as I'm concerned, his was one of the greatest stories of the last century. I am most proud to be a minor footnote in his grand narrative.

The journey from my hometown of Gloucester, New Jersey, to my current appointment in Orlando, Florida, has been a journey I could never have imagined. Only a God who is far greater than you and I could have envisioned the lifelong path my story has taken. It has been my honor to travel his road with his Spirit guiding my footsteps. That's my story and I'm sticking to it. Now, if you'll turn the page we can talk about a different narrative, one that enables us to learn how narrative preaching all began.

A Foreword by Clayton J. Schmit

EVERY TIME I TELL a story, whether in a sermon or in private life, I see how my listeners lean in. They are engaged. They want to hear how the story ends. Sometimes you get that "I could hear a pin drop" experience. I have learned that the "pin-drop" happens not so much because people are being extremely attentive. It happens because, for a brief moment, they stop breathing. Some stories can take your breath away.

When these things happen during my stories, they happen not because of any special powers of mine to tell stories. These special moments happen because of the inherent powers of story. Story-telling is natural to all people. My father was a gifted story-teller. I wish I had his talent for bringing humor out of the most ordinary human experiences. But, story-telling is something we can improve upon as we seek to communicate the experiences and the meanings of our lives.

Telling the Bible stories is what Christian people are about. From parents and grand-parents, to Sunday School teachers, to preachers: all have the same goal in mind for the people they guide in the faith. They want their audiences to know the stories about Jesus and about how God has been at work in people's lives for millennia. To tell a Jesus story is to preach the gospel. Narrating the scriptures is central to the practice of faith.

In the past few decades there has been intense conversation among those who study and teach homiletics relating to "narrative preaching." The term has come to mean several things. One meaning is that a sermon can be designed to move upon the long narrative arc of the entire scriptures; it becomes one more point on that arc and seeks to be consistent with its trajectory.

A sermon made up of good stories can also be called a narrative sermon. It links story to story, unfolding the good news in a chain of episodes that culminate in a meaningful expression of God's love. Garrison Keillor once spoke to us during my seminary days. He used this form so effectively, I remember his message clearly today.

A rarer form of narrative preaching is found in sermons where the preacher creates a fictional event that, as it unfolds, contains the focus and intent of a scriptural passage. These sermons usually do not quote the text or even make reference to it. They invite the listener to stay in the fictional story and gather from it the biblical truths it unfolds. The story makes a biblical message come alive in a fresh way through the imagined experiences of the characters in the story. William Faulkner was a writer whose work often functioned in this way.

Narrative preaching can also mean that the sermon is designed to unfold in the *shape* of a dramatic story: the beginning introduces an issue or problem; that issue becomes complicated (the plot thickens); a solution to the problem is sought; the problem finds resolution. It is fascinating to note that this kind of sermon can be designed without a single story or illustration; yet it meets the qualifications for a narrative sermon because of its dramatic form. That form is typically very engaging. People will lean in to hear how the sermon resolves the scriptural problem being addressed.

This book is about yet another form of narrative sermon: preaching from *within* the story.

Jeff Frymire is a master story-teller. Like my father, he has an eye for humor and drama. Jeff's wonderful story about Elijah from Tishbe (see chapter 8) came about as a surprise. Jeff was working with me as I taught a preaching course at Fuller Seminary in Pasadena, California. He was working on a PhD in preaching at the time. In my class, the students' first practical assignment (one which I borrowed from my mentor, Richard Lischer at Duke Divinity School) was to prepare a simple telling of an Old Testament narrative. They were not to do a lot of textual research, nor were they to write a carefully crafted story. They were simply asked to stand, speak an Old Testament story from memory, and get used to speaking before their peers. It was intended as an uncomplicated "ice-breaker" exercise.

The students would often ask for an example so that they would know how to prepare this assignment. On this occasion, I turned to Jeff and said, "Say, you are a good story teller. Why don't you start our next class with an Old Testament narrative example?" Jeff happily agreed. He came to class with this delightful story about Elijah, the man from Tishbe, the man from nowhere. Though it was captivating, Jeff actually failed in his assignment. I was hoping to provide the students with a simple example that they could easily emulate. What Jeff gave us was a masterpiece of exegetical discovery, character and plot development, and impressive narrative performance. Students loved the story. But, they soon complained: "Wait a minute. Is that what you expect *us* to do?"

In *Preaching Inside the Story*, Jeff Frymire teaches us to do more than a simple telling of the biblical story. He gives us the building blocks for telling a biblical story that proclaims the good news from inside the story itself. Often, it is a reimagining of the story from the perspective of one of its characters. This is what most listeners might expect when they hear the term "narrative preaching": it brings the biblical event to life in a story, without adding preacherly commentary and exhortation. Jeff lets the Bible story speak for itself and he encourages us, at least occasionally, to do the same. No one is better suited to teach this than Jeff, the master story-teller. Imagine getting a lesson on story writing and story-telling from Mark Twain. That is what we get in this book.

We also get something more: Jeff also offers theological, philosophical, and neuro-scientific explanations as to why the human person is intensely interested in the telling and hearing of stories. We are, as Jeff says, wired for story.

Those of us who dare to learn to preach from inside the story may soon find that people will be leaning in on the front edge of their pews. The sermon story will captivate them, just as all stories do for people who are hard-wired to hear stories. That includes all of us. Enjoy this tale, told by a master-story teller, of how to preach inside the story.

Clayton J. Schmit
Epiphany 2, 2022

An Introduction

Inside a Narrative Preaching Journey

> *Christian preaching has to do with telling The Story, and doing so with a sense of history, a settled faith-perspective, and an acquaintance with God who is at work in human history. The Christian preacher is a steward of The Story, a person entrusted to administer biblical truth as a steward of the God and Father of Jesus Christ, an agent intent and eager to see the consequences of that telling effected in personal and social history.*
> —James Earl Massey[1]

THIS IS A BOOK that invites the reader to take a journey into the fascinating world of narrative preaching. Specifically, it is designed to open a door that leads the reader on a journey into the kind of storytelling that is often left out of too much of our modern approach to preaching. It is an invitation to spend time journeying through the literary location of biblical narrative where narrative preaching lives. For more than a decade I've been taking my students on just such a narrative excursion and it has provided profound experiences. I have watched novice preachers and seasoned pulpiteers find a breath of a fresh wind in their preaching approach. Considering the transformations and exciting changes I have seen in others, I now invite you to take a similar journey with me.

What might you need for such an adventure? All you really need is your Bible, an open mind, and a willingness to trek through the world of narrative storytelling; an inclination to venture into a kind of biblical

---

1. Massey, *Stewards of the Story*, xv–xvi.

storytelling that has been a staple of preaching long before Jesus stood on a mount to deliver his beatitudes or dazzled a crowd with parables of good Samaritans and prodigal sons. This journey can fundamentally change how you preach as well as how your congregation hears and understands the word of God. It is a journey into how to tell *The* Story . . . *His* Story. Interested? Then come, journey with me.

While my own journey has spanned the course of more than four decades of a pastoral/preaching life, the idea of this book arose soon after I had finished my PhD at Fuller Theological Seminary in 2010. My friend and mentor, Dr. Clay Schmit, suggested that it might be time to rewrite my first book. Clay thought that it might make an intriguing project since I had written *Preaching the Story: How to Communicate God's Word Through Narrative Sermons* prior to attending Fuller. That book was intended as a practical guide to narrative preaching born out of decades of pastoral experience as a local pastor. Going through the academic rigors of a PhD in homiletics had provided a certain gravitas to my practical experience in the pastorate. So, with the benefit of a doctoral education and research insights gleaned from papers and a dissertation, Clay suggested it was worthwhile writing project to consider. I thought about it for a while but decided to turn my energies to the classroom and teaching—after all, that was my first love. So, for the last decade, first at Princeton Theological Seminary and now at Asbury Theological Seminary, I have revelled in the joys of the classroom and the challenges of teaching preaching at a graduate level.

But after having developed and taught numerous Narrative Preaching classes at both institutions, it appears to me an appropriate time to reconsider the basic thrust of my mentor's insightful suggestion. However, rather than rewrite my original book, I've taken on the challenge of trying to put down on paper the fundamentals of my approach to narrative as a homiletical discipline. My goal has been to write a useful treatise that will introduce students of preaching to the world of narrative, narrative preaching, and a storytelling approach to preaching. I am seeking in this writing to answer some basic questions, questions such as: "What are the origins of the narrative sermon?" and "Is creativity a valid hermeneutical principle when it comes to exegeting a narrative text?" My sense is that many preachers have been hesitant to try a narrative approach to preaching for three specific reasons: (1) they have not been provided with a firm understanding of the historical, theological, and biblical origins of the storytelling/narrative approach to the sermon nor its validity; (2)

too many preachers and preaching professors have leaned heavily into the science of homiletics and have moved too far away from the art of preaching, resulting in a dearth of solid, exegetical models for narrative preaching; (3) as a result of such leanings, preaching and preachers have not been provided with an understanding of how creativity functions in the inspiration of the Holy Spirit in the sermon. My goal in this work is simple: I want to give preachers permission to use their God-given creativity in the service of biblical preaching through a storytelling approach to narrative.

At the same time, I am attempting here to continue the work I started in *Preaching the Story*. I have endeavored to put into words the practical realities of the preaching experience I have been leaning into a narrative vein for more than four decades. I have been fortunate to benefit from more than 30 years of local preaching as a pastor in the Church of God (Anderson) and from more than 15 years in the academy teaching these concepts. I have been invited to share these insights in numerous conferences, conventions, and seminars that I have led on the subject of narrative preaching. In addition, my current position as a member of the pastoral team at my home congregation (Solid Rock Community Church, Kissimmee, Florida) has afforded me the opportunity to preach regularly in a local congregation while pursuing the passion of teaching at the graduate level. It has kept me firmly grounded in the kind of local preaching that is the heartbeat of the church and allowed me to continue to explore the depths of narrative preaching.

Furthermore, as Dean of the Chapel at Asbury Theological Seminary in Florida, I am afforded numerous times during the school year to preach in a seminary setting to aspiring and committed pastors who are seeking more knowledge and understanding of the things of God. I feel that God has afforded me the unique opportunity of having a foot in both worlds: the world of the local pastorate and the world of the preparing preacher; the realm of the preaching pastor and the realm of the academic; preaching to laity and to ministers. My intent with this work is to share insights from both domains to assist those who live in one or both of these worlds.

While working through my doctoral program I became almost exclusively narrative-based as a preacher.[2] A few years back I took on the

---

2. I should note that I was an interim pastor, preaching weekly during almost the entire time of my PhD work. I am grateful to both congregations (Church of the Foothills in Pasadena and the Church of God in Santa Ana) for the opportunity to refine

challenge of being, yet again, an interim pastor for a congregation searching for a new pastor. As part of that assignment, I was required to preach weekly for nearly six months. After completing the task, I spent some time reviewing the sermons I had preached during those six months. It reaffirmed what I already knew . . . I am a narrative preacher and narrative preaching can be successful in most any situation. Specifically, I realized how strongly I have been influenced by the works of Fred Craddock and Eugene Lowry.[3] I note this because it has been some fifty years since Craddock and Lowry published their seminal works on preaching in an inductive and narrative form. As I engaged in my review and use of these homiletical giants, I took note of how I had applied Craddock and observed how I had subtly tweaked Lowry's approach, I began to wonder if it might not be time for someone to revisit parts of the premise of Lowry's groundbreaking work and see if there might be some small contribution that could be made to Lowry's original work, insights, and research. I pray that this work adds to the ongoing conversation concerning what Lowry so ably began in the 1970s.[4]

It is not the scope of this work to be a historical treatise on the history of preaching. However, in the course of my research I found some valuable evidence on both the Jewish and Greek origins of a narrative, story-based approach to preaching. These Jewish roots, found in the Exilic struggle to worship without a temple, and the Greek origins of the narrative principles of storytelling espoused in Aristotle's *Poetics* have formed the foundation for this entire work.[5]

The juxtaposition of these two sources lead me to another concern: Is narrative preaching merely an application of the principles that Aristotle taught centuries ago on drama or is it a unique form of preaching that owes its roots to the struggles of the exiled Hebrew people and their desire to worship God?[6] And if, as I suspect, Aristotle (or at least

my preaching during my doctoral journey.

3. Specifically, Craddock, *As One without Authority*; Lowry, *Homiletical Plot*.

4. While not my primary focus, I hope that this conversation will add something to another of Lowry's books, Lowry, *Homiletical Beat*.

5. Aristotle, *Rhetoric (and the Poetics of Aristotle)*.

6. To put this into historical context, the exile of the Jews began in the early years of the sixth century BCE (circa 588) and ended when they returned to Jerusalem around 520–515. On the other hand, Aristotle lived during the fourth century BCE (384–322). By comparing these dates, it can rightly be inferred that the move toward a more narrative approach was a Jewish idea before Aristotle codified it during his lifetime. Ultimately, philosophers such as Coleridge, Hume, and Kant determined that

his principles) comprised a significant influence on, or distillations of, the whole genre of storytelling and narrative, and if this whole genre of preaching really did develop in the Post-Exilic nation of Israel, and if the storytelling/narrative preaching genre was further established in the New Testament world of Jesus, then how does that connection influence not only preaching today but also how we understand the biblical texts that provide the foundations of narrative preaching?

While there is much in this book that scholars and students can and will debate, this one thing seems blatantly obvious on its face—Jesus was a storyteller in the Aristotelian mode and he utilized principles conceived in the synagogues of the exile. If anyone loved the narrative/storytelling sermon approach favored by Aristotle's teachings and by some of those in exile in Babylon, it was Jesus. That should drive us to understand the roots of narrative. It should influence how we preach and even whether or not we should be preaching narratively.

As the book developed, I decided to place it in two sections. *Section One: Journeying into Narrative* provides the foundational and academic work needed to produce a narrative philosophy of preaching. This section is the result of my research and pedagogical work over the past dozen years. It is intended to allow students to grapple with the key questions concerning a narrative approach to preaching and preachers to understand the philosophical and theological underpinnings of a narrative approach. *Section Two: Journeys in Narrative Preaching* is the practical application of these ideals in the pulpit. The chapters in this second section are examples of narrative sermons and are written in storytelling form, thereby providing the reader with a practical experience of what Section One has been teaching. To tie the two sections together, I have explained and related the sermons in Section Two with the issues explored in Section One.

As the writing began to take form, I struggled with fundamental questions regarding the narrative sermon. It appears that the answer to these questions has not yet been agreed to by all those in the academic world of homiletics. These critical questions are:

- What is a narrative hermeneutic?

---

narrative/storytelling is the way in which human beings communicate, who they are, and what they know. Therefore, it should not surprise anyone that narrative/storytelling principles are divine in nature or, at least, used significantly by the Bible, its authors, and its characters.

- How does our inherent understanding of how stories affect us influence preaching?
- What critical questions require preachers to delve into how narrative texts differ from non-narrative texts?

Five Questions

As I wrestled with these fundamental notions there emerged in my thinking certain foundational concepts that guided my research and provided a structure for my work in narrative.

Question #1—How does one begin a journey into narrative preaching? Chapter 1: "My Journey into Narrative: Questions for Storytellers" seeks to help the reader explore the narrative journey through my own testimonial journey and exploring the roots of the sermon in and through the rise of the Jewish tabernacle. In part, it delves into the fascinating world of Midrash and how the rabbis developed a preaching style in the exile that would influence preaching down through the ages. Ultimately, it gives a series of biblical examples to back up the notion of a narrative/Haggadah methodology to biblical preaching.

Question #2—What does a narrative hermeneutic look like? In chapter 2: "The Journey Intensifies: Toward a Narrative Hermeneutic," I explore this issue. This chapter looks at the foundational understanding of how one approaches a narrative interpretation of texts and of sermons. Beginning with an overview of the narrative quality and quantity in scripture, the chapter traces the difficulty that a narrative hermeneutic has faced throughout centuries of scientific certainty and interpretive definitiveness. The bulk of the chapter is a development of a new kind of narrative hermeneutic that incorporates a series of narrative sensibilities that are different than the hermeneutics of certainty. The chapter provides a key template for a hermeneutical approach to preaching and introduces the reader to issues in regard to Performance Theory in preaching.

Question #3—Why do stories appeal to us? Any journey into narrative requires the reader to explore how the brain functions in storytelling. In chapter 3: "The Journey into the Mind: We Are Wired for Stories," I invite the reader to learn how our brains are created for stories; how they are wired for stories. It takes a novice reader on a journey into the vast and fascinating world of neuroscience and what it can tell us about the creative/narrative experience of the mind. The application of this research applies what we can learn about how the brain works to its impact on both preaching and listening to sermons. Rather than using the popular terms of "left brain-right brain" to explain creativity, my research has shown that the brain has a particular kind of neurobiological response to storytelling that involves creative learning skills, multiple parts of the brain, and the uniqueness of memory. When storytelling is combined with or utilizes these aspects of creativity, the brain goes through specific kinds of responses that reveal how our brains are wired for stories. These insights are designed to give encouragement to those who seek to be creative by preaching from a narrative/storytelling perspective.

Question #4—What are the basic elements of story and why do they matter? Preaching from the Inside the Story takes a voyage into the philosophy of stories in chapter 4: "The Journey into Stories: A Philosophy of Stories." It breaks down the basic elements of story as described by Aristotle. This provides the necessary nexus for the work of Eugene Lowry who based his work on Aristotle's emphasis on plot in storytelling. His "The Homiletical Plot"[7] sparked a renewed interest in the workings of good storytelling and the basic building blocks laid out by Aristotle: plot, character, thought, diction, melody, and spectacle. This chapter provides an opportunity to engage the work of Lowry afresh and anew. It is intended to give an even more robust understanding of Aristotle and how Lowry's approach (and the approach of other kinds of narrative preaching such as third-person and first-person) can benefit from deeper insights into the basic formula of narrative/storytelling.

Question #5—What does this all mean for preaching? Section One concludes with "Narrative Journey, Narrative Sense: Learning to Preach from Inside the Story." Chapter 5 provides the essential basis for how one accomplishes the title of the book, how to preach from inside a story. It is designed to help the reader develop both a narrative sense for preaching and a storytelling lens for communicating narratives. It explains how to enter a story and how concepts such as analepsis and prolepsis aid in preaching narratively.

In order to provide a well-rounded methodology of narrative preaching, *Section Two: Journeys in Narrative Preaching* contains a series of narrative sermons that I have preached in the past. Having said that, the reader may find that they present more like short stories than sermons. If that is the case, then I have succeeded in what I set out to do.

---

7. Lowry, *Homiletical Plot*.

After all, narrative sermons are really the "kissing cousins" of the short story.[8] The only difference between the generic short story and a narrative sermon is that the text for the narrative sermon arises out of the biblical story rather than the imagination of the writer.[9]

This section opens with an introduction to the idea of third-person and first-person narrative sermons along with an example of a Lowry Loop design. It attempts to give a brief and overarching view of the different kinds of approaches one can use in these unusual and special kinds of sermonic structures. Rationale is also provided as to why third-person, first-person or the Lowry Loop were used.

The opening example is of a first-person sermon. Chapter 6: "The Journey into Grief: Moses' Mother Mourns," is the more "traditional" approach to first-person preaching using a single character's perspective. In the case of this sermon, however, that person is an implied character, Moses' mother. I put traditional in quotation marks because I preached this sermon at Princeton Chapel while serving as a postdoctoral teaching professor. It was well received but challenged numerous stereotypes, namely the fact that I am a man and preached a first-person sermon from a woman's perspective. I note in the chapter that no costumes were used nor were any kind of visual or introductory explanation given in order to prepare the congregation for what was about to be done. I've included it here as an example of the power of narrative to overcome stereotypes. The application section of the chapter looks at how this sermon develops a narrative sense and a narrative storytelling lens.

Chapter 7: "The Journey Toward Assurance: Mary and Joseph Wonder" is a first-person sermon that is able to be done dialogically by a man and a woman. Together they present the story of Mary and Joseph and the events surrounding Jesus' birth. Its inclusion here is to provide the reader with a different kind of first-person experience than chapter 6. It is a different kind of creativity in structure but follows the same principles laid down in Section One and utilized in chapter 6. The application

---

8. For a more detailed discussion of that principle, see the excellent work of McKenzie, *Novel Preaching*.

9. In that sense, this work approaches narrative in a significantly different way than some others have viewed the creative, narrative, storytelling-based sermon. See Troeger, *Imagining a Sermon*, for a different approach than mine. More than a polemic against others approach this work is really an answer to the call by Dr. James Earl Massey for others to explore the narrative/storytelling-based sermon as part of a comprehensive biblical and exegetical discovery. See Massey, *Stewards of the Story*.

section looks at how this sermon incorporates insights about neuroscience and narrative.

Chapter 8: "Journey from Tishbe: Elijah, the Man from Nowhere" is an Old Testament *haggadah* story using the text of Elijah, his calling and his confrontation with King Ahab. I've included it in this volume because it is the narrative piece that put much of my academic career into motion. I first shared this at the request of my mentor Clay Schmit for a classroom example as to how to tell an Old Testament story. Later he asked me to share *Tishbe* at a meeting of the Academy of Homiletics. It was well received by that professional guild of preaching professors and especially by the Dean of Princeton Theological Seminary (James Kay) who, as a result, would become interested in hiring me for their vacant Postdoctoral Teaching Fellowship. I've shared this story in lots of places and even on several continents at Clay's behest and it has remained a positive example for use in the classroom. It fits the need for the book, but I confess to including it for sentimental reasons as well. The application section details how this sermon is the product of a narrative hermeneutic.

Chapter 9: "The Journey at the Altar: What Was Zechariah Expecting?" provides an opportunity to explore how the Lowry Loop should function. It was initially preached at the chapel at Princeton Seminary and was well received by both students and faculty (and much discussed). Analysis is provided that breaks down each step of the Lowry Loop and how each step functions in the development of a narrative sermon in the Loop structure. The application section explores a fresh look at the Lowry Loop principles.

The final example, chapter 10: "The Journey of Jesus the Storytelling Savior: Jesus and His Teaching Method" concludes this section with a New Testament haggadah concerning, appropriately, the storytelling Jesus. It seemed a proper conclusion to a work about storytelling. The concluding sermon brings the section to a fitting conclusion with a third-person account of why Jesus used stories as the basis for his teaching. The application section looks into the connections between Jesus and Aristotle's dramatic principles.

The epilogue (and the book) ends rather abruptly. It is intentional. The epilogue: "The Journey Continues: The Ongoing Development of Narrative Preaching as Storytelling" is designed to remind readers that understanding narratives is an ongoing pursuit. It highlights two ongoing truths about narrative preaching. It encourages the reader to keep working on narrative—to continue the journey. My intent is that this chapter will be an encouragement to the reader to be a more narrative/storytelling preacher.

Ready to take the journey? Good! Then let's begin at the start.

SECTION ONE:

A Guide for the Narrative Journey

1

My Journey into Narrative

Questions for Storytellers

> *Preaching has become a bye-word for long and dull conversation of any kind; and whoever wishes to imply, in any piece of writing, the absence of everything agreeable and inviting, calls it a sermon.*
>
> —From A Memoir of the Reverend Sydney Smith[1]

> *In modern language, the word sermon is used in secular terms, pejoratively, to describe a lengthy or tedious speech delivered with great passion, by any person, to an uninterested audience.*
>
> —From Wikipedia

WHERE WE BEGIN

How did we get here?

How did we get to the place where the preaching of the good news of the gospel of Jesus Christ is considered by the culture as "tedious speech"? What has caused ministers to preach the gospel in such a way that a called, ordained, and trained preacher of that gospel would define the very act of preaching as a "byword" for dullness?

---

1. Holland et al., *Memoir of the Reverend Sydney Smith*, 1:43.

How in the world did we sink to this low point where a sermon is used as a way of talking about things that are disinteresting? Paul may have called it "the foolishness of preaching" but he never insinuated that preaching was supposed to be delivered dully to an uninterested audience! How did we get here?

As a seminary professor of preaching, I have often told my students that boring preaching is a sin. I believe that. I think it takes hard work to turn the greatest story ever told into something like the definitions above. And yet, for all too many parishioners and "Nones" (those who were once involved in the church but now have left), their definition of preaching matches closely to the popular notion proposed by Wikipedia. How did we get here?

What is missing in our preaching that has turned the story of David and Goliath into a one-dimensional cartoon about a boy vs. a giant; how have we turned the life and death struggles of Ruth and Esther into something that merely references marriage or position; how have we reduced these timeless narratives so that the power has been excised out of them and replaced with points, deductions, and analogies; why do we gut the power of narrative and replace it with a preacher's musings? Have we become so jaded and unmoved by these amazing stories that we fail to realize they are real stories about real people doing real things? Why do we, instead, relegate the life altering realities of biblical people's lives to flannel boards, two-dimensional characterizations, and poorly animated cartoon stories? Why have preachers wandered so far off the biblical path of narrative stories that we have replaced them with deductive points and principles that too often have to be shoehorned into the biblical text?

How did we get here?

Maybe most confusing of all, considering our culture and its emphasis on movies, television, and theater, why do we not have a greater appreciation of the power of stories and the efficacy of narrative in the pulpit? Why shouldn't the creation story be infused with unimaginable power? Why isn't the exodus event dripping with fear and exultation? Why wouldn't the story of Lazarus being raised from the dead astonish us and fill us with the same kind of unprecedented awe that Mary, Martha, and the citizens of Bethany experienced? What have we done to the Bible?

How did we get to this point?

A GUIDE FOR THE JOURNEY

When I first began in ministry, I asked my senior pastor, Forrest Plants, what he was preaching on Sunday. He told me his text was the fall in Genesis. I asked him what his goal was in the preaching of that text. His answer was revelational. "I want them to taste the apple."

There is something of the purpose and focus of narrative preaching that cries out to respond to his preaching goal and say, "Yes and Amen." At that time, I didn't understand his goal. Now I do. What was Rev. Plants trying to say about preaching? He was saying:

Make it vivid.
Make it real.
Let the listener experience the story in fresh ways.
Make the sermon anything but dull and uninteresting.

If these kinds of issues have been stuck in the back of your mind and you've been too afraid to ask them out loud, then welcome to this journey into narrative. And, if it is any help whatsoever, let me give witness and testimony to how my journey began and how it flourished. Maybe it will provide some helpful mile markers along the way of your journey. This is how I got from where I was to where I am today; from how I approached a sermon back then to how I approach a sermon today; from how I started understanding the rudiments of narrative storytelling to the place where I preach almost exclusively in the narrative vein. This is how I got from where we seem to be to where I am today.

THE JOURNEY

My journey into narrative started, literally, at my mother's knee. My Mom was a storyteller. Admittedly, her stories were always long, involved, all-over-the-place retelling of events that she had seen, heard, or known. She loved "rabbit trails" and would get caught up in extraneous details. She would start out saying, "It was Monday. No. It was Tuesday. Oh, right, it was a Thursday afternoon just before sunset." On and on she would go, going to great lengths to cover not only the main story but every possible permutation of it. And yet, she had the ability to grab your attention as the drama unfolded in front of you and hold it for the longest time. Maybe it was the picturesque language she used or all the details she incorporated, but I found her storytelling mesmerizing.

When I was a young teenager, I received a portable tape recorder for Christmas. Along with it came a microphone and a package of cassette tapes to use for recording. Back then, that was quite a novelty. One of the best memories I have of my mom is sitting on the couch and interviewing her about her life, recording it on my new toy, and listening to her spin her yarns. Oh, how I wish I still had those tapes and could hear her tell her stories one more time. It has been more than 40 years since I have been able to hear her voice. I miss her . . . and I miss her stories.

As you can tell, I get my interest in narrative honestly. I am the son of a storyteller; the child of someone who taught me by example the power of stories. I cherish that heritage. I quickly realized after being called to ministry that my greatest teaching/preaching/leadership strength was in the ability to tell stories well. Even more than that, I possessed an innate ability to know if a story was a "good" one, one that had "legs" (i.e., the potential to hold the interest of a congregation of listeners). Maybe it was all those hours spent listening to my mom on the couch. Maybe it was just the way my brain was wired. Either way, I knew early on that I was a storyteller at heart. And while you may not believe it yet, you are too.

THE STORYTELLING ART

Storytelling is an art. There are scientific principles to storytelling that we will discuss later, but more than a science, storytelling is an artistic virtuosity. There's an inventive skill inherent in humans to tell tales and weave stories. Before cultures were literate they had strong and effective oral storytelling skills. Walter Ong notes that of the "3000 languages spoken that exist today only some 78 have a literature."[2] More than writing, literate societies we are a composition of oral cultures that first learned how to tell stories before they ever envisioned writing them. The result is that human beings are more storytellers than they are story-writers.

Jesus was a prolific storyteller, a true artist when it came to crafting parables. Which leads to a question I've always wondered about preaching: Why is Jesus' example of preaching not followed by most preachers? While storytelling may be an art form, the truth is that we are all storytellers, artisans, verbal picture makers. It's in our DNA. We have all learned from the earliest of ages to tell stories. And we all love to hear stories. Ong notes that there is something called the "interiority of sound" that

---

2. Ong, *Orality and Literacy*, 7.

allows us to experience stories viscerally. He writes, "Sight isolates, sound incorporates."[3] So if we are natural storytellers and if we are excited by the interiority of sound when listening to stories, then why not follow in the footsteps of the greatest storyteller of all time?

When I took my first pastorate and began preaching weekly (actually, twice on Sundays—one in the morning, one in the evening) I struggled to find stories/illustrations to add to my preaching. I compensated for not having a lot of illustrations at my fingertips by being drawn to the narrative sections of Scripture for preaching. I found that the stories of Jesus in the Gospels were foundational; the journeys of the disciples in Acts were bedrock; Genesis and Exodus anchored the history of the events that shaped Israel; everything from Joshua to the I & IIs (Samuel, Kings, and Chronicles) to storybooks like Jonah, Esther, and Ruth appeared to be rich with the kind of narrative building blocks I loved to preach. Hosea, Nehemiah, Joshua, and Judges were compelling stories of people's lives and their struggles with sex, marriage, leadership, sacrifice, loneliness, conflict, and obstinance. Paul's letters all had a backstory to them in Acts that spoke to church conflicts, spiritual development, sinful attitudes, and human needs. The subjects seemed endless and fascinating. Even the book of Revelation with its dragons, angels, and strange creatures appeared to be a story of epic proportions worthy of any J.R.R. Tolkien novel. I had no shortage of stories to find, exegete, and preach. The arc of my preaching was set. I was a narrative preacher.[4]

FOUNDATIONS FOR NARRATIVE PREACHING

The foundation for this kind of storytelling-based preaching began during my college years at Anderson University where I had the great privilege of having Dr. Marie Strong as my Bible professor. I took her for New Testament Survey (often called Introduction to the New Testament in other colleges and seminaries) and the first day of class she gave this

---

3. Ong, *Orality and Literacy*, 70–73.

4. My theology of narrative/storytelling preaching is pretty simple. A narrative/storytelling sermon is based in a text and in its context. It is not stringing together a series of stories from other sources as you "drive by" the text. Narrative preaching is an exegetical exploration of a narrative text and its context and exposing the truth of the biblical passage in a storytelling fashion rather than a 3-point structure. Narrative preaching believes that the biblical writ is about real people, with real feelings, being in real relationships, and experiencing real interactions with others.

disclaimer: "You will all get frustrated in this class because we were going to study *about* the New Testament rather than really study the spiritual *content* of the New Testament." She told us we would spend a lot of time in the Gospels and the book of Acts as background/context for the writings of the New Testament. We would not be delving into what the Gospels and the book of Acts were actually teaching, nor would we be doing a deep dive into the doctrine and theology taught throughout the New Testament. She proceeded to take us on a long journey tracing the movements of Peter and Paul through Acts, the places they went, the churches Paul helped to begin, and the key conflicts that took place among them and in the missionary movement of the first-century church. Rather than being frustrated by all this minutia, I was enthralled. It was like taking a historical journey with a master storyteller at the helm. At that time, I was a fairly young Christian; an undisciplined believer; a novice reader and student of the Bible. Dr. Strong made the New Testament come alive to me in ways it had never been. I saw how it all connected. I was mesmerized and I have been fascinated by Scripture ever since.[5]

As a result of knowing the stories behind the books of the New Testament—their writing and context—I fell in love with the Bible. My love for the Word started out as a blind date but has developed into a comfortable evening with a good friend whom I had gotten to know and who knows where I came from and where I'm going. From that point forward, when I opened the New Testament, the words of Matthew, Mark, Luke, John, Paul, James, and Peter took on new meaning. I was hooked! This Bible was a great story!

NARRATIVE EVIDENCE

The evidence of how much Dr. Strong and her teaching had affected my thinking came during my first senior pastorate. One Sunday I announced

---

5. Some years later, while pursuing my MDiv degree, I had a similar experience with Dr. Robert Branson as he unlocked the joys of the Old Testament. It was revelational to someone who was in ministry but never really had the background to understand the thread of revelation that marches through the totality of the Old Testament. Without these two professors and their passion for the Bible I fear I may have gone through my preaching ministry with too few handles to help form people through my sermons. I owe them both a great debt of gratitude for what they poured into my life. For those interested in a flavor of both of these scholars, here are a couple of suggestions from their writings: Strong, *Basic Teachings from Patmos*; Branson, *Judges*; Branson et al., *Discovering the Old Testament*.

my intention to preach through Paul's letter to the Romans. My wife loved the book and my objective was to do a deep dive into the theological underpinnings of Pauline theology, to grapple with the intricacies of the heavyweight subjects of salvation and adoption, and to mine the depths of the greatest thinker of the apostolic age. I jumped in with both feet. It lasted three weeks. I remember declaring to the congregation that I wasn't ready to take on such weighty matters and announced a new series based on one of the narrative sections of Scripture. I was a narrative preacher or at least a preacher that was more comfortable *in* story than *out* of story.[6]

It should be noted that while I couldn't figure out how to read Romans narratively at that early juncture of my ministry, I have now learned how to read even the densest theological books in the Bible in a narrative way (see note below). I have learned the secret of re-narrating a text in order to understand its context and meaning. But at that early point in my ministry, I stopped fighting who I was and how I thought. I realized I was my mom. That narrative helped my preaching greatly but it also brought up at least one major caution.

STORYTELLING CAUTIONS

After preaching one Sunday morning, my wife Joanie and I were headed home in the car. I asked her about the sermon and what she thought of it (I had not yet realized that if I asked that question, she might actually tell me the truth). Joanie inquired about one of the illustrations I had used and wondered about where I found it. I was excited about her question because I loved the illustration (go figure!) and felt really good about how I had told it. I told her I had found it in a book I was reading that week and thought it was a great illustration. Joanie quickly agreed it was a great story and I had told it extremely well. Then came the backhand side of the compliment.

---

6. It would take me some growing and seminary education to be able to fully grasp the depths of Christian theology from the pulpit. This story occurred during my first pastorate, when I was just about to begin my seminary journey. As the years went by and my education and maturity in the faith increased, I found myself more comfortable preaching the depths of theology and doctrine, though I still found that narrative was, for me, the best vehicle for that type of preaching as well. I did not find it mutually exclusive in my preaching to have people understand doctrine while at the same time taste the apple—they could do both. See Wil Willimon's work in chapter 5 of Green and Pasquarello, *Narrative Reading, Narrative Preaching*, 107–16. .Another example of how to approach a non-narrative text in a very narrative way is Wright, *Paul*.

"It was a great story" she said. "Of course, it didn't have anything to do with your sermon, but it was a great story."

As deflated as my ego was at that moment, I was still able to hear the wisdom of her critique and realize that she was absolutely correct. I recognized that day that I was more interested in a good story than in a good sermon. In reality I think I believed at the time that good stories were more important than good sermons because stories were more memorable and sermons, at least my sermons, were more forgettable. I was less concerned with mining the biblical text/context for the narrative than I was in finding an illustration that would enable me to become a storyteller rather than just an expository preacher. I had yet to figure out that the Bible was the best story and the best illustration (and source of illustrations) a preacher can have.

I fear this is way too common among those preachers who have abandoned strong exegetical content and settled for more stories and illustrations than biblical depth in their sermons. Too many preachers are putting a sermon together as a "string of pearls"—a series of stories, illustrations, and anecdotes they hope will create a better sermon than one that plods through the text and becomes tiresome. I must admit that at that point in my life I probably agreed with the Wikipedia definition of preaching at the beginning of this chapter: *"a lengthy or tedious speech delivered with great passion, by any person, to an uninterested audience."* What I would find out in time is that biblical texts, well narrated and well applied, would give me hope that my preaching could break the rancid mold of tedious speech. And, yes, it can help you overcome that, too.

One reaction to my wife's insight was that it motivated me to develop a library of stories from which to choose stories that would relate to my sermon. As happenstance would have it (or God's will would unfold) I had a member of our small congregation volunteer to be my secretary. Sally was invaluable in so many ways during those early years. Around the same time that my wife had given me the insight about my illustrations Sally arrived at the office and asked for my notes from Sunday's sermon. She took the illustrations I had used in the sermon, typed them up individually on some 3x5 notecards, gave me a file cabinet, and told me to always give her the illustrations I was thinking about using or had used. She told me, "I think you're a good storyteller and I want you to have good stories at your fingertips." Soon we figured out a simple filing system and codes to use to organize the file. Today, that fledgling file cabinet holds thousands of sermon illustrations on most any subject needed. I no longer have to shoehorn a story into my sermon. There is one in the file that will connect most directly. It gave me a chance to explore different genres of preaching while still having illustrations at my fingertips that fed my narrative abilities. It was important that I learn how to do all the exegetical work on the text necessary for what James Earl Massey called, "real preaching."[7] What I learned in this phase was to distinguish between telling stories and doing exegesis on a text and how the two could be formed together into a sermon.

Sally's prophetic word over my preaching came true and that system served me well for many years. It helped to bring me to Fuller Seminary and a PhD program in homiletics to explore even grander understandings of narrative preaching. While there, I was able to dig deeper into the nuances of narrative preaching philosophy and creativity theory. Two events early on in my sojourn at Fuller would change everything about my understanding of narrative and further impact my preaching. These are more than just autobiographical nuances; they help for the foundation for narrative.

STORYTELLING RISKS

During my first year I was taking a seminar with my mentor and friend, Dr. Clay Schmit.[8] During a break in the class Clay was talking about his Introduction to Preaching class and one of the upcoming assignments for it. He told us that he always required each student in the class to take an OT story/text and tell it in five minutes without notes or Bible in hand, without points or sermonic structure, and to do it in the style of "don't preach, just tell the story."[9] As we were sitting on the porch, Clay looked at me and said, "Hey, you're the storyteller. Why don't you work up an OT story and tell my class?" I agreed (it was a great opportunity and a

---

7. Massey and Thompson, *Designing the Sermon*.

8. For those unfamiliar with Dr. Schmit's work, here are a few of his titles: Schmit, *Too Deep for Words*; Schmit, *Public Reading of Scripture*; Schmit, *Sent and Gathered*.

9. I later talked this over with Clay after I noticed that, during my time of being a Teaching Assistant with all the other professors who taught preaching at Fuller, he was the only one to require this assignment. In addition, I found that his students were, on the average, better at the preaching task than students in other sections. Considering they all taught the same material and all taught it well, I came to the conclusion that there was something about this assignment that helped students significantly in their preaching. Today, I require this same assignment and have found that students receive a great deal of help by doing it.

great affirmation to be singled out by my mentor) but as I planned the story, I had some trepidation. After all, I was in a PhD program and had just agreed to address serious MDiv students preparing for the preaching ministry. Would my concept of storytelling hold up? Did the narrative principles that I had learned and used during my pastoral ministry have the kind of intellectual and biblical gravitas to pass muster at the graduate school level? Looking back, I wonder if I wasn't really facing a moment of self-doubt and asking, "Was my storytelling approach to preaching viable?" A negative answer to that query would set back my whole graduate program just as it was getting underway.

I mention this story to emphasize the point that being a narrative preacher in the pulpit is to wrestle with self-doubt. So many examples of three-point deductive preaching abound that to preach in a narrative style often requires risk. You wouldn't think it would be that way considering the fact that telling stories is so natural to human beings, that it's what we do, and that we all share our stories by turning most every conversation into a campfire time of tales from our history. But examples of narrative preaching are often rare in our pulpits. I have a good friend who is one of the more dynamic preachers in the pulpit today. He is a powerful preacher with a strong narrative style . . . and yet he always has three points, sometimes even having multiple three-point sections in his preaching. He reflects what I have found that preachers who have narrative abilities and skills feel that they have to couch them in a non-narrative, three-point structure. It takes risk to break out from the mold of the traditional deductive style of preaching. But the risk is worth it, especially when you consider the audience to whom we preach.

FEAR VS. NATURAL STORYTELLING

So far, we've tiptoed around the subject of you being a natural storyteller. I've hinted at it numerous times. But maybe it's time to address the elephant in the room. Some of you have been convinced from before you opened this book that you really aren't a good storyteller. Maybe you purchased this book in order to help you understand how to become a better narrative preacher. But I have a slightly different question, one that is broader than the one you may be asking. My question is this: are we all really storytellers? More precisely, are you a natural storyteller? It's obvious I think you are but, let me make my case in full.

As human beings we think in story, learn in story, create realities and truths through stories, and define ourselves by the stories we tell. It would seem that telling stories should be the easiest thing for a human being to do. It is, after all, natural and normal to communicate through stories. We do it all the time. Theorists and philosophers alike have argued that we are created this way, that story is the natural way in which we process information.[10] But what prevents us from exploring this in the pulpit is fear. Fear of failure, experience, examples, and the naked fear of speaking to others in an unfamiliar way from the pulpit.

Everyone has experienced the fear of public speaking in one way or another. The sweats, butterflies, and panic that ensues when you stand in front of an audience is one of, if not the greatest fear human beings face. Ask any standup comedian what it feels like to stand in front of strangers and all you have is one story after another after another. You have to make the audience laugh, cry, smile, applaud, and relate in some way to the things you tell. It's hard . . . it's very hard. When I teach students or pastors about narrative preaching and they come to the insight that this is hard to do, that it takes extra time and preparation, I am always reminded of the deep and insightful words of Tom Hanks in *A League of Their Own* when he tells his star player who is about to quit the game of baseball, "It's supposed to be hard. If it wasn't hard, everyone would do it. The hard is what makes it great." Don't let the fear of something new or something out of your comfort zone prevent you from exploring the wonderful world of narrative.

When I finally shared my Old Testament story with Dr. Schmit's preaching classes, Clay was so enamored with the story that he has asked me to share it not just once but on numerous occasions, everywhere from a gathering of homileticians in Tanzania to a meeting of the Academy of Homiletics in Minneapolis.[11] The narrative story I shared that day

---

10. Philosophers such as Immanuel Kant, David Hume, and Samuel Taylor Coleridge all explored the concept of imagination as the basis for all learning. Together they all agreed that our ability to imagine words and concepts formed the foundation for all learning. In essence they were affirming the idea presented here that we are all-natural born storytellers who imagine conversations rather than just hear them. Their seminal works would be: Kant, *Critique of Pure Reason*; Hume, *Treatise of Human Nature*; Coleridge and Shawcross, *Biographia Literaria*.

11. Clay gave me an opportunity to share *Elijah, the Man from No Where* narrative at the Academy of Homiletics in front of colleagues and peers from all over the nation. It was so well received that I later got an interview at Princeton Seminary, in part, because the dean remembered me sharing that narrative years earlier. It is safe to say

about Elijah and his prophetic calling taught me a lot about storytelling. It taught me how important a good opening is, how important a solid, repetitive theme line is, and it taught me afresh and anew how a powerful story told with fresh eyes and heard with fresh ears can transform an encounter with Scripture and place everyone in the very midst of the biblical narrative. Realizing how powerful stories from the Bible can be, it reinforced in me the admonition to "just tell the story" because the story is powerful in itself.[12] It is that revelation about the power of story that allowed me to overcome my reticence and fear about narrative preaching and set out on a path of storytelling in preaching. And as I've watched my students over the years, it's the same leap of faith that they have to take in order to enter the narrative world. All I can tell you is that I find an unexplored freedom and joy in narrative that is worth the journey. I encourage you to find that same strength to begin your own journey into narrative.

THE TRUSTING STORYTELLER

Another significant experience took place when I was about halfway through my PhD and found myself at yet another Academy of Homiletics conference. As a third-year grad student I was a part of the background, an amateur member of a professional guild. No one knew me and I had no real network to rely on for help. But I was an older student and if my years of being a senior pastor had taught me anything it was that you made your own connections and you had to build your own network. And so, at a reception during the annual meeting, I decided to have an intentionally accidental meeting with one of the leading members of the Academy.[13]

At the time, Tom Troeger was a professor of preaching at Yale Divinity School and a very prominent member of the Academy. Tom had hosted a reading group earlier in the day dealing with issues related to

---

that without that narrative and Clay's unwavering support of my narrative approach to preaching, the arc of my seminary career would have been quite different.

12. While I always think stories can lose something by being written down (at least my stories) I have included this story in the second half of this book, chapter 8. It is entitled, "The Journey from Tishbe: Elijah the Man from Nowhere."

13. The Academy is a guild of preaching professors that meet yearly to share understandings, encourage good homiletical pedagogy and create networks of friends and colleagues for collaboration and the development of quality preaching.

Imagination in Preaching. While I was unable to attend the discussion group, I was interested in talking to him about one of the papers they had discussed at that meeting. The paper was intriguing to me because my dissertation was going to deal with issues of creativity, originality, novelty, as well as imagination in preaching. The paper I wanted to discuss was one of the most imaginative and creative papers I had ever read at the Academy. I saw Professor Troeger go up to the makeshift bar to obtain a refill on his glass of wine and decided I needed one too (even though I don't drink!). I greeted Professor Troeger and he noticed my nametag and greeted me by name. He was looking for the right wine and I was looking for the right introduction to a conversation. I inquired about the paper his group had discussed that day and we were off and running.

The paper was by Alexander Deeg, a German homiletician and international member of the Academy. He had submitted a fascinating paper on "Imagination and Meticulousness" in preaching.[14] I began a discussion on the paper with Professor Troeger and he responded by asking me some questions about the issues covered in the document. He quickly realized that, regardless of who I was (a mere student at the time and not a professor), I appeared to have a deeper grasp of the issues surrounding creativity and imagination than most. From that "chance" encounter would come an invitation from him to come and spend a week with he and his wife in Connecticut where I could devote time to attending preaching classes, chapels, the library, and conversations with him. It was an invitation that would help forge my academic life and my understanding of the rich, deep connection between imagination, creativity, and my growing understanding of narrative. It was an important step in my journey into narrative preaching. During our evening conversations in front of the fire Tom warned me that doing this kind of preaching and using this particular matrix for sermon preparation and practice would be dangerous. Not everyone would be encouraging of my approach. In the circles I ran in it would be viewed with a particular kind of skepticism. I understood what he meant but am eternally grateful for his encouragement and rich hospitality.

That "chance" encounter would reinforce within me that it was not just precarious to be a storyteller in the pulpit but that it even requires risk to take the journey toward narrative. What risk, you may ask? I had to risk sharing my own understandings about narrative; I had to risk

---

14. Deeg, "Imagination and Meticulousness."

revealing how much I hadn't yet worked out about creativity, originality, and novelty with two mentors who had a greater grasp and more experience with these subjects than I did; I had to risk falling on my face in front of respected mentors in order to get from where I was to where I needed to be. Like telling the story of *Elijah the Man from No Where* I had to stand in front of students, professors and even the Academy of Homiletics and offer my thinking in the marketplace of ideas. What I learned in the end was that all my mentors, even ones who were committed to a three-point, deductive style, encouraged me to follow this scholarship. I discovered that my colleagues in the Academy responded better than any audience I have ever spoken in front of and their response, both corporate and personal, gave me hope. And since that time, my students at Princeton and Asbury have given wonderful affirmations and insights that helped embolden me in my pursuit of narrative. In the process they helped change my life. I learned all over again the old adage, "Without risk there is no reward."

I often remind my students who are venturing into the world of narrative or attempting their very first narrative sermon; or who are taking on the task of trying a sermon in a third-person structure; or, even more out of the box, preaching as a first-person character in the biblical story; or those who dare to preach a sermon for the very first time in a mode other than the deductive model we all know; I tell them that I understand the risk they are taking. I pray that this testimony of my own story convinces them that I really do understand. All of us who have made the move to narrative have known that fear and understand what it is like to make the leap. Like most things in life, doing something new can be scary, but it can also change your life forever. That's what the journey into narrative did for me. And I am writing this book out of a conviction that it can change your preaching as well. I believe that. I really do.

NARRATIVE HISTORY

The next major step for me came after graduating from Fuller and spending time as a Post-Doctoral Teaching Fellow at Princeton Theological Seminary. It was at Princeton that I was called upon to develop and teach a course on Narrative Preaching. That was a new task for me. Although I had preached narratively and done work at Fuller and in the pulpit in storytelling, I had never taught a course on the subject. I was allowed the opportunity to put my theories into a syllabus and teach them in a classroom of outstanding students. The reaction of those students to the principles I am sharing here was one of the most helpful and encouraging events of my life. Their reinforcement enabled me to see not just how these principles would stand up to academic rigor, but I saw how they helped transform the thinking and preaching of these developing preachers.

After my two-year post-doctoral fellowship was finished, I was called to a tenure track position at Asbury Seminary in Orlando (a post I have held for a decade and continue to gratefully serve the needs of my students). A few years into my tenure I was asked by our library technology person, Wes Custer, to be the guest speaker/presenter at a Library Association meeting he was hosting at the seminary for some Christian schools. Wes had done so much to help and support my teaching and chapel ministry at the seminary that there was no way to say no, so I readily agreed. But what do you teach to an eclectic group of librarians?

For whatever reason, my thoughts returned to that paper by Alexander Deeg. I really hadn't done much with that since I was at Fuller, so I decided to explore with them the issues related to Haggadah and Halakah that Deeg had written about in his paper. It ended up a fascinating and insightful discussion. It all began with an exploration of Psalm 137 and the context of going into Exile:

By the rivers of Babylon,
There we [captives] sat down and wept,
When we remembered Zion [the city God imprinted on our hearts].
On the willow trees in the midst of Babylon
We hung our harps.

For there they who took us captive demanded of us a song with words,
And our tormentors [who made a mockery of us demanded] amusement, saying,
"Sing us one of the songs of Zion."
How can we sing the Lord's song
In a strange and foreign land?

If I forget you, O Jerusalem,
Let my right hand forget [her skill with the harp].
Let my tongue cling to the roof of my mouth
If I do not remember you,
If I do not prefer Jerusalem
Above my chief joy. (Ps 137 AMP)

After spending years exploring the issues surrounding narrative preaching, I realized that in this rather plaintive psalm about Jewish prisoners being marched into exile there were important issues related to narrative preaching. When you're on an ancient "Trail of Tears" how do you sing the songs of Zion? How do you worship your God when the holy city has been destroyed? Even more poignant, how do you worship the Lord when the temple is devastated, the land has been salted to prevent crops being grown, and the central worship idea of animal sacrifice by the priests on behalf of the people is no longer an option? As I read the story of them hanging up their instruments because they had nothing to sing and praise God about, I started to feel the anguish these Israelite captives must have felt at that moment. It was heartbreaking.

HAGGADAH VS. HALAKAH

As I delved deeper into the Psalm and the context of the Jews in Babylonian exile, I discovered that the eventual solution of the exiles was one of powerful simplicity and creative expression. With the temple sacrificial system gone they created an alternative called the synagogue. Synagogue worship gave them a place to sing the songs of Zion, pray the prayers of hope, and it introduced the enclaves in exile to the concept of the sermon as a central act of their worship experience (replacing animal sacrifice as the lynchpin of their worship rituals).

But as Deeg explained, there developed two methods of preaching in the synagogue, two approaches to the sermon. One was called Haggadah and the other Halakhah. Church historian O. C. Edwards gives a concise definition of the two:

> **Halachic/Halakhah** interpretation is an *analytical process* aimed at deriving rules and principles, stating clearly what is involved in the observance of Torah. **Haggadic/Haggadah** interpretation is freer, more creative, analogical, and *homiletic*, and involves stories and examples.[15]

As I pondered Deeg and Edwards' words I came to realize that the origins of narrative vs. expository sermon approaches could be traced to the synagogue in the exile. There the didactic, three-point, logic-based sermon followed what Deeg referred to as Halakhah principles—analysis, finding rules/principles, and turning them into points. But Deeg also

---

15. Edwards, *History of Preaching*, n22–23 (italics and bold mine).

noted that, for others, the Haggadah approach followed what we now call the narrative sermon process—creative, analogic, and story based.

As I prepared for the Library Association meeting, I realized that I had stumbled upon this origin story of the narrative sermon. The exilic Jewish worship services featured reading from the Torah and preaching from those texts as the primary focus of worship, replacing the celebration of sacrifices. That realization lit a candle in my mind as to how the sermon could be conceived and perceived as a worship element. As is true today, some exilic sermons were deductive, point driven, and followed principles derived from logic (Halakhah). But there were other synagogue sermons that concentrated on the story itself, the plot ideas contained within the narratives of the Jewish Bible, and the character studies so essential to storytelling (Haggadah). I sensed I was onto something. I couldn't help but wonder if the germination of the division between these differing sermon approaches (Halakhah vs. Haggadah or, if you prefer, expository vs. narrative) was a direct result of the new worship setting of the exile, the loss of the sacrificial system of the temple, and the struggle to find the blessing of God in captivity? If so, what implications might that have for what we understand the sermon to be today?[16]

THE SYNAGOGUE INFLUENCE

As I made this case to this small group of the Library Association, I took them on a journey to explore what I hadn't known and what they might never have considered. After explaining how the synagogue came about in captivity, I noted that the synagogue movement did not die out at the end of the exile but became a thriving enterprise during the New Testament period. I reminded them that it was most probable that Jesus was more affected by the synagogue in Nazareth than the temple in Jerusalem. So much so that when he was a 12-year-old and failed to join the caravan

---

16. The synagogue became a place to remember the Law and to receive instructions about how to live in captivity. Recovering the final instructions of Moses to the Exodus community, synagogue worship followed his admonition, "You shall read this law before them in their hearing. Assemble the people—men, women and children, and the foreigners residing in your towns—so they can listen and learn to fear the Lord your God and follow carefully all the words of this law. Their children, who do not know this law, must hear it and learn to fear the Lord your God . . ." (Deut 31:11–13). Without sacrifices and altars, the reading of the Law and the sharing of Scriptures became central to exilic worship with the sermon becoming an integral part of synagogue worship. For further information see Stott, *Between Two Worlds*, 122–23.

his parents were a part of as they left Jerusalem, when he was frantically found three days later by Mary and Joseph, they discovered him in a most interesting, unusual place for a 12-year-old and doing a most interesting and remarkable thing for a young boy from a non-priestly heritage. Jesus was in the temple engaging the elders. Amazing as this story was, I was in for an even more surprising discovery about where he was in the temple.

The text notes, "After three days they found him in the temple courts, sitting among the teachers, listening to them and asking them questions." (Luke 2:46 NIV) The first thing I noticed about this simple verse is that the scene presents an unusual posture for temple interaction with priests. There were outer courts and porches where folks would gather and do these discussions and priests might wander into these outer courts a few at a time. But it was uncommon to find a group of priests sitting around having these discussions in one of the outer courts. As a whole these gatherings of priests were restricted to meetings of the Sanhedrin or to the inner workings of the temple. I wondered where in the courts of the temple would exist such a place where a 12-year-old might engage in listening to and asking questions of the priests? This sounded more like the synagogue than the temple. It reminded me of those exilic gatherings that formed the first synagogues. What was this gathering?[17]

Further research revealed that the synagogue was not only alive in Israel during the ministry of Jesus but that it was prominently featured in Jerusalem with some 200+ synagogues in the temple city. I delved further into this research and discovered that tradition holds that one of those synagogues was in the temple itself. Could it be that the boy Jesus, reared in the synagogue in Nazareth, found himself in a familiar setting inside the temple in a synagogue gathered for discussion, Bible study, preaching, and storytelling? And could it be that his penchant for storytelling and parable yarns was fostered in these Haggadah sessions one would find only in the synagogue, even if it was in the temple?[18]

---

17. For more on the origins of the synagogue see Bacher and Dembitz, "Synagogue." Batcher and Lewis mention the fact that synagogues located in the temple arise out of halakic tradition, though the tradition does not specify where or how those synagogues operated.

18. O. C. Edwards expresses this in his chapter concerning Synagogue Sermons. He reminds us that "most scholars still think the synagogue originated during the Exile in Babylon" and I agree. However, Edwards notes that it may well be that the establishment of the synagogue was much later, during the Hellenistic period. After all, the very word synagogue is Greek rather than Babylonian or Hebrew in origin. The clear implication is that the Halakhah and Haggadah sermon approaches developed

COMMENCING YOUR JOURNEY

So, armed with an experiential reality, a biblical understanding, and a historical foundation, I embarked anew on this ongoing journey into narrative, a journey into exploring an effective way of communicating the gospel in the twenty-first century from inside the story. If modern day preachers are to avoid the scathing critique of Rev. Sydney Smith and not condemn our sermons to the ash heap of boredom, then maybe we should explore this narrative thing; this inductive concept of preaching; this storytelling-based approach to the art of homiletics; this Haggadah rather than Halakah?

What I have learned about narratives and stories is that, when they are written down, there is always more to the story that is *un*written than what *is* written. Stories exist in the words they use and in the "white space" between the words. There is always more to a story than what you first read. There is more to Moses' confronting of Pharaoh than just, "Let my people go." There is more to John the Baptist in the wilderness than just crying out, "Repent for the Kingdom of God is at hand." There is more to Jesus than just telling the woman, "Go and sin no more." The stories are in the telling and in the art of telling them and there is always more about the story that you don't know. In a narrative, Haggadah approach to Scripture God invites the reader to discover what Paul Harvey used to call, "The Rest of the Story."[19]

Let me give you one example that comes from the rabbis who loved Haggadah. In one section of the Talmud, the rabbis were commenting on Gen 22:2 where God is testing Abraham in preparation for the command to sacrifice his son. The biblical text reads, "Then God said, 'Take your son, your only son, whom you love—Isaac—and go to the region of Moriah.'" The rabbis questioned the repeated statements made by God. They wondered why God approached Abraham in this manner. They would ask, "Why does God say, 'Take your son' then add, 'your only son'

---

outside of Israel in the exile and in the Hellenistic influences that are the reality of much of the New Testament. For more of Edwards review of the history see Edwards, *History of Preaching*, 8–11. For additional understanding of the Hellenistic influence on the synagogue see Levine, *Judaism and Hellenism in Antiquity*.

19. Ong refers to this concept as "Voicing" though he chooses to use oral art forms or verbal art forms as his preferred expression. His critique is of the use of the term "oral literature" as though that could somehow express the idea of orality vs. literature. The key is that oral expressions give voicings to the story rather than the mere reading of the text. See Ong, *Orality and Literacy*.

and finally conclude with, 'whom you love'"? Only after repeating these three, seemingly redundant descriptions of Abraham's son does God add the name of the son, Isaac. Why so repetitive? Wouldn't it have been sufficient for God to say, "Take your son Isaac to Moriah"?

Sensitive to the realities of narrative voicings and storytelling principles, the rabbis suggested that rather than a monologue Genesis 22:2 is really a dialogue between God and Abraham with Abraham's responses missing. They suggested the full conversation might look like this:

> GOD: Take your son.
> ABRAHAM: Which one?
> GOD: Your only son.
> ABRAHAM: But I have two.
> GOD: Whom you love.
> ABRAHAM: But I love them both.
> GOD: Isaac.
> ABRAHAM: Ah, and where shall we go?
> GOD: Go to the region of Moriah.

There is always more to the story than meets the eye. There is always discovery that occurs as one tells a story rather than when one reads the story. Storytelling does not change the story of Abraham and his conversation with God but it does flesh out the dynamics of that story. It recognizes that a lot of the story is found in-between the lines. That is the subject of the rest of this book. That is the synopsis of why I took this journey into narrative. It is my testimony of one person's journey into narrative. But it is only the beginning. There is so much more to discover. Has this whet your appetite? Care to accompany me on your own journey into narrative? If you are intrigued then turn the page. Your journey is about to commence.

2

The Journey Intensifies

Toward a Narrative Hermeneutic

> A sermon is like music, not music in a score but in the live performance, where bar is heard after bar, theme after theme, and never all at once. A sermon is like a play, not a printed book but the action on a stage, which moves from a first act through a second to a third and the drama is not seen all at once. A sermon is like a story told aloud, where each sentence has gone forever into the past before the next is spoken.
>
> - H. Grady Davis[1]

If the Levitical priests in the synagogue helped to develop the narrative sermon through Haggadah, then what are the principles upon which a biblically authentic narrative hermeneutic should be based? Are there approaches to a narrative text that can aid in helping to develop narrative sermons? This chapter seeks to suggest some basic hermeneutical approaches that will serve the preacher who looks at a narrative text and seeks to bring understanding from the story to the sermon.

---

1. Davis, *Design for Preaching*, 168.

NARRATIVE QUALITY AND QUANTITY

The narrative quality of Scripture is unmistakable. Arguably, the Bible is the greatest storybook the world has ever known. Stories abound in Scripture from the narrative of Adam and Eve in the garden to the visions of John the Revelator about worship in heaven. Jesus at his core was a storyteller who used parables, metaphors and stories to communicate the nature of God and the fundamentals of the kingdom. In a similar way, the book of Acts sets the stage for the letters of Paul in the New Testament by detailing the stories of his adventures throughout the Mediterranean, his establishing of new churches in the region, and the events that occurred during those missionary journeys. Even in the poetic musings of the Psalms, there are stories that are rooted and grounded in the history of Israel and the narrative of David's life.[2] From start to finish, the narrative quality of the biblical revelation is filled with characters, plots, drama and spectacle. It is accurate to say that the Bible is God's Storybook.

Such statements also beg the question, "What is the narrative quantity of Scripture?" Colin Harbinson has written, "Approximately seventy-five percent of Scripture consists of narrative, fifteen percent is expressed in poetic forms and only ten percent is propositional and overtly instructional in nature." He laments that these figures seem to be reversed when it comes to preaching and that only ten percent of our modern-day approach to the pulpit comes in a narrative form. Harbinson suggests, "We have reversed the biblical pattern."[3]

In a similar way, Richard Eslinger's research has taken on the two areas where scholarship suggests that there is no real narrative quality in wisdom literature and apocalyptic writings. Eslinger writes, "Proverbs can be found, interestingly, that may either undergird or undermine specific biblical narratives."[4] While this is hardly dispositive about wisdom literature being narrative, it does suggest that there are parts of Proverbs that can be tied to a narrative event. Using Beardslee as his basis, Eslinger

---

2. The Historical Psalms are numerous where the psalmist is reviewing or celebrating some aspect of Israel's history. Psalms such as 78, 105, 106, 135, and 136 fall into the category of historical narratives while others (44, 66, 89, 107) have a more individual or personal historical reflection. There are Royal Psalms, many of which are instructive about things like the king's coronation, marriage, etc. Then you have psalms that connect more directly to the life of David as a shepherd (Ps 23) or when he was grieving as both a father and a king when his own son, Absalom, deposed him in a coup (Ps 3).

3. Harbinson, "Restoring the Arts to the Church."

4. Eslinger, *Narrative and Imagination*, 22.

further suggests that a proverb can imply a story, even if the subject is the story of God and his kingdom.[5]

The concern about apocalyptic literature being non-narrative seems even more curious. After all, the book of Revelation is highly narrative and so are major parts of Daniel, including his visions in chapters 7–12. Regardless of one's view concerning apocalyptic literature, these two books are but a small sliver of the total biblical writ and if even they produce sections and chapters that are narrative, it would seem to strengthen the case for Scripture being a majority narrative book.

If these figures are correct, and I certainly believe they are, why do preachers fight against the basic nature of the biblical story? If narrative is central to both the quality and quantity of Scripture, why is there not a greater production of "real" narrative, biblically centered preaching in our pulpits? What is it that prevents so many in the modern pulpit from delving into narrative preaching? Is it merely our historical experience that makes us overly comfortable with preaching as it was presented to us when we were growing up? Where does this hesitancy originate? Maybe we should blame Sir Isaac Newton.

THE STRUGGLE FOR CERTAINTY

Isaac Newton was the most influential physicist of his day or, for that matter, of the centuries that followed. His basic laws of motion affected everything that human beings knew about their surroundings.[6] They provided great certainty to a human race whose knowledge of how things worked or why certain reactions took place was limited. Newton's Laws were felt well beyond the scientific community and helped usher in an age of certainty or what we refer to today as "Modernity." Archimedes, the ancient Greek scientist, once penned the statement, "Give me a lever long enough and a fulcrum on which to place it, and I shall move

---

5. Beardslee, "Uses of the Proverbs in the Synoptic Gospels," 65 as found in Eslinger, *Web of Preaching*, 72–73.

6. For those who need a brief refresher, his three laws of motion are: Newton's first law of motion states that an object continues in its state of rest or of uniform motion unless compelled to change that state by an external force. It explains what we call inertia and why things move the way that they do. Newton's second law of motion states that if a net force acts on an object, it will cause an acceleration of that object. This helps explain the movement of everything from planets to billiard balls in a game of pool. Newton's third law of motion is probably the most well-known and simply states that for every action there is an equal and opposite reaction. Maybe that in itself explains the preponderance of non-narrative preaching today.

the world." Newton's Laws added certainty to Archimedes' claims. Rene Descartes, the famous mathematician, philosopher and scientist stated that we were thinking machines with his philosophical axiom, "I think, therefore I am."

As the Age of Enlightenment dawned on western civilization, the pulpits of the churches in the western world embraced this certainty principle by "elevating" preaching to the discipline of homiletics, a discipline that should be able to explain what we know and how we can know it with a kind of absolute certainty. The effect of this on the church was felt in numerous ways. The First Great Awakening under Jonathan Edwards (1730s and 1740s) was an unusual move of God. The Second Great Awakening at Cane Ridge (1801) was a divine visitation rarely seen since Acts chapter 2. These grand movements were part of the moving and mystery of God. Only God could bring about an Awakening, a revival. However, by the middle of the nineteenth century, the key to revival was no longer mysterious, it was certain and sure. Evangelist Charles Grandison Finney told believers revivals were not miracles but the result of "the right use of appropriate means."[7] Finney simply told folks to do certain steps and revival had to come. The church world, even as it celebrated the miraculous visitation of the Holy Spirit, was operating in Newton's sphere of certainty.

Preaching embraced this kind of certainty. In a Cartesian world, the influence of Plato ascended and preaching became about reliable sources of knowledge and provable ways of knowing. Narratives and stories could not compare to principles, syllogisms, and points of assurance. Preaching had to fit into modernity's quest for absolutes. Sermons became rooted and grounded in points that sounded like certitude. Preaching from Calvin to Wesley used syllogistic formulas to teach congregants that, "If God this . . . then God that . . ." The transformation from a narrative sourcing for sermons to variations of "three points and a poem" was well under way. From the scholasticism of Erasmus at the dawn of the Protestant Reformation to the proclamation of the Puritans and their plain style of preaching, value was attached to didactic models and preaching became both an art and a science—but mostly a science.[8]

---

7. Finney and Finney, *Lectures*, 7–8.

8. An excellent resource for the history of Modernity in preaching is Edwards, *History of Preaching*, 391–469. He has two chapters devoted to preaching and the "Dawn of Modernity."

The problem with preaching the certainty of modernity is that narratives present to us a different way of knowing and understanding the world around us. The challenge to preaching today is to preach truth without having to base that truth on the certainty principle that is being challenged in a postmodern era.[9] It's not that we should stop preaching certainty, but narrative preaching reminds us that the basis for our preaching must be the certainty of our faith *not* the provability of our facts. This questioning of Newton's certainty principle gives greater reliability to narratives, in general, and narrative preaching specifically. How? Because the power of story is that narratives carry with them a kind of certainty that is inherent *in* the story not in the extrapolation of principles *from* the story.

Narratives have a point of view that is granted to them from the author of the story being shared. Barbara Lundblad writes, "Thus, a parable does not simply have a point—the parable itself is the point, and its narrative quality invites the reader's participation."[10] This point of view also provides within it a framework for how to respond to the story. As a result, stories tell truths in certain ways and set up responses in a specific manner without using Newton's certainty principle, without saying that this point of view is certain. They avoid the pitfalls of the postmodern distrust of absolutes while at the same time providing a reliable framework for understanding truth.[11]

Fred Craddock championed this revolution in homiletical approach in his seminal work, *As One Without Authority*.[12] He argued in favor of sermons as discovery rather than the propositional outlining of certainties that is the feature of didactic sermons. Discovery, a key principle in the development of plot, occurs in the mind and understanding of the listener as the story unfolds. Rather than being an empty vessel into which points are poured, the listener becomes an archeologist accompanying the preacher in the discovery of wisdom found in the ancient artifacts of the biblical account. The guides for this journey of discovery are the Holy Spirit and the word of God. These guides combine to keep the centrality

---

9. See Smith, *Desiring the Kingdom*.

10. Lundblad, "Narrative Theory," 203.

11. I am indebted to the work of Gregory Currie on the *Philosophy of Stories* for these insights. While his work is based in the world of literary criticism, he has much to say to us about how to use the storybook nature of Scripture. See Currie, *Narratives and Narrators*.

12. Craddock, *As One Without Authority*.

of the story in focus as the preacher and listener explore a world that is vastly different than their own. At the same time, narrative stories are able to reflect on the world and culture in which both the preacher and listener dwell.

APPROACHING A NARRATIVE EXEGETICALLY

What constitutes a narrative approach to a text? While there are numerous thoughts and approaches to narrative, the question here is "What might constitute a narrative hermeneutic?" The following methods are designed to give preachers and students of the Word a series of approaches that can supplement the basic exegetical process used by most preachers and serious exegetes of Scripture.[13] While the list is extensive, it is by no means exhaustive. Preachers should feel free to add to this list as their experience and insights into narrative grow over time.

WHAT NARRATIVES ARE ABOUT

Narratives are about real people doing real things in real situations . . . even if they are not. When Jesus tells the parable of the prodigal son, Enlightenment preachers look to cobble together truths and principles because they know that this is a story, a parable Jesus made up. Narrative preachers have a different approach. Even if they don't know the name of the prodigal, the place where he lived or the land where he went and lost his inheritance, the story is still real. It represents what happens in a real family when there is conflict and trouble over roles, rights, and responsibilities. I once had a seminary professor who speculated that the story of the good Samaritan was so powerful and vivid because it really happened to Jesus. He proposed that Jesus was the man in the ditch and that the events were more autobiographical than they might appear on the surface. I don't know if that is exegetically defensible, but it is narratively possible. As mentioned above, authors have perspectives for the stories they tell—even Jesus. Regardless, a narrative hermeneutic

---

13. If the reader is in need of knowing what kind of basic steps are needed for a truly exegetical process of understanding a text, there is none better than Long, *Witness of Preaching*, 69–116. Other books that can provide a strong exegetical framework are Broadus and Weatherspoon, *On the Preparation and Delivery of Sermons*; Demaray, *Introduction to Homiletics*; Massey and Thompson, *Designing the Sermon*; Wilson, *Practice of Preaching*.

approach a parable as a real story that represents real situations and real people because *narratives are about real people doing real things in real situations . . . even if they are not.*

I once had a student respond to a lecture I did about how exegesis creates a homiletical perspective from which to view the text with a rather pointed question. My example included some exegesis concerning historical, political, and cultural background relating to the Jews enslaved in Egypt based on Exod 1:1–14. After I described the background of the text his question was, "But what if I don't believe in the historicity of Exodus?" Well, the next 20 minutes of class was taken up as the students began a lively discussion about their various views of the historical reliability of the Old Testament. After class, I discussed the question with some of the teaching assistants who were PhD students in preaching. One responded, "Well, you still have to preach the text as text." I pondered that for some time. My initial response to the student's question had been to tell him that if all you preach is what you don't believe then you really don't have anything to say. People come to church to hear a word from God, a word of hope and help. Preaching your doubts and proclaiming your intellectual negatives will not help your parishioners find hope for their lives and situations. But was that the best answer?

The idea of "preaching the text as text" had some resonance with me. While I choose to believe the historicity of Exodus, the idea of preaching text as text made more and more sense to me when it came to other stories in Scripture. For instance, in the parables of Jesus, the question is not whether Jesus ended up in a ditch and was rescued by a Samaritan, but that such a story has a purpose and a point of view in the mind of Jesus. Not only is Jesus trying to answer the question, "Who is my neighbor?" to the satisfaction of a teacher of the Law, but he is trying to frame a story that can carry the weight of the truth he seeks to impart. Without explaining the story's meaning, Jesus conveys the reality that if a hated Samaritan can act more neighborly than a temple priest or Levitical official, what might that say about the meaning of who really is my neighbor? As a result, the parable is still a narrative about real people doing real things in real situations . . . even if the parable is *just* a story.

This reality about stories is one of the most significant actualities about narratives. Stories have strength in them that is able to carry the weight of truth and certainty without the baggage of empirical claims of absolutism. In the same way that actors, readers, authors, and movie watchers know that there is no such person as the wizard Gandalf, the troublemaking Huck Finn, or the dashing Rhett Butler, they also know that what each of them presents and represents is true. Whether it's Gandalf's moral and ethical clarity or Huck's youthful exuberance or Butler's larger than life personality, we all know people who have those qualities. In many ways, we come to see them in ourselves or in our congregants as we prepare and preach the Word. The concept of "real" becomes more illusory than we first think and we begin to see reality in narratives beyond what lies flat on the page. That is why narratives are about real people doing real things in real situations . . . even if they are not.

Undoubtedly there are those who will claim I am advocating that the Bible is not true or that it is not historically accurate. Far from it! Instead, I am suggesting that the issue of truth is in the story not in the historicity argument. Children of Newtonian certainty and Enlightenment surety will struggle with this, but it remains the guiding principle of narratives in the Bible. Biblical stories are strong enough to carry the heavy weight of truth without trying to manifest that truth in a propositional claim that reduces the size, weight, and impact of the story. That's why stories are true. That's why narratives are about real people doing real things in real situations . . . even if they are not.

WHERE NARRATIVES BEGIN

While the issue of studying a text in context is a tried-and-true principle, it must be noted that narratives stretch that axiom more than other types of texts. The truth is that narratives don't start at the beginning of the story. This comes on the heels of what narratives are about. If stories carry the weight of divine truth, then the discovery of that truth requires a greater understanding of the contextualization than the immediate narrative on the page. Most preachers delivering a propositional sermon on a narrative text provide only minimal background on the text surmising that they must concentrate on the text rather than the context. Stories, however, don't act like that. They force the preacher to deal with the origins, ancestries, and roots of people, places, culture, geography, and events. Context is more than just what precedes and follows a narrative. Context is the very heart of a story because every story has a backstory that informs and affects the events of the narrative text.

What the student with the Exodus issue struggled to grasp was that the story of Moses and the exodus has a real backstory and that story has its roots in the political and social realities of a xenophobic Egyptian culture. The statement that a new king had come to power that did not "know" Joseph is a very pregnant statement. It speaks not of "knowing" in the sense of Joseph being an acquaintance or of the new pharaoh understanding Joseph's contributions and influence but in the perceiving of him and the Jews in ways other than how previous pharaohs viewed him. It has its roots in the idea of a new king, which was more than just the old king dying and his son taking his place. It has to do with the changes of houses in Egypt and the rejection of all things non-Egyptian. It has to do with the old pharaoh being of the Hyksosian dynasty that ruled Egypt for generations but were originally from Canaan rather than being from pure Egyptian blood. It has to do with the overthrow of a ruling house in a xenophobic coup that decried the need for hyper nationalism and led to Jewish enslavement rather than political favor. It has to do with Joseph and his family. Exodus begins in Genesis because narratives don't start at the beginning of the story.

The Last Supper does not begin with the meal any more than it ends when they leave the upper room. The conversion of Saul may have happened on the Damascus Road, but it began with the stoning of Stephen and was fueled by what it meant to be brought up and trained as a Pharisee. The truth is that these realities are not ancillary to the stories but central to them. That's why context should not be referred to as background but should be viewed as discovering where the story really begins. Like a river that begins high on a mountain and slowly builds speed and power as it flows down the mountain, stories gain gravitas and significance when they are connected to their own beginnings. That is why narrative preachers know that narratives don't start at the beginning of the story.

WHAT NARRATIVES SAY

One of the struggles preachers have with narrative is this foundational concept that narratives are more than what is written. While this should seem obvious to anyone who has read a novel and imagined the story in their "mind's eye," it is a difficult premise for some to embrace when it comes to Scripture. Preachers in the certainty mode are quick to offer concerns and cautions that such a viewpoint will bring harm to the Scriptures by reducing their divinely held authority. They often jump to the admonition of John at the end of Revelation:

> I warn everyone who hears the words of the prophecy of this scroll: If anyone adds anything to them, God will add to that person the plagues described in this scroll. And if anyone takes words away from this scroll of prophecy, God will take away from that person any share in the tree of life and in the Holy City, which are described in this scroll. (Rev 22:18–19)

While the warning is true and sobering and should be heeded by all preachers, it is also true that one can argue that this caution does not relate to what narratives say. Let me explain why . . . but to do that we have to sojourn into the world of what is called "Performance Theory in Preaching."

Performance Theory in Preaching

Performance Theory suggests that both a sermon and a text are only brought to completion when they are "performed," by which I mean preached or read. Charles Bartow describes scriptural texts and sermons as "arrested performances" that only come to life in proclamation.[14] Performance Theory suggests that speaking the Word aloud allows the one speaking to give voice to the whole text and not just the words printed on the page. In a highly charged passage such as David and Goliath, the words of both characters are emotionally spoken. When Goliath first encounters the boy David, he expresses an emotion akin to disgust. The text says, "Am I a dog, that you come at me with sticks?" (1 Sam 17:44). But the verses surrounding Goliath's reaction help us to understand more about that statement than just the words. Goliath despises the Israelite army, King Saul, and the scrawny child David and curses the boy. Any reading of that text must include the concepts of disgust and cursing that Goliath feels and is attempting to express when he calls the future king "a dog."

In Performance Theory the way one expresses words is as crucial as the words themselves. Expression in reading is the way in which the lector interprets the meaning of the story for the listener. It is not enough to say that Goliath is disgusted or that he feels disdain towards the young boy, it must be portrayed in the reading. Why? Simply put, it is because narratives are more than what is written. They are filled with emotions,

---

14. Bartow, *God's Human Speech*, 53–94.

feelings, gradations of expression and intent, sarcasm, irony, spite, and empathy. Readers and preachers of texts should be well versed in vocality, tonal qualities, pitch, emphasis, pace, use of inflection, volume and other speech qualities that help express what the text is really saying. To know a text in its exegetical sense is give expression not just to what the words may mean but also to what the words express.[15]

Thomas Boomershine suggests that the writers of the Gospels were not composing words but sounds. "They assumed that persons who read their writings would read them aloud."[16] Preaching and Scripture reading are oral/aural arts that cannot be limited to words on a page (literature) as the only medium of true expression.[17] It's hard to imagine God saying, "Let there be light" in a monotone and unemotional manner in the same way that Jesus could not have uttered, "It is finished" without having a tinge of victory and a dash of anguish in his tone. How did Nathan say, "You are the man," when he confronted the adultery of King David? What was the tone of Job as he cried out to God concerning his own suffering and God's inaction? The way these statements are expressed is more than theatrics or rhetorical flair but offers an essential key in bringing meaning to life.[18] The real challenge of Scripture reading is to bring sense to sound, to bring meaning to expression. As Boomershine suggests, we hear stories because they are communicated in sounds that help us recreate the story in our own mind. That is part of the reason that narratives are more than what is written. There is a narrative sound to Scripture that is as important to its meaning as the literate words are, especially when considering the tonal qualities that accompany the public reading of stories.

---

15. While there are many texts concerning these qualities, one that combines the issues of Performance Theory, preaching and creativity would be Childers, *Performing the Word*, 57–77. Others that are helpful are Jacks, *Getting the Word Across*; Rang and Lee, *How to Read the Bible Aloud*; Ward, *Speaking of the Holy*.

16. Boomershine, *Story Journey*, 41.

17. For the concept of preaching as an oral/aural art, see Bartow, *God's Human Speech*, 9–24. Also, for a discussion of the differences between literacy and orality see Ong, *Orality and Literacy*.

18. Richard Ward expresses it this way: "These connotations suggest that performance describes a coalescence of thought and enactment within a communicative event that is charged with liveliness and engagement. This would situate performance at the very heart of human interaction, since thought is not fully realized until it is embodied and enacted through expression." Ward, "Performing the Manuscript," 237.

While these concepts are true for any text or reading, it is fair to say that they are even more crucial in narratives because of all the *unspoken* things that take place in stories. One of the reasons that stage plays and movies are so popular and effective is that directors, playwrights, screenwriters and actors all know that the eye catches more than the ear. We often determine mood and intent by facial expression rather than just verbal expression.[19] Authors write narratives based on what they see not just on what the listener hears. A narrative is often an event that took place in the past that is then written down afterward. As such, the author is "seeing and hearing" the narrative even while they are "writing" the story. It is fair to say that the author sees and hears more than they can put down on paper. To communicate the fullness of a narrative text, it is incumbent upon the preacher/lector to share as much of what the author sees and hears as possible. This is the heart of what we talked about in haggadah in chapter 1. The rabbis saw and heard the voice of God and the movement of divine agency in the stories of the patriarchs and in the history of Israel. In their minds and hearts, everything was in the story because narratives are more than what is written.

To understand a narrative in its fullness the lector/preacher must not only hear the story, but they must experience and envision the story. They have to give weight to what the text is really saying and not just to what the words are on the page. Bartow speaks of this concept as "turning ink into blood" and it is a vital component of narrative expression.[20] The ink on the page must be returned to the flesh and blood sensibilities that inspired the narrative in the first place. It is this concept that is at the heart of storytelling. Storytelling itself allows for the preacher to indwell the text and to come to an understanding of it.[21]

One of the best definitions concerning performance theory comes from Richard Ward when he parses the etymology of the world performance. "Derived from the Old French *par* and *fournir*, performance literally means, 'to perfect' or to 'carry through to completion.'"[22] When

---

19. Childers quotes the well known instruction of speech communication theorist Albert Mehrabian that 55 percent of all the meaning derived from a face-to-face setting is communicated by the body (lips, face, brow, eyes, gestures, posture, etc.) while only 38 percent comes through the tone of the voice. Even less, 7 percent, is attributed to the words that are spoken. See Childers, *Performing the Word*, 57.

20. Bartow, *God's Human Speech*, 53.

21. Bartow, *God's Human Speech*, 4.

22. Ward, "Performing the Manuscript," 237.

preaching in a narrative vein, the preacher is charged with carrying through to completion the story related in the biblical text. One of the primary ways to understand a completed performance is to embrace the truth that narratives are more than what is written.

WHAT NARRATIVES SEE

In the preaching event, preachers experience the story differently than the listener. Preachers must remember that narratives are panoramic rather than episodic. To the listener, the narrative is episodic, unfolding and plot based. While the preacher knows this is how narratives are received, they must also be aware that the view from the pulpit of a passage is panoramic, fully revealed rather than episodic, partially exposed. The preacher must remember that they see the whole picture, whereas the listener sees only the unfolding story. This is crucial for understanding the nature of the narrative you are preaching. Joel Green writes,

> To speak of "the narrative of Scripture" is to make a theological claim that takes us beyond the warrants of any one of the books comprising the Bible, or even what might be strictly authorized by one or another of the Bible's Testaments. It is to insist that the whole of the Bible is, in Christian engagement, more than the sum of the parts, and that we can and should account for a theological presumption behind and woven into this collection of books.[23]

One age-old adage for preachers is that their sermon preparation should "always keep the end in mind." That is good advice not just for sermon preparation but also for a narrative hermeneutic. One primary advantage of having exegeted the text is that you begin to formulate a panoramic view of the text. You see how it begins, how it ends, how the plot twists and how the characters react. You see beyond the episodic moment of the text and see how it leads to other moments, issues, relationships, tragedies, victories, and the revelation of God's handiwork. As a result, narrative preachers begin to understand that narratives are wholes, not mere holes filled in by stories. Preachers in the narrative vein experience the whole story rather than merely investigating a single serialized moment.

---

23. Green and Pasquarello, *Narrative Reading, Narrative Preaching*, 28.

At the seminary where I teach, students are required to take a class entitled, "Biblical Narrative." The thrust of the class is to enable the students to see the Bible as a whole story and not just separate books unrelated to the overall purpose of God. Rather than view the Old Testament as thirty-nine different books by multiple authors or the New Testament as twenty-seven separate writings divided into history, epistles, and apocalyptic literature, the course encourages students to see the Bible as a whole, as an extended story that furthers the redeeming work God began in Genesis. This is crucial for good exegesis of texts. Texts have an antecedent as well as an immediate context. Texts have an impact on the future not just the present. Narratives, therefore, don't start and stop as much as they ebb and flow. Even when the Gospels suddenly move from one scene to another, they are not leaving the intended story. The next scene furthers the narrative toward its ultimate end, which is to tell the story of God and his redemptive work in the world. Aristotle was the first to explain this natural structure and focus of narratives.

> Now a whole is that which has a beginning, middle, and end. A beginning is that which is not itself necessarily after anything else, and which has naturally something else after it; an end is that which is naturally after something itself, either as its necessary or usual consequent, and with nothing else after it; and a middle, that which is by nature after one thing and has also another after it. A well-constructed Plot, therefore, cannot either begin or end at any point one likes; beginning and ending in it must be of the forms just described.[24]

Therefore, when a biblical narrative moves from one episode to another, it is the responsibility of the narrative preacher to know and understand how the *whole* story (beginning, middle and end) relates to itself and that the preacher does not sacrifice the greater story by getting stuck in a single rabbit hole. Even if you concentrate on only one scene in a narrative, you must still know the whole and not just the hole you are concentrating upon. After all, narratives are panoramic rather than episodic.

When the author of First Samuel wrote the story of David and Goliath, it was imperative that the reader realize that he wrote the whole story and that it has a precedent and an antecedent. The precedent is that David does not appear on the scene in some divinely miraculous, incarnational

---

24. Aristotle, *Rhetoric and the Poetics of Aristotle* 1450b 26 (p. 233).

way. David has been introduced to the readers of the story already and he has been anointed to become the king of Israel. It is David's right and responsibility to be at the battle and face the giant, especially if the present king (Saul) will not.

The author also wants us to realize that King Saul has been cowering in fear of Goliath for more than a month. Daily the giant has challenged the Jewish troops and neither Saul nor his fellow soldiers show any gumption to face Goliath. The author also tells the narrative in such a way that the readers have already seen this fatal flaw in King Saul. His cowardice should come as no surprise to anyone who knows the whole story. After all, when they went to crown him king, they found Saul hiding amidst the luggage (1 Sam 10:21–22). This foreshadowing allows the reader of the whole story to prepare their listening audience for what is about to happen and why God brings the boy-king-in-waiting to the battlefield in the first place.

In the same way Goliath is not merely a physical giant but the manifestation of the ongoing struggle and conflict that has plagued Israel ever since they first conquered the promised land. The call to face Philistine aggression is not new—it has happened throughout the book of Judges. The establishment of a monarchy sought by the Israelites during the weak tribal confederation of the Judges is supposed to solve this problem. But the same misunderstanding persists despite the miraculous interventions that God orchestrates throughout the Judges' rule. The lesson? God is the one who fights and wins battles. It is not armies or military might that will determine the outcome of the battle but the will and intervention of the God of Israel. Over and over again God determined, from Joshua to Gideon to Deborah to Samuel, that it is not by power nor might, but by God's will that Israel would achieve victory.

Everyone in the story seems to have forgotten that lesson except the boy who challenges Goliath. While this grants to David a great advantage, it is equally true that David's greatest advantage is that he knows God's will is found in wholes not holes. David knows the narrative, the longer and more complicated story of God's will for his life. He knows he will not die at Goliath's hand, for God has told him he will be King of Israel. Whatever that may mean or however it may happen, David knows that a giant warrior in the Valley of Elah will not derail God from accomplishing his will. In the same way, this is the advantage narrative preachers have because they always see the whole story and not just the hole. Narrative preachers know this powerful truth that narratives are panoramic rather than episodic, they are about wholes not holes.

WHAT NARRATIVES DO

Finally, narratives are about disruptions and those disruptions hold the meaning. Screenwriter Syd Field has stated what dramatists, playwrights, storytellers, and authors have all known since the days of Aristotle. "All drama is about conflict. Without conflict there is no action; without action there is no character; without character there is no story. And without story there is no screenplay."[25] Conflict is at the very heart of a good story. Jesus knows this all too well. That's why his famous stories are all about conflict: The prodigal son (conflict over inheritance and freedom); the good Samaritan (conflict brought about by reactions to the man being beaten, robbed, and left for dead); the lost sheep, the lost coin, the lost son (conflict brought about because someone or something is lost); the sower (conflict over what happens to seed in different soils); the tenants (conflict between the landowner and the tenants who refuse to pay). In each story and in all the parables the power of the parable emits from the conflict, the struggle, the confusion, the clash, the disagreement, the encounter, or the divergence of what happens there. While resolving the conflict is the ultimate point of the parables' teaching thrust, it is the disruptions brought about by dramatic encounters that makes the story relatable and interesting. Conflict provides the basis for the listener to say, "What's going on? What's about to happen next?" This is what narratives do. This is why narratives are about disruptions and those disruptions hold the meaning.

Disruptions are at the heart of narrative, because they lead to the revealing of causation. Disruptions happen for a reason and finding the roots and results of their cause is what comprises the plot. Disruptions lead to action. That is why Fields is right to say, "Without conflict there is no action." Once the conflict is revealed, the plot follows the action. For Aristotle, plot is king. "We maintain, therefore, that the first essential, the life and soul, so to speak, of Tragedy is the Plot . . . "[26] The plot of a narrative is found in the disruption of the story and the causation for that disruption.

---

25. Field, *Four Screenplays*, xvii.
26. Aristotle, *Rhetoric and the Poetics of Aristotle* 1450a 39 (p. 232).

The following drawing (referred to as Freytag's Pyramid) shows how you can diagram Aristotle's concept of plot.[27] The exposition is merely the setup or prelude to the narrative. The exposition can be as simple as what Jesus does in the parable of the prodigal son (A man had two sons and the younger one came and said, "Give me my inheritance") or as complicated as the beginning of John's Gospel (the whole of John 1 is designed as the set up for who Jesus is and what he has been sent to do). According to Freytag's Pyramid, the plot springs into full action once the inciting incident occurs (i.e., once the disruption/conflict occurs). The actions that take place (rising, climax and falling) all follow after the disruption in the

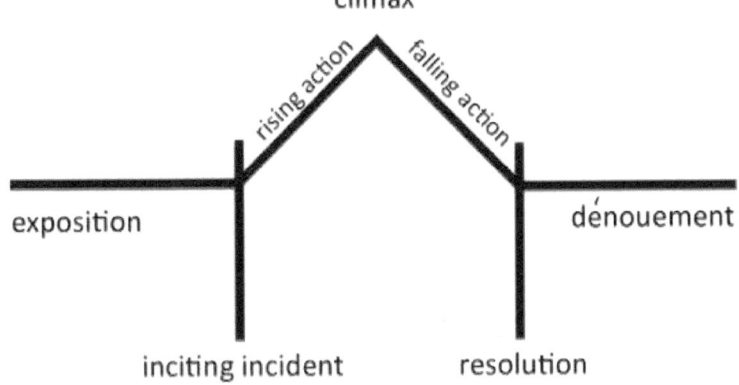

flow of the story. Actions are often reactions to the inciting incident. For instance, once Jesus interrupts the Passover meal by washing the feet of the disciples, everything in the story becomes a reaction to this unusual and powerful symbolic action. Peter doesn't believe Jesus should kneel and humble himself in this manner; Judas is confronted about selling out Jesus to the Pharisees; all the disciples are made to feel uncomfortable and ashamed so they cry out, "Is it I?" The meaning of the story is a result of the disruption at a very standard, liturgical meal. The power of foot washing is in the disruption of the traditional liturgy of the Passover meal. Conflict and the reaction to it are powerful components of any narrative because narratives are about disruptions and those disruptions hold the meaning.

Homiletically, this view of narrative can be seen in the work of Eugene Lowry. When Lowry proposed the sermon structure that has come

---

27. Gustav Freytag bases this diagram upon an analysis of Aristotle's Poetics and his understanding of how Aristotle views Plot. See Freytag and MacEwan, *Freytag's Technique of the Drama*.

to be known as the Lowry Loop, he helped many a preacher realize that disruptions are key to narratives. His first movement in the Loop is titled, *Upsetting the Equilibrium*. Lowry's students came to refer to this as the "Oops!" The whole premise of the Loop is based on finding a disruption in the text, something that makes you go, "Hmmm?" His other way of describing this experience is to refer to it as an "itch." What Lowry knows is that all drama is based on conflict. Something goes wrong, there is causation, there is intrigue and suspicion, unfolding of a plot and a final resolution of the narrative—the itch is scratched and, in Lowry's terms, the Oops is turned into an Aha![28]

Even Lowry's second movement, referred to as *Analyzing the Discrepancy*, capitalizes on the importance of disruptions. In the Loop it is not enough to point out the problem—you have to complicate it further. To do this, you follow the hurdles in the plot of the story. As the plot is disrupted and conflict ensues, the outcome of the narrative is held in doubt. Tension rises until a key to resolution is found in the text. But the emotion of the event is not completed just because the key is revealed. In both Freytag's Pyramid and Lowry's Loop, the climax is not the completion of the story. The tension rises and falls, but it only dissipates as the plot runs headlong to its ultimate conclusion and resolution. The disruption is not a scene in the story, but it is the controlling factor throughout the entire narrative. Screenwriter Michael Tierno puts it succinctly, "Plot is soul."[29] This is why narratives are about disruptions and those disruptions hold the meaning all through the plot.

One day I was discussing the Lowry Loop with my mentor and friend Clay Schmit. We had both taught a class where students had to preach a Lowry Loop structured sermon. While I was convinced that the key to successfully producing a Lowry Loop sermon was found in the "Oops and Aha" movements, Clay was convinced that the real secret was in how well the preacher could complicate the problem by continuing to analyze the discrepancy (what is called the "Ugh").[30] As the years have unfolded and I've gained more experience with the Loop and heard more

---

28. Lowry, *Homiletical Plot*, 19.

29. Tierno, *Aristotle for Screenwriters*, 31–32.

30. Each movement of the Loop was given shorthand titles by Lowry's students. Upsetting the Equilibrium became "Oops!" while Analyzing the Discrepancy became "Ugh!" The Key to Resolution became the "Aha!" The final two movements, Experiencing the Gospel and Anticipating the Consequences became "Whee!" and "Yeah!" A longer and more detailed analysis of the Lowry Loop is the subject of chapter 9.

student sermons, I've come to appreciate the wisdom of that insight. If I were to reimagine the way in which the Loop is taught and preached, I would urge my colleagues in the Academy and in the pulpit to produce sermons that spend more time in the first two legs of the Loop than in the latter two movements. As a timeframe goes, more than half (maybe even two-thirds) of a Lowry Loop sermon should be given over to Upsetting the Equilibrium and Analyzing the Discrepancy. The reason is simple. Narratives are about disruptions and those disruptions hold the meaning.

REVIEWING A NARRATIVE HERMENEUTIC

As mentioned in the beginning of the chapter, the hermeneutical principles proposed here might not be exhaustive but it is a place to begin. Others may find additions to this list that will help engage even more of the narrative experience. The hope is that this list can form a foundational basis to talk about what a narrative hermeneutic should entail. In this instance, I've proposed the following five principles:

1. Narratives are about real people doing real things in real situations . . . even if they are not.
2. Narratives don't start at the beginning of the story.
3. Narratives are more than what is written.
4. Narratives are panoramic rather than episodic.
5. Narratives are about disruptions and those disruptions hold the meaning.

It may be that some of these principles will seem counterintuitive to many preachers. Don't worry. Work on them anyway, for there is another foundational truth about narratives that will perk up your ears: human beings are wired for stories. Read on.

3

The Journey into the Mind

We Are Wired for Stories

> *"When you want to motivate, persuade, or be remembered, start with a story of human struggle and eventual triumph. It will capture people's hearts—by first attracting their brains."*
>
> Paul J. Zak[1]

If you are unaware, there is a powerful truth about narratives and stories that is neuroscientifically verifiable. That truth is this: our brains are wired for stories. The human brain is constructed in such a way as to form, create, share, listen to, and engage with stories. This is not an accident of nature or the evolution of how human beings think. It's how God made us, how he made our brains. He created the human brain and hard wired it for stories.

THE BIBLE AND REMEMBRANCE

The Bible is full of prompts from God for us to "remember." God desires for us to remember the Sabbath and keep it holy. God promises Noah he will remember the flood and not repeat that kind of judgment.

---

1. Zak, "Why Your Brain Loves Good Storytelling."

God called Moses to go back to Egypt and to "remember his covenant." Remembering is a function of the brain as well as an *aide-mémoire* for spiritual maturity. The Jewish community was urged to use the mind to remember their covenant with God as well as his goodness toward them. Jesus told the teachers of the Law, "Love the Lord your God with all your heart and with all your soul and with all your *mind*." Indeed, remembering the covenant and the actions of God in the past was essential to all the major festivals of the Jewish year:

- Passover—remembering Israel's deliverance from Egypt
- Unleavened Bread—remembering how God redeemed them from slavery
- Firstfruits—remembering God's bounty in the promised land
- Weeks/Pentecost—remembering the giving of the Law
- Trumpets—remembering the calling of God on the nation
- Atonement—remembering our sins and atoning for them
- Booths/Tabernacles/Ingathering—remembering the giving of the tabernacle and the struggles of the wilderness years

Memory and remembrance are constant directives in both the Old and New Testaments. The Bible reminds the Christian community to remember God's love in numerous ways: the sacrifice of Christ on the cross, God's blessings bestowed through the Holy Spirit, the resurrection of Christ from the grave, and his Second Coming. The very act of communion is designed, like these Old Testament festivals, to be a time when the participant remembers what God has done in the past so that they can celebrate what God is doing in the present.

This biblical concept is bound up in a single Hebrew word, *zakar*.[2] The simple and obvious definition of *zakar* is that it means remembrance. But a deeper dive into the etymology of the word suggests that it is properly translated as if one is remembering a physical action: *to be brought to remembrance; to be brought to mind*. The word possesses the force of causing something to be remembered. In each case, remembering is an action taken by someone or pressed upon someone by an outside entity. The Bible appears to affirm that memory (or the connections made in memory) may have a divine origin. God is the outside force that is acting

---

2. The Hebrew word is זָכַר and is found in Strong's H2142. It is a primitive root that occurs more than 230 times in the Old Testament.

upon our minds/memories to communicate his will and convert those insights into truth. God acts upon our brains and helps us to make connections in our minds between what is happening, what has happened, and what God can do, and then he brings those connections into focus. In this scenario, memory has a divinely inspired function or, at least, becomes a primary tool used by God to lead us into a deeper spiritual formation.

If memory is a divinely used neurological function, then preachers (and Christians in general) ought to understand the workings of the brain as it relates to memory. For our purposes, this concept of memory and the brain is crucial to know how narratives work, how God uses them, and how human beings perceive them. To do that, we must look at some aspects of neuroscience and the brain. You need not be a brain surgeon to follow or understand this material (Lord knows I'm not!). You will find that God has created our minds in such a way that your brain and mine are wired for stories.

THE NEUROBIOLOGY OF STORYTELLING

In 2014, neuroeconomist Paul J. Zak reported the results of research he compiled concerning narratives and the brain. In a laboratory experiment, Zak and his team mapped the effects on the brain of a chemical called oxytocin. Oxytocin has been referred to as the "human bonding or empathy chemical."[3] Its effects have now been linked to what motivates people to react and respond to everything from pleas for money to how we feel about James Bond saving the world from all those pesky villains. Zak describes what oxytocin does this way: "Oxytocin is produced when we are trusted or shown a kindness, and it motivates cooperation with others. It does this by enhancing the sense of empathy, our ability to experience others' emotions." What Zak describes in laboratory terms some are describing as the "neurobiology of storytelling."[4]

This neurobiology of storytelling is being examined and applied to everything from advertising toothpaste to evaluating motion pictures to the psychology of memory. What business leaders and advertising executives want to know is how our brains respond to stories they use in commercials and sales presentations. Educators are using this new area of

---

3. Weldon, "Your Brain on Story."
4. Zak, *Why Your Brain Loves Good Storytelling*, 2014.

neuroscience to try and understand how students learn and gain insight into new areas of learning. But what this neurobiology of storytelling can teach preachers is simply this: our brains are wired for story.

The Boulenger Study

Neuroscientists are discovering what preachers have known for centuries. Our brains are far more engaged by narratives and storytelling than they are by the recitation of facts. Recently, a French cognitive scientist, Véronique Boulenger of the Laboratory of Language Dynamics in France, performed studies on the brain using functional magnetic resonance imaging techniques (fMRI).[5] Her findings revealed that when a subject's brain is scanned using fMRI technology, it reacts differently to narratives than it does to facts. In her test experiment, people were given the sentence "John grasped the object" and their brain functions were monitored using the scans. Boulenger found that a subject's brain reacted to facts in a very specific, normative, and limited way. The brain perceived that the sentence was simple, basic, objective information. Each subject's mind noted what the information was and sent it to the appropriate lobe in the brain to be filed away in memory. There was nothing spectacular or unusual about how the brain reacted to the sentence. It did so in the kind of muted, matter-of-fact way the brain does millions of times each day.

However, when Boulenger and her team offered a different kind of sentence, one that painted a simple narrative like "Pablo kicked the ball," the brain suddenly reacted measurably differently to the story-nature of the sentence. The first thing researchers recorded was that the motor cortex of the brain (that part of the brain that deals with physical/motor responses) was suddenly engaged. It's not that the person involuntarily moved their legs or jumped up and began imitating the physical action of kicking the ball. Instead, the area of the brain that would normally do just that (tell the body to kick the ball) was suddenly engaged. The motor function of the brain "kicked in" as soon as someone told a "story" about Pablo's act of kicking. Boulenger concluded that the brain, upon hearing that Pablo kicked the ball, activated that part of the brain that would normally be involved only if the subject were physically doing it. The test subject had a visceral, physical reaction in their brain to the beginning of a story. Her conclusion? Narratives affect us physically as well as mentally.

5. Paul, "Your Brain on Fiction."

Secondly, Boulenger found that when the narrative was changed to Pablo hitting rather than kicking the ball or using his hand or arm in some way to affect the ball, a different part of the motor cortex became involved. Instead of the part controlling the feet, it was the part of the motor cortex that controlled the hands or arms. In other words, when you tell someone a story that involves movement (arms flailing, legs kicking, lips kissing, shoulders pushing, bodies jumping, etc.), the action in the story actually engages the listener's brain in some kind of mental movement or mental-physical action. The listener feels the ball and, in her mind, is physically acting upon it. This helps explain why music gets you to swaying in your mind and a good story puts you on the edge of your seat.

> Through these studies and others, it can be concluded that the human brain does not distinguish between reading or hearing a story and experiencing it in real life. In both cases, the same neurological regions are activated.[6]

Not only do we hear stories, we feel them; not only do we listen to storytellers, we experience their narratives as though we were there; not only do we relate to stories, we act them out in our memories and our brains. Apparently, our brains are so connected to stories that it does not distinguish between what it hears and what it experiences. Our brains connect the two. Why? It's simple. Our brains are wired for stories.

This is how we initially related to stories in the Bible. We physically and emotionally experienced the story of Jairus losing his daughter, or the woman suffering from 38 years of having continuous menstrual bleeding, or Jesus' suffering as he hangs on the cross. These stories remain powerful for preachers and listeners alike because we all feel them and experience them afresh and anew every time we hear them. We *feel* stories we hear and tell. As a result of oxytocin on the brain, stories not only move us but we are also moved by them.

The Spanish Study

In a 2006 study, Spanish researchers found that the same stimulations that stories had on motor functions in the Boulenger study were found to occur in parts of the brain that are activated by smell. Researchers used

---

6. Rush, "Science of Storytelling."

stories incorporating words that stimulated the part of the brain that is triggered by strong smells, the olfactory cortex. When the researchers used neutral words like chair or key, the olfactory regions remained unaffected. But when they introduced words that have a strong connection to the sense of smell (i.e., coffee or perfume), these words activated the olfactory cortex. The researchers found that subjects heard the word coffee then smelled the beans roasting. It seems that our brains are wired not just to experience the physical activity of a story, but they are wired to smell the smells and hear the sounds of a story.[7] Our brains are wired for stories.

This is significant not just neurologically but also narratively. Modern readers of the Scriptures forget that we live in a very sanitized world. Soaps, air fresheners, perfumes, regular bathing, fresh meats and produce, and refrigeration are all part of our lives and culture in first-world countries (and many third-world ones, too). Our experience with smell is vastly different than generations living a century or two ago, let alone a couple millennia ago. The biblical world is a world of smells and fragrances that were pungent and filled the air. Imagine worshiping at the temple with all the animal sacrifices that were done there. The temple was not a pristine place with all that blood, smoke, and burning. Large gatherings of people so common in Jerusalem, in the public ministry of Jesus, and in the gathering of armies when Israel went out to fight were full of odors and smells that signaled what kind of event was taking place. In Jerusalem there was a trash dump called Gehenna that burned day and night. The smell from that burning garbage heap is part of every story about Jerusalem in the New Testament. Part of understanding the context of stories is to remember that feeding pigs or sacrificing the fatted calf; walking for miles and miles or experiencing a famine; or being in Egypt when frogs, locusts, flies, and water turned to blood all produced an odor that made it quite distinctive and often triggered memories for each person. The Spanish Study helps us to realize that we can help modern day listeners experience ancient days by triggering memories of smells that create a distinctive interaction with the biblical context. Psychologists will tell us that smell is a powerful trigger for our memories.

---

7. Paul, "Your Brain on Fiction."

The Emory University Study

Today, researchers are looking at how things like metaphor (picture words that create images and tell a unique story in a phrase) can cause other areas of the brain to be stimulated. Recently, a team from Emory University reported that the sensory cortex is stimulated by metaphors that involve texture or touch. A metaphor such as, "The singer had a velvet voice," or "He had leathery hands," did far more to stimulate the sensory cortex of the brain than more bland or neutral phrases like, "The singer had a pleasing voice," or "He had strong hands." Apparently, stories don't just cause us to have physical reactions to actions they describe, but they cause visceral reactions even to something like metaphor that merely describes a physical object. Our brains react to action and to physical description, to smells and the memory of what something feels like.[8]

Stories affect the brain in ways we rarely imagine. Stories are powerful tools that have the ability to involve more than just memory or understanding. Narratives engage the whole person, the whole brain—not just some small portion of the mind. Does this not explain the power of preaching biblical narratives or of teaching biblical stories to children? It also helps explain the methodology of Jesus speaking in parables and stories. Jesus knows the power of a narrative and how it involves the whole person and not just a small part of her brain. Does this not help us to know, in non-neurological terms, that our brains are wired for stories?

Elizabeth Phelps Study

Not only have these studies increased our understanding of how memory involves our brains, but over the course of the last half-century those who have been studying how memory works have discovered how our brains respond to narratives. This neurological investigation of memory has discovered that different lobes of the brain interact not only with the story being shared, but they react differently with other parts of the brain. Elizabeth Phelps has researched two specific areas of the brain—the amygdala and the hippocampus. Phelps research detailed how the interaction of human emotion and memory affects the brain. When someone tells a story that produces emotion in the brain (joy, happiness, sadness, confusion, etc.), the mind also connects these emotions with similar feelings

---

8. Ludlam, "Hearing Metaphors Activates Sensory Brain Regions."

that have been experienced before by the listener. From a neurobiological view, there are two different parts of the brain, two medial temporal lobes, which begin to interface when someone is telling a story.[9] What happens when they do provide some significant insights into how our brains are wired for stories.

The first lobe that stories engage is the amygdala. The amygdala processes emotions both great and small. What Phelps learned in her research was that stories connect the amygdala (where emotions are processed) to a second lobe of the brain, the hippocampus. The hippocampus acts as a huge storage bank for the brain, a kind of internal hard drive for our memories. It not only stores memories but also controls how we retrieve them. Telling and listening to stories "fire up" both of these areas of the brain. Phelps found that storytelling bridges the gap between our emotional reactions to a stirring narrative and the memories we possess of our own stories. This is why the story of a little girl who is dying can so affect our emotions even though we don't know the person or have any specific connection to her. Fueled by the amygdala's emotional understandings, our hippocampus areas connect the little girl's plight with some memory of ours that relates to the situation. Maybe we connect it with the death of a parent or a recent run in with a little girl who was having struggles with her motor skills. However it happens, and in whatever way the hippocampus connects the present with the past in a narrative, our emotions are stirred by the power of story connected to memory.

I experienced this in 1979 after my father died of a sudden heart attack. I found myself dealing with a deep sense of grief in the days and weeks following his passing. My wife would look over at me sitting on the couch watching TV and wonder why I was crying. It was hard to explain at the time, but something in a commercial or in the plot or dialogue of a television show would trigger a memory of my dad. I could be laughing at a sitcom one moment and in tears the next. I now know that when the story being told connected with memories I retained about my father, tears would flow. The strangest part of the process was that the stories being told on the television show rarely related directly to my dad or to his death. No one else connected them to him but me. They triggered my memories and made connections no one else possessed. If something had a distinctive smell or an image connected in my mind to my dad, or if some phrase brought back memories of how my father use to speak,

---

9. Phelps, "Human Emotion and Memory," 198–202.

or if a word reminded me of a conversation my father had with someone else that I overheard and remembered, then the connection was instantaneous and powerful and it was strong enough to move me to tears.

I learned during those difficult weeks and months of mourning that we don't always hear stories as the writer, screenwriter, storyteller, or preacher intended them. When we hear stories, we feel them deep inside us, in places the storyteller cannot go. They touch off memories and connect to other lived stories the author has never experienced. I found that simple things like commercials or basic lines of dialogue in a comedy would allow me to experience grief afresh and anew not because they were funny or sad but because they connected to something in my memory that caused me to feel happiness or sadness. Our brains are built in such a way that when we hear a story, whether the function of the story intends to or not, we relate to it in instinctual ways. We do this because our brains are wired for stories.

GOLDBERG AND NOVELTY IN THE BRAIN

One of the most fascinating understandings of how the brain functions in story comes from the work of Elkhonon Goldberg.[10] A Russian neuroscientist, Goldberg was launched into this area nearly half a century ago while still a medical student at the University of Moscow. What neuroscientists had observed for decades was that traumatic brain injuries affected people in different ways depending upon which hemisphere (which side) of the brain was damaged. The prevailing thought in the neurological community was that someone with left hemisphere damage, especially to the frontal lobes of the brain, would be devastated by the injury. Goldberg notes that neurosurgeons were often reluctant to even operate on the left hemisphere of the brain for "fear of affecting language."[11]

The left hemisphere of the brain was considered the "dominant" hemisphere while the right hemisphere was not nearly as important, even being referred to in older medical texts as the "minor hemisphere." The higher functions of the brain are located in the left hemisphere: math, rational thinking, language, and those processes that enable the routine functions of everyday living. For years, neurosurgeons who operated

---

10. Goldberg, *Executive Brain*.
11. Goldberg, *Executive Brain*, 42.

primarily or exclusively on adults documented how injury or surgery on the left hemisphere would be devastating, but surgery on the right hemisphere could still allow the patient to function. As long as the damage didn't affect the left side where motor and language functions resided, the person's thinking, movement and memory abilities could be managed without a fully functioning right hemisphere.

During his student days Goldberg was increasingly drawn to the work of neurosurgeons and their understanding of brain function. Eventually, he became part of a discussion with some pediatric neurosurgeons at the Burdenko Institute of Neurosurgery. They spoke about unusual results that had been noted in brain surgery on very young children. These neurosurgeons noted that damage to the right side of the brain was particularly devastating to young children, whereas damage to the left side appeared "relatively inconsequential." This was the exact opposite of the standard understanding for adults. The curious reversal of symptoms intrigued Goldberg. What caused the difference in children and adults? Why is the problem reversed based upon the age of the patient? Does the brain function differently as a whole unit when it is young than when it is old and, if so, how? In what way? It is a puzzle that has occupied Goldberg's research and writing ever since. Eventually, he developed his findings into something called the Novelty-Routinization theory.

NOVELTY-ROUTINIZATION THEORY

Goldberg's research found that the right-left brain dichotomy assumed by neurosurgeons failed to fully comprehend the unique ways in which children learn and, by extension, the ways in which adults absorb information.[12] Goldberg realized that to young children, all learning is novel or new. It is fresh information that comes with revelation and insight into the mind of a child. As of yet, children have not developed a storehouse of memories and routines on which to depend. They must learn things from scratch, so to speak.

"Malachi, don't touch that oven, it's hot."

"Sammy, don't stand in that puddle, you'll catch your death of a cold."

---

12. As a result of Goldberg's study and other advances in neuroscience and the brain, neuroscientists no longer refer to the idea of Left Brain—Right Brain when talking about things like creativity or learning processes. As Goldberg found, it does not accurately reflect the complicated nature of how our brains function.

"Elliot, if you drop that glass it will break."

"Evie, Eliana, Mahalia, and Wesley, if you don't stop that, one of you will get hurt."

Children learn nearly everything based upon the mere novelty of the information. Adults, on the other hand, have a large storehouse of learning that they can access through memory, thereby allowing much of their learning cycle to be based upon routine rather than novelty. We know how to tie our shoes, which side of the street to drive upon, and how to sip a really hot cup of coffee. We do these things without "thinking" because we have experience of them. They are not new or novel to us. They have become routine and we do them every day. They are ours, they belong to our memories, and they are not novel or new. They are part of who we already are.[13]

This dichotomy between novelty and routine is not just the difference between being a young child or a middle-aged adult but also forms the basis of Goldberg's understanding of the brain. An adult has already learned so much information that they depend upon their storehouse of memory for just about everything. Should the left hemisphere of their brain be damaged, they cannot access the "file cabinet" of routine information that allows them to know how to drive a car or cross the street safely. However, in young children the file cabinet is largely empty. They operate not so much by routine but by novelty, imagination, and creativity. Since these functions reside in the right hemisphere, a traumatic brain injury to their left side does not rob them of routine (since they have relatively little), but an injury to the right side would prevent them from learning new and novel information, which for a child is just about everything. This is the difference between what scientists refer to as *cognitive routine* (knowing what you know) and *cognitive novelty* (learning how to do things you don't know). It helps explain why an injury to the brain hemispheres differs in its effects upon small children and grown adults.

---

13. While far more complicated than this statement, it does help us to understand why an Alzheimer's patient or an elderly woman suffering from dementia is able to recall with great accuracy what happened decades ago but cannot recall what they had for breakfast.

LEARNING AND NOVELTY

Another way of putting Goldberg's theory is to say that all learning is based upon change. When we see things differently or observe something new, that information produces a change in how we see and understand the world, a change in our routine understanding of things. While adults may tweak the information in the file cabinet of their memories and routines, children are learning whole new worlds of how things work and how to comprehend and understand what is really going on around them. Put the brakes on their ability to learn new things and you have permanently stunted their intellectual, social, and emotional growth. What children need in order to learn are novelty, creativity, and originality—they need the right side of their brain to function at peak levels. Stated another way, they need the ability to hear stories and learn from narratives.

Lisa Cron, in her aptly entitled work "Wired for Story: The Writer's Guide to Using Brain Science to Hook Readers from the Very First Sentence," makes the case that stories are more crucial to the human species than almost anything.

> Story, as it turns out, was crucial to our evolution—more so than opposable thumbs. Opposable thumbs let us hang on; story told us what to hang on to . . . Story is what makes us human, not just metaphorically but literally. Recent breakthroughs in neuroscience reveal that our brain is hardwired to respond to story; the pleasure we derive from a tale well told is nature's way of seducing us into paying attention to it.[14]

Every parent involved in raising a young child has observed Cron's point. I have seven grandchildren and I'm proud of every one of them! As young children, their parents would put *Veggie Tales* on the television and they would be enraptured. Bob the Tomato and Larry the Cucumber would enthrall Evie or Mahalia. If you put on a Curious George cartoon from Netflix, it will get an instant reaction from Wesley or Eliana. And don't even get me started on the importance of Thomas the Train to Sammy! These animated stories have the goal of teaching life lessons to the young children they are designed to reach (though my grown sons, Jonathan and Joel, know all the dialogue to *Veggie Tales* and can sing along with the songs—go figure). These educational stories are filled with facts and routines that will help children navigate their growing and

---

14. Cron, *Wired for Story*, 1. Obviously, I am also indebted to her for the title and emphasis of this chapter.

developing worlds. However, my grandchildren are not just learning facts and routines. They are learning how to navigate life by listening to a story told through the imaginative lens of a talking tomato, a happy cucumber, a curious non-verbal monkey, and a train that is constantly learning lessons. Why is it so magnetic for children to be drawn to a video, even the same one over and over? Why did I devour the latest Robert Ludlum novel or read the "Rise and Fall of the Third Reich" well into the night, far beyond when I needed to be asleep for work the next day? Because children and adults are wired for story.

LIGHTING UP THE BRAIN

Children learn in story and are educated by narrative. It lights up their brains. Eventually, information taught by videos or read in books will be transferred to the storage bins of my grandchildren's memory and included in the filing cabinets of their brains. *Veggie Tales* will become part of the routines that help them to understanding life. At some point, it will join with their left hemispheres to create a brain in which Bob and Larry will become the entryway to certain kinds of knowledge and Curious George will become the portal to routines that will govern some of their day-to-day lives. As Goldberg rightfully concludes, "Novelty and familiarity are the defining characteristics in the mental life of any creature capable of learning."[15]

What Goldberg's research into the brain teaches preachers is that stories combine both novelty and familiarity in an engaging way. If a preacher chooses to preach on the parable of the prodigal son, they can assume that most of those in attendance will have a previous connection with that very popular narrative. They may have read it in Scripture or heard it in a Bible study or sermon. Maybe they were first exposed to the prodigal son when they listened to Bob and Larry in "The Wonderful Wizard of Ha's." Regardless of how they were exposed to the story, they "know" something of it. Some more mature Christians in the crowd have had extensive interaction with the narrative of the prodigal over many years, even decades. Yet, if the narrative is told well and comes to them from the unique perspective of the preacher, it is received as something fresh and new. How can that be? Because stories light up our brains.

---

15. Goldberg, *Executive Brain*, 42.

NOVEL FRAMEWORKS OF UNDERSTANDING

Neuroscience tells us that we are comforted by the familiarity of the information from a story already stored in the brain—in the hippocampus. But as the story unfolds through the preacher, the emotions of the prodigal or the father or the elder brother are connected to something in the listener's own memory banks. As a result, a familiar story takes on a novel framework of understanding and the congregation sits there listening to the preacher tell the story as though they were hearing it for the very first time. Indeed, in many ways, it is the first time they have experienced it in quite this way. There is something satisfying about the comfort of routine combined together with the excitement and emotion of novelty. It may be because stories inform and activate both the right and left hemispheres of our brains or that they touch and connect the amygdala and the hippocampus. Either way, the brain lights up in a particular way when it is presented with the combination of familiar and original stories. Maybe that's why narrative preaching excites both newcomers to the church and the seasoned saints that have heard it all before. Or it may be that our brains are wired for story.

IMPLICATIONS OF NEUROSCIENCE ON PREACHING

With these recent advances in neuroscience affecting the way in which we understand how the brain reacts to story, it may be time for us to update some of our attitudes about stories, narratives, and our approach to sermons. I would offer several suggestions that can be implied from this neuroscientific research. These are not meant to be exhaustive but they are instructive for preachers.

Sermon Beginnings

First, as Lisa Cron suggests, the first words you say in a sermon are what trigger the functions of the brain. It seems that too little attention is given to the first words preachers say in a sermon. I've heard preachers give announcements or meander to their sermonic opening rather than give credence to the idea that the brain is ready to be engaged by the narrative of Scripture. Preachers in certain traditions are prone to spend an enormous amount of time thanking whatever dignitaries or special groups are present. It seems like a wasted opportunity to engage the brain creatively. Research has shown that listeners will make up their minds in the time it takes to utter a single sentence whether or not they will listen for the rest of the sermon. Malcolm Gladwell stresses the importance of relying on first impressions claiming that they are more accurate than we give them credit. Instinctively, people make up their minds long before we as preachers get to the "meat" of our sermon or the story. Gladwell claims that his book is all about those first impressions that we form and how they are more often than not reliable, even more reliable than months of research and hard data can provide.[16] He notes that the part of the brain that allows for people to leap to conclusions (like whether or not the sermon is going to be interesting enough to listen to) is found in the adaptive unconscious. It is our internal computer "that quickly and quietly processes a lot of the data we need in order to keep functioning as human beings."[17] If it is true that our brains are wired for stories, then it is equally true that stories need to have an interesting beginning that grabs our attention and causes us to want to hear the rest. In sermons, it means that we have less than 10 seconds to capture the listener's attention. What you say first will have a greater impact on the hearer's decision to listen than we have previously thought.

Building a Homiletical House

Maybe we should stop thinking about illustrations (another form of stories) in sermons as just additions to the sermon. In my classes on preaching, I have often used an analogy about constructing a sermon structure by comparing it to the building of a house. (1) The foundation of the sermon is the Word of God. Sermons should be built on a text, on a scriptural foundation. (2) The framework/walls of the house are built out of the exegetical work with the text. What does the text really mean? What is the text revealing? Exegesis, which is anchored to the foundation,

---

16. Gladwell, *Blink*, 3–8.
17. Gladwell, *Blink*, 11.

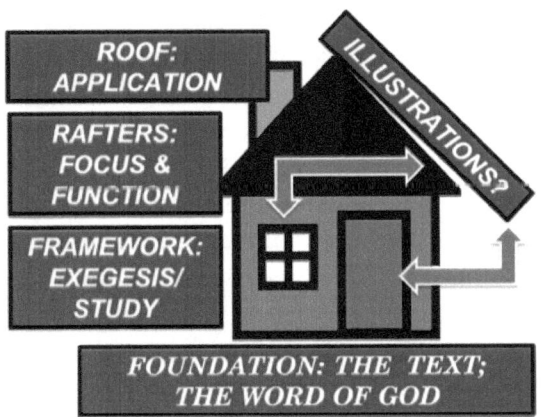

allows the preacher to build an understanding of the word of God based upon the textual tools, insights, and revelations received during this process. (3) Next comes the rafters that hold the frame together. The rafters of preaching are what holds the structure together or what Thomas Long calls, the focus and function of the sermon.[18] (4) The roof, which is the application of what has been discovered in the text, is placed firmly on the walls and connected to both the exegesis of the text and the foundation of the word of God, the roof/application process holds the structure together and brings stability to the whole sermon. After showing them the house, I ask the students, "What is missing from the house?" They can quickly see that it is missing windows and doors. (5) That is the function of illustrations. Stories in a sermon allow the whole structure to breathe. Narratives allow light and a breeze to flow through the whole message. Without well-placed illustrations, connected to the structure of the walls, a sermon is either stuffy and rigid or fails to give the listener a chance to breathe and see what is really happening. Like a door, stories give listeners a place through which to enter a sermon, which is why so many sermons begin with an illustration. Just as you would enter a house by the front door an opening illustration unlocks the entrance to a sermon offering. In a similar way, closing illustrations allow the listener to interact with the sermon and its message, close the door, and complete the message. Stories, narratives, and illustrations are not ancillary to preaching, they are foundational to good preaching.

---

18. Goldberg, *Executive Brain*, 99–116.

Our Brains Hunger for Stories

Considering the impact that stories have on the brain, it is of some surprise to me that preachers fail to take advantage of the storybook nature of so much of the Bible. As has been noted earlier, some 90 percent of the Bible can be classified as narrative in structure or form. All the Old Testament historical books, as well as the Gospels, Acts, and much of Paul's letters are filled with narrative sections that are foundational for our faith. Abraham, Moses, David, Esther, Ruth, Nehemiah, and Ezra are all incredible stories that allow a wealth of preaching material. Jesus' miracles, parables, and the story of the church in Acts are treasure troves of powerfully formed narratives. You can follow the exploits of Peter, Barnabas, Timothy, Aquilla and Priscilla, and catch a real glimpse of the advancement of the first-century church. Yet, the first instinct of too many preachers is how to break these narratives down and take away the power of their narrative quality. Three-point expository sermons certainly have a place, but if we are to have a truly lasting impact on contemporary listeners maybe we should allow the stories to remain more narrative in our sermonic form instead of merely distilling them into propositional statements of what we think is truth. If the purpose of exegesis is to "let the text speak," shouldn't we allow stories to speak as stories? Goldberg's research indicates that our brains are not only wired for stories but are hungry for them. The brain gobbles up a good story like a hungry person gobbles up a good steak or a bowl of vegetable stew. Why fight the natural instinct of the brain? If you want to reach the next generation with the gospel then may I humbly suggest that stories are the best way to engage and introduce new listeners to old stories while engaging old listeners with old stories told in new and fresh ways.

Follow the Rules of Narratives

Finally, it would help to improve the general malaise of preaching if preachers understood what a story actually entails. Most preachers have a sense of what makes a story a story but rarely do they have a solid understanding of the basic elements of story. Narratives follow certain rules. These rules are rarely, if ever, violated by Jesus when he tells the gospel in parables. The rules of narrative have been followed for centuries by playwrights, novelists, screenwriters, and the writers of both the Old and New Testaments. Knowing these rules opens up the world of narrative in new and exciting ways. When you understand the foundation of story and how stories unfold, it allows you to not only craft sermons that have a stronger connectivity with your listeners, but it also allows you to better grasp the meaning and development of the Scriptures themselves—at least the narrative parts.

In reality, the rules of narrative are employed in many non-narrative sections of the Bible, including the Psalms, Proverbs, Daniel, James, and Revelation. It can also be argued that every book of the Bible arises out of a narrative experience. Just read over the opening section of a commentary that explores the issues of who wrote the book, to whom it was written, the historical situation, and the condition of the author when they wrote the book and you will find that all the books of the Bible have a narrative background that is crucial to understanding the book itself. I would argue that preachers should begin seeing stories as the heart of our preaching and not the additions we attach at the last minute. To be an effective narrative preacher, you have to know the philosophy behind the telling of stories and the development of narratives. It may seem a weighty subject to take on at this point of a narrative preaching book, but I believe you are ready for just such an exploration. The next step in the journey is awaiting you.

4

The Journey into Story

A Philosophy of Stories

> *At about that same time Jesus left the house and sat on the beach. In no time at all a crowd gathered along the shoreline, forcing him to get into a boat. Using the boat as a pulpit, he addressed his congregation, telling stories . . .*
>
> *The disciples came up and asked, "Why do you tell stories?"*
>
> *Jesus replied, "You've been given insight into God's kingdom. You know how it works. Not everybody has this gift, this insight; it hasn't been given to them. Whenever someone has a ready heart for this, the insights and understandings flow freely. But if there is no readiness, any trace of receptivity soon disappears. That's why I tell stories: to create readiness, to nudge the people toward receptive insight. In their present state they can stare till doomsday and not see it, listen till they're blue in the face and not get it. I don't want Isaiah's forecast repeated all over again:*
>
> *Your ears are open but you don't hear a thing.*
> *Your eyes are awake but you don't see a thing.*
>
> Matthew 13:1–3, 10–14 (The Message)

Any philosophy of stories must begin with the insights given by Aristotle. His diagnosis of the key elements of drama has gone largely unchallenged over the course of centuries. In *Poetics*, Aristotle lays out the six elements that comprise the development of a story.[1] His frame of reference is the epic poetry of his time and any dramatic presentation of it. But, as we have seen, Aristotle and Plato have had a significant effect on all philosophical thinking (including preaching). While Platonic thought has greatly influenced the sciences and how the scientific method is understood, Aristotle has had a deep impact on the arts, particularly when it comes to understanding the fundamental structure of what comprises a narrative. We now get to move beyond Halakha and Haggadah. Now we get to meet Aristotle.

It may seem odd to engage an ancient Greek philosopher when it comes to building a theology of narrative preaching, but it is not an exaggeration to say that Aristotle's insights are essential to any philosophy of stories or, for that matter, to any theology of preaching. Therefore, let us begin by exploring the six elements of a story according to Aristotle. As we shall see, the order is extremely important:

1. Plot
2. Character
3. Thought
4. Diction
5. Spectacle
6. Melody

Most readers can readily see the meaning of most of these elements in a play or movie. In *Poetics*, the foundational document for these basic building blocks of story, Aristotle covers them in only a page or two. However, they are so significant to a philosophy of stories that each one deserves to be investigated in some detail. Let us begin with the primary element of story which is plot.

---

1. Aristotle, *Rhetoric and the Poetics of Aristotle*, 223–66. Hereafter, any references or quotes will use the customary four-digit numbers used to refer to Immanuel Bekker's edition from 1837. This is the process followed by scholars such as Bywater in his 1909 translation.

ELEMENT #1: PLOT

First and foremost, Aristotle believes that the heart of a story is to be found in the plot. "We maintain, therefore, that the first essential, the life and soul, so to speak, of Tragedy is the Plot."[2] By plot he simply means the series of actions that take place in a story and the order of their unfolding. Plot carries the action in a story, a narrative, or a tragedy. Aristotle's contention is that how such events are arranged and ordered unveils the essential skeleton of the story while at the same time revealing its meaning. To follow the plot is to follow the action and the intent of the author/storyteller. Plot is king and cannot be ignored when determining any approach to narrative understanding or narrative preaching. Plot is a multifaceted idea and holds within it several key aspects that affect its development. The first of these is called causation.

Causation

E. M. Forster once asked whether the following constituted a story: "The King died and then the Queen died." His conclusion was that it constitutes a story but not a plot. To Forster the key ingredient of a plot was to force the audience/reader to wonder, "What's next?" In Forster's famous example, what the "story" lacks is a plot. And what creates a plot? Plots must have causation.[3]

Causation is the action that initiates tension, brings about meaning and requires that the story continues forward. In this example, you have two facts that are seemingly related (both the king and queen die) but no plot forms because, in both instances, the sentence lacks causation. The story has no plot because it lacks conflict. All the sentence does is report tragic facts. The King died (a fact) and then the Queen died (another fact) but nothing else is included. As a result, no plot is developed because the story ends (Forster might argue it has never begun). There is nothing to require the reader to say, "What's next?"

What stories need to develop are conflicting ideas. Plot and engagement are found in complications, conflicts, something that creates a puzzle to be solved or provides a connection with the story that can cause the relationship to flourish. Forster's problem with this simple story of

---

2. Aristotle, *Rhetoric and the Poetics of Aristotle* 1450a 39.
3. Forster, *Aspects of the Novel*, 86–88.

the king and queen is that there is nothing that complicates the basic reporting of the death of two persons. What plot accomplishes is to immediately create interest in the future. Stories (and the plots they introduce) want to cause the reader's hand to thrust in the air asking questions like:

- How did they die?
- Why did they die?
- Did someone kill them? If so, who did it?
- Did someone have it done?
- Did they both die of natural causes?
- Was there something nefarious in their deaths?

In other words, causation. Something has to happen to connect the events and begin to roll the story forward. If there is nothing to further the story or to create mystery and discovery, there may be a detective's case file entry but there is no plot.

But what if you added an element of mystery? What if the story had even the simplest of implications? What if the aspect of having to discover something was introduced into this simple sentence? What if you added causation? For instance: *"The King died and then the Queen died of a broken heart."* Now you have the beginning of a plot. Not only do you have facts (two people died) but now you've added a conundrum to be investigated and a causation to be discovered. The simple introduction of the queen's broken heart introduces another series of intriguing questions that cry out to be further explored. Knowing the circumstances of the queen's death prompts the reader to ask:

- How did the king die? Did he die of natural causes? In battle? By sickness? Was it a suicide? Murder? A plot against the throne?
- How did the queen's broken heart come about? Was it uncontrollable grief? Did she find out something about the king after his death that destroyed her notion of who he really was and what their relationship was really like? Was she lonely, depressed, or suicidal?
- Did the king die heroically? Tragically? Senselessly?

The simple insertion of causation prompts questions about the relationship of both people that require further investigation. The reader now wants to know what the real relationship was between the king and queen. As a result, what causation accomplishes is to make the reader desire to know more. It makes you want to ask the author more questions:

- What was their marriage really like? Were they madly in love or was there tension in the palace?
- Did she grieve because there was no heir to the throne so that her own position of power and stability were threatened?
- Did the king die as a result of a hostile takeover and the queen died knowing that the conquering new king would kill her anyway?
- Where does this story take place? Is it in a culture where the queen had to be sacrificed in some kind of horrid ritual?

It's not just that circumstances surrounding the king's death are unknown—those can be either factual or speculative. However, the introduction of causation as a key element in plot further prompts speculation about the circumstances of the queen's own death.

- Was her death caused by depravation (by not eating or even by suicide)?
- Was it the longevity of their relationship that brings about her demise (she couldn't live without him either because of love or how long they had been married)? Or was there something more nefarious afoot?
- Did the circumstances of the king's death prompt the queen to suffer deeply in her soul and she died not only of grief but also of guilt? In other words, did the queen have a hand in the death of the king? Did she participate in a plot that she now regrets?
- Is this a Shakespearian tragedy in that the queen inadvertently set in motion the tragedy of her husband's untimely death?

The introduction of mystery requires the author of the story to answer questions that arise in the mind of the reader. This is what plot does to stories. Plot invites listeners/readers to participate in the development of the story, in the how's and why's of what happens. Causation allows the author to provide a future for his story. Causation not only enhances plot, but it allows the plot to have sustenance, some form of food for the journey of discovery. When you introduce conflict (or mystery or uncertainty) into a story you require the development of a future and that gives birth to a plot line. And for Aristotle, just as it is for Forster, plot is king.

But it is not only causation that allows plot to develop. There is an even more essential area for stories that plot allows us to explore. Plots are, by nature, unfolding.

Unfolding

Both Aristotle and Forster imply that plots are unfolding. As a literary element, plot does not happen all at once but is revealed over the course of the story. By nature, plot is made up of a series of episodes that reveal the meaning and the action of the story. Stories are naturally layered with revelations and insights, plot twists and turns, resolution possibilities and choices. The term used to express this is that stories are not static but are always unfolding.

One example of the unfolding nature of plots can be found in the biblical story of the prodigal son (Luke 15:11–32). In the parable, Jesus uses different scenes as a method of telling the story. Here is an episodic breakdown of the unfolding story of the parable:

- *Scene One*—the confrontation between father and son over the inheritance. (Note: the conflict occurs at the beginning of the story. Jesus is following the Aristotelian principle of causation by putting the inciting incident at the beginning of the narrative.)
- *Scene Two*—the journey of the son from the family farm to a foreign land. Scene Two includes his loss of money, the famine that breaks his bankroll thereby contributing to his descent into poverty, and his ultimate humiliation and loss of funds.
- *Scene Three*—takes place on the pig farmer's land and includes the realization by the prodigal that things would be better if he swallows his pride and returns home as a servant. Scene Three includes the climactic realization of the prodigal.
- *Scene Four*—begins with the reunion event between father and son and climaxes when the father moves his prodigal son from confession of sin to the celebration of his return Scene Four includes the function of the parable, which is to describe salvation by grace.
- *Epilogue*—occurs away from the celebration between the elder son and the father (which creates another possible unfolding scene in itself). The Epilogue is similar to the dénouement of Freytag.

Each scene in the story builds the story and carries the listener through the plot. Each episode further complicates, reveals, or helps resolve the initial conflict that occurs between the father, the son, and the inheritance. This is a prime example of why plots are unfolding because they reveal some insights while not revealing everything all at once. Plots like to "tease" the reader/listener into engaging with the story and staying with it until the end. As a result, each episode gives more and more clues, understanding, and insight into how the narrative will ultimately be resolved. If causation gives a story a future, the unfolding nature of plot propels the reader into that future and beyond. To create this forward momentum the plot becomes unfolding by creating twists and turns.

Twists and Turns

While these movements and plot developments are founded in causation, they are thrust forward by twists and turns in the story. Twists and turns complicate the plot and cause the reader to be transformed into a treasure hunter. This is how the reader helps the author to complete the story. Readers (or listeners in a sermon) help the story to find completion not by changing the plot but by enhancing the elements of the plot. Plot enhancement is found in twists and turns that arise in the story and keep the plot fresh and exciting. For instance, in the prodigal son story there are numerous twists and turns that propel the listener forward into the unfolding future of the narrative and into the intricacies of the Plot as it is revealed. Here are some of the twists and turns that are possible at every stage of the development of the plot. Maybe you can add some more to the ones listed here.

- *Opening Twists and Turns*—What causes the son to leave the farm? Was there conflict between him and his father, or was the break due more to the impatience of youth? Was the father a hard taskmaster and the son chafed under his strict hand?
- *Developmental Twists and Turns*—What causes the prodigal to lose his inheritance? The story gives clues but not a definitive understanding. Was he immoral, foolish, or just not wise in the ways of the new world he had entered? Did he gamble the money away on "wine, women and song?" Did some disreputable people pretending to be friends fleece a stranger and take advantage of a naïve and trusting prodigal? Did he lose his money because of a character flaw

(licentiousness) or because of a character trait (trying to buy affection and friendship)?

- *Rising Action Twists and Turns*—What causes the son to find work on a pig farm? Is it the result of the famine, the loss of all his inheritance, the realization that his "friends" are really leeches, or a combination of some or all of these? Is it a sign of his depression (he has nowhere else to go to survive) or a loss of his faith (a Jew feeding pigs)?
- *Climactic Twists and Turns*—What causes the son to return to the father? Is it desperation because he is hungry? Is it social humiliation because he would rather face the disappointment of his family than the embarrassment of facing his friends? What does it mean when the text says, "He came to himself"? Is it self-realization? Divine revelation? Maturation? Desperation?
- *Falling Action Twists and Turns*—What causes the reaction of the father? Is it concern for his son? Surprise that he's alive? Gratitude that the boy has finally come to his senses and come home? Love? Relief that his parenting approaches that caused the rift have been overcome? Pure joy?
- *Resolving Action Twists and Turns*—What causes the reactions of the elder brother? Is he jealous? Is he disappointed? Was there a previous tension between them that has been exacerbated by his brother's leaving and cannot easily be dismissed by his return? Does the elder brother have some internal issues of jealousy or disappointment that haven't been resolved? Is this a retelling of the Joseph and his brothers from Genesis?

Answering the causality questions begins to reveal the twists and turns of the plot. As each twist and turn is revealed, the ultimate understanding of the plot unfolds. When Jesus begins the story of the prodigal by telling us that, "There was a man who had two sons," he instinctively follows the rules of plot that Aristotle taught. Jesus is setting up the story, preparing the hearer to engage with a narrative that will follow along a line of revelation, providing a future for the parable, bringing into the story causation, making it unfolding, and filling it with twists and turns. In every way that matters, Jesus is exploring the basic building blocks of plot that Aristotle expressed.

68 PREACHING FROM INSIDE THE STORY

Freytag's Pyramid

Another way of seeing this process is to return to Gustav Freytag's analysis of Aristotle's understanding of plot.[4] As you may recall, Freytag divided them into a simple diagram relating the five parts that comprise a plot and three crises that allow stories to unfold.[5] Take a look at the following popular diagram of what Freytag wrote and then we will take a look at what each of his five steps and three crises' moments means in the development of what Aristotle described as plot:

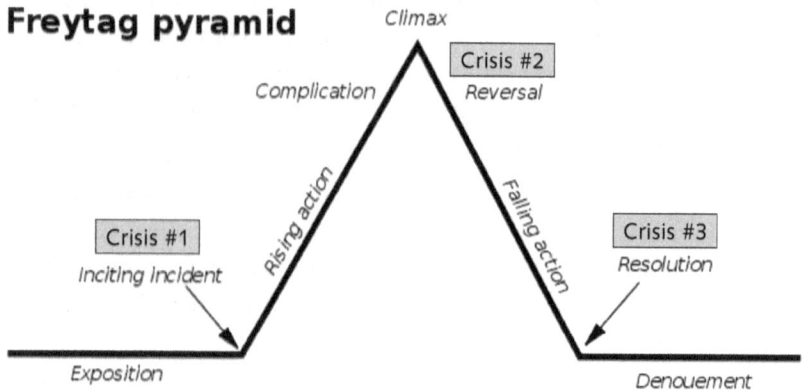

What Freytag laid out is a visual expression of how plot works. There is (1) an *Exposition* ("A father had two sons"), followed by an *Inciting Incident (Crisis #1)* ("Give me my inheritance"), which results in (2) a *Rising Action*—the tension that is created when questions arise about what is going to happen in the story ("squandered his wealth in wild living"), that culminates in (3) a *Climax* ("He came to himself"). The climax initiates a sudden and complete *Reversal of Tension (Crisis #2)*, which does not alleviate the tension but results in (4) a *Falling Action*, which moves the story

---

4. I've actually followed the pyramid mechanism in the process of explaining twist and turns in the plot. The use of the terms Falling Action, Climax, and Rising Action were taken directly from the diagram. The phrases "Opening and Resolving Action" are implied in the same diagram. Even the idea of twists and turns is implied in the directional analysis of Aristotle's principles as expressed in Freytag. This whole section is designed to give the reader the background understanding that has enabled the author to make the claims that have preceded the explanation of Freytag's Pyramid.

5. Freytag and MacEwan, *Freytag's Technique of the Drama*, 114–15. While I have used a more common, detailed diagram of Freytag's Pyramid, his basic structure is set out on pg. 115 under the heading "Five Parts and Three Crises of the Drama."

toward its ultimate conclusion ("So he got up and went to his Father"). Ultimately the tension is relieved through *Resolution (Crisis #3)*, which solves the issues brought up by the *Inciting Incident* that created the plot in the first place ("For this son of mine was dead and is alive again")! Finally, the whole story is wrapped up and brought to a conclusion by (5) the *Denouement* ("My son, you are always with me, and everything I have is yours"). This is what Freytag meant by five parts of a story and three crises that form the basics of the plot of a story.

In conclusion, the elements of plot can be found through the introduction of causation, the sequencing of events in the unfolding of plot developments, the twists and turns as the story is told and the resolving of the questions raised by causation in the manner described in Freytag's Pyramid. It is easy to see why Aristotle taught that plot is primary since it is the skeleton upon which the entire story is enfleshed.

We should note at this point that while plot is king in Aristotle's thought, it is not the only element that is essential in telling a story. In each of the following elements there are essential ideas related to the philosophy of stories. Each one is in descending order of importance for the story. Nothing is more important than plot, but there are five additional elements that are indispensable for how stories develop.

ELEMENT #2: CHARACTER

The second most important element in narrative/story is character. Aristotle intends for a double meaning to be understood here. In his *Poetics*, character is not just a person in the story (i.e., the prodigal, the father, the elder brother, etc.) but what the character does that reveals their internal character (what Aristotle calls "moral purpose"). If plot follows the action of the story, then character is the conduit through which the action and moral motivation of the plot unfolds. Stories explore not only what is about to happen but why it is about to happen. Narratives reveal motives.

Motives

Characters add an ethical or moral dimension to the story. Characters discover, divulge, and reveal what the motives are behind the actions in the plot. These revelations provide meaning, depth, and understanding to the actions of the characters and the plot of the story. In Forster's query about the king and queen, the plot is developed when the author can attribute motives to the actions of the character. Hence, you have the exploration of how the king really died (suicide, murder, illness, on the battlefield) and the development of the queen's true feelings toward the king, possible reasons behind those feelings and insights into what may be her fate as the surviving spouse of a monarch. All of these lend motives to the characters' internal moral compass as well as fleshing out the nature of each character. If plot is key then character is the lock that plot opens and motives are the lock pins that the key turns inside the characters inner thoughts.

Motives tell you why a character acts the way she acts. Motives are essential to action because it fills in the "why" of what takes place. Why does one character in the story do the right thing and another character in the same situation in the story always does the wrong thing? You begin to look to motives for answers or, at least, shades of meaning in their morality meter. This is one of the reasons that we struggle with plot developments for which provocation is hard or impossible to ascribe.

For example, it is easy to understand why a mother does what she does to protect her child from a dangerous predator, but it is much more difficult to decide why a tornado follows its path and destroys one house but not another. Since hurricanes, tornadoes, and the like are called "acts of God," we tend to ascribe reason to them from the only character we can think of—God. Because we get so used to explaining events/stories in terms of motivation, God gets blamed for lots of things that theologians have debated for years![6] In the same vein, you can watch how media outlets struggle deeply when they report horrific events but cannot find the motives behind them. Someone commits suicide and doesn't leave a note or any real clues as to their action; a criminal commits a random act of violence with no apparent reason or relationship to their victims. These acts are called "senseless violence" because we do not have the ability or information to assign motives. Motives help us to understand the "why" of plot. They also add another dimension similar to what causation adds to plot—it adds morality to the characters' intentions.

---

6. This is described in theological circles as theophany. Theophany comes from the Greek *theophaneia* and refers to God's appearance. This has led to its theological connotation that theophany is the place where we seek to "see" the hand of God in events or ascribe to him some kind of purpose and direction.

Morality

Characters are moral beings and they act so as to reveal their own character. As a result, what they do and why they do things reveals not just motivation but the moral and ethical reasons behind why they do what they do. Characters form the conduit through which both plots and subplots occur. If morality (the sense of what is right and wrong) forms the foundation of motives, then the best way to understand plot is through the morality of the people that are moving the story forward. However, the only real way to understand a character's motivating principle is by understanding their inner character. Aristotle's principles associate the moral sense of stories to moral choices and understandings of characters. Without character there is no moral basis for the story. Without morality there is no basis for the plot to unfold since plot is based on conflict and conflict arises out of motives and morality that become action.

Let's turn, once again, to the example of the prodigal son story. In the parable, the prodigal squanders his inheritance in loose living (a moral judgment); the father runs to his son, embraces, and kisses him (a moral act of love, grace and redemption); the elder brother is angry and refuses to attend the party for his younger brother (thereby revealing his moral foundations and concerns). Every action of a character also reveals their character. Every reaction to the story's plot reveals the motives and morality that makes up what Aristotle means by character. These decisions about morality contain issues for the plot to consider. They have both effects and affects.

Effects and Affects

Because the characters' actions reveal motives and morality, Character has an effect on plot in three ways. First, as we have already noted, characters help to carry the action forward so characters have an effect on a person's internal character and affect that character's motives and morality. So, in some sense, character and plot are intertwined. If plot is action, then the characters become the medium through which most action occurs or is reported. Without characters it is most difficult to express action in a story. While moviemakers have the advantage of creating special effects and camera angles to express the movement of plots, storytellers and preachers have little opportunity to use such devices.[7] As a result, the preacher is almost exclusively reliant on characters in the story to further the plot of the narrative.

Secondly, because characters reveal the character of the characters in the story, they also deeply effect and affect morality. This is true of "good" characters (moral) and "bad" characters (immoral). Both have an influence on the meaning of the story and, therefore, the plot of the story. In the story of the prodigal son, the father represents the good character in the story. He is moral, upright, grace-filled and redemptive towards both of his children. The prodigal represents the transformative character. He begins headstrong and independent, moves to immoral behavior and returns to his father in repentance and humility. He represents both the immoral and moral sides of human beings. The elder brother seems to represent the bad character, complaining to the father about sibling rivalry, judgmental attitudes, and presenting a picture of an unforgiving attitude toward his brother. If the prodigal represents the process of repentance and salvation and the father represents grace and the forgiveness of God, then the elder brother represents the unyielding Pharisaic commitment to the jot and tittle of the Law. Each character not only reveals morality and motive, but they help shape the total meaning of the story and in some significant ways, the plot of the story. In other words, they produce both effect and affect.

Thirdly, because characters carry the moral reasons behind plot twists and turns, characters effect and affect motives. Morality is not just about good and bad, ethical and unethical behavior but about the reasons and rationales characters use to justify their attitudes and actions. Human beings feel justified in taking the course of actions they take even if they are immoral. The prodigal felt "justified" in leaving his father and family because he had a series of motives that allowed him to rationalize actions that might negatively impact his family. The so-called "friends" of the prodigal were motivated by certain beliefs and practices that allowed them to take advantage of the prodigal in ways that left him broke and destitute.[8] The elder brother lived by a series of principles that gave him

---

7. Students of Aristotle will quickly note that he uses the idea of Spectacle in his Poetics and that will be addressed later in this chapter. While storytellers may use props or sets on occasions, it is not the function of this book to encourage the wide use of such materials for preaching. They are often unnecessary and encourages the congregation to think you are acting rather than preaching.

8. Mark Allen Powell has a fascinating story about how the prodigal story is

the moral high ground when talking with his father about the prodigal's immoral abandonment of the family and the father's lack of appreciation for the elder brother's faithfulness and moral certitude. Each of these character actions effect and affect the story, the internal dialogue of characters in the parable, the twists and turns of the characters in the narrative, and the ultimate morality of both the characters and the plot itself.

Clashes and Complications

Character adds a crucial dimension to plot that all preachers and storytellers need to be aware of, if they are not already. In stories, characters are inevitably pitted against one another. It is this clash of characters that allows plot to reveal character. There are times when characters may face some kind of trial that challenges the morality of the character (i.e., the prodigal facing the pigs). There are other times when the plot follows the conflict between characters (the conversation between the father and the elder brother). Out of these clashes and complications arise both morality and motives that effect and affect the plot.

- How will the father treat his wayward son? How he responds to his son's return will affect the prodigal effect the plot.
- How will the son behave towards the father he once rejected? Will his new found humility be viewed as genuine or another manipulative gesture?
- How will the elder brother resolve his issues with his younger brother? He has choices to make before he talks to the father. He is informed by the servants of his brother's return. What choice of action/reaction will he make?
- These clashes and complications are at the heart of a dramatic story.

So, when a character interacts with the plot, she affects the plot in dynamic ways. It's not just a furthering of the story, but clashes are how stories become complicated. Complication is at the heart of storytelling. Notice Freytag's Pyramid. The plot does not really kick in until the inciting

---

affected by social location theory. In one of the interpretations he uses, the students felt that the sin in the parable was not the prodigal's loose living but the attitudes of the friends and community that took advantage of the prodigal's wealth and generosity. In this interpretation of the story it is the community that sins rather than the prodigal. See Powell, *What Do They Hear?*

incident. What is the inciting incident? Simply put, it is the introduction of conflict and clashes. Inevitably the conflict complicates relationships, questions the motives of the characters involved, and reveals and refines the character of the characters in the story.

In the parable of the prodigal, it is revealing not just what each one does but how the character of each actor is revealed in the clashes that take place and the complications that result.

- Is the father good or bad? Forgiving or a push over? Unfair or gracious?
- Is the prodigal immoral or naïve? Changed or just tired of being hungry? Repentant or manipulative?
- Is the elder Brother surly or justified?
- Does he hate his brother or is he more disappointed in his father's reaction to his brother's return?
- Is he more concerned with the inheritance than he is about his brother's welfare?

As you hear stories or read them in the Bible or listen to narrative sermons based upon biblical texts, you instinctively look at the clash and complication of character and characters in a story to teach you about morality, motives, causation, unfolding, twists and turns, and the overall effects and affects on plot and character.

As we have noted, Character is an integral aspect in revealing plot. But as we have described above, exactly how do characters reveal the struggles, trials, and difficulties that help character complicate plot? The answer is twofold: first, they reveal these things by their actions, which is why character moves plot forward; second, in stories you also have an advantage over other forms of communication because you get to know the thoughts of the characters, which is the third element of Aristotle's process.

ELEMENT #3: THOUGHT

Stories are able to let the listener/reader know what the characters are all thinking. As a result, Aristotle's concept of thought is really more about the inner dialogue and inner turmoil characters experience.

The Inner Dialogue

Since actions are rarely expressions of simple processes, stories allow the listener to hear a person think, to eavesdrop on the complicated rationale of their inner dialogue. Thought is the narrative device used in all kinds of literature (including the Bible) to allow the reader to "listen in" on the hidden discussion that all human beings employ. Descartes' axiom that gave fuel to the Enlightenment (I think, therefore I am) has implications for this Aristotelian ideal. Thought affirms the Platonic idea that human beings are thinking machines. What Aristotle proposed is that our internal dialogue influences who we are as well as what we do. To understand both plot and character, we are invited to hear the inner dialogue of those who are taking action in the narrative.

Thought is used in preaching to give expression to what a character is viewing, interpreting, and doing. Preachers employ this all the time by telling the listener what is happening in the mind of a character. For instance, preachers may say, "The prodigal feels so bad about how his life has turned out that he leaves his job on the pig farm to return home to his father." While this interpretation of the story may seem to be an expression of plot, in reality it is an expression of thought that employs an understanding of his inner dialogue. How do you know that the prodigal "feels bad" in the story? It may seem obvious from the unfolding of the plot, but the preacher/storyteller has turned the listeners' understanding of plot into the internal dialogue expressed by thought.

Inner Turmoil

In these moments when preachers interpretively turn thought into description, the audience becomes privy to an inner turmoil that may or may not be seen in the outward expression of the story. In truth, the entire scene at the pig farmer's ranch is revealed in the inner turmoil of the prodigal disguised as an outward monologue. In Luke 15:17–19 the prodigal begins to "speak" his thoughts.

> When he came to his senses, he said, *"How many of my father's hired servants have food to spare, and here I am starving to death! I will set out and go back to my father and say to him: Father, I have sinned against heaven and against you. I am no longer worthy to be called your son; make me like one of your hired servants."*
> (NIV; italics mine)

Jesus, in telling the parable of the prodigal, employs thought as a rhetorical and storytelling device to express the inner turmoil experienced by the prodigal as he finally comes to his senses. "Reading minds" is a normal way for storytellers to share the inner turmoil of the characters in the story. It is important that preachers realize that conflict, the essence of what enables plot, can occur just as easily in the inner turmoil of a character as it can in the outward action each character takes.[9] Aristotle notes the differences between the older poets/storytellers like Aeschylus and Sophocles who used only action to show plot (since the older forms of poetry did not utilize dialogue between characters), and his own "modern day" playwrights (like Homer) who are beginning to use thought and dialogue to express plot.[10] As a result of this change, Aristotle understood that without thought there would be large gaps in the movement of plot. Therefore, it is important for storytellers and preachers to reveal the inner turmoil of characters through thought in order to express plot movement and complication.

Writers often use this device to hide the resolution of the story in order to sustain tension. Anyone who has ever read Sherlock Holmes knows that Sir Arthur Conan Doyle did not reveal the inner dialogue of Holmes until the very end of the book. He would rush around asking odd questions or making strange observations until he was ready to solve the crime. Then he would weave all the odd occurrences and actions into a single narrative that he had been "thinking" about all along, but the reader was not privy to in the story. Doyle has turned plot development into thought understanding by revealing the inner turmoil of trying to discover who done it.

Similarly, a television show like *Psych* (NBC, 2006) gives insight into the thought processes of the main character by highlighting with special effects the observations that Shawn Spencer is making. He "sees" things others overlook and when the special effects let you in on what it is that he sees and its potential significance, the audience begins to think with him about what it may mean for solving the crime and explaining the conundrum. Plot has been turned into thought and the inner struggle to understand what is really happening allows the audience to experience his inner turmoil.

---

9. Rosenstein, "On Aristotle and Thought in the Drama," 552–53.

10. Aristotle, *Rhetoric and the Poetics of Aristotle* 1448a 25.

Similarly, in *The Homiletical Plot*, Eugene Lowry employs these Aristotelian ideas into a preaching form. Lowry argues that preachers should employ the idea of thought and its influence on plot in an inductive approach to a biblical narrative.[11] In such preaching structures the sermon is designed to start at the point of conflict (Lowry calls this "Upsetting the Equilibrium;" his students gave it the shorthand of *"Oops!"*). The third major shift is called "The Key to Resolution" or the *"Aha"* moment when the real answer to the Oops is revealed. However, in-between those two lays something called the *"Ugh"* or what Lowry described as "Analyzing the Discrepancy." This movement in his structure is designed to further complication of the story and take full advantage of the concept of thought by accessing the inner turmoil of the characters in the story.

I was once told that the secret to the Lowry Loop was the ability of the preacher to hold the tension of the *"Ugh"* as long as possible.[12] One of the most effective ways to hold that tension is by revealing the thought process and the inner turmoil of the characters in the story. The preacher can describe in detail the kind of internal dialogue and debate that is going on in the mind of the character. Homiletical expression can be given to what struggles are foremost in their inner turmoil? What additional factors in the culture and background of the characters further complicate the story and can be revealed in the inner turmoil of the characters? To accomplish this the preacher must be able to reveal the thoughts of the characters in inner turmoil.

Revealing Thoughts

One of the more interesting ways the Bible accomplishes thought is by directly connecting expressions of thought to narrative actions, thereby revealing the inner thoughts of the character that might normally be hidden. For instance, Ps 3 is not merely a hymn but, according to its

---

11. Lowry, *Homiletical Plot*.

12. I am indebted to my friend and mentor, Dr. Clay Schmit, for this insight into the Lowry Loop. After I encouraged him to require students in his Creative Preaching class to preach one of their sermons in the Lowry Loop form, his evaluation was that the ability of a preacher to hold the tension during the Analyzing the Discrepancy phase was critical to the listener because it heightened the sense of anticipation and engagement with the story. To allow that tension to be dissipated too soon by moving quickly to the Key to Resolution let off the steam of the Oops too soon, much like taking the lid off a teakettle squanders the heat needed for boiling.

prescript, "A Psalm of David. When he fled from his son Absalom." What you have in Ps 3 is the thought of David concerning the narrative that is found in 2 Sam 15–18. It is a valid exegetical interpretive position to say that you cannot fully understand the events of Absalom's conspiracy and David's overthrow without revealing the thoughts of David expressed in Ps 3 since it was penned in reaction to the king's overthrow. Revealing thoughts expresses not only the inner turmoil of David but also the depth of his faith in God.

It is here that most preachers and listeners tend to push back against Aristotle. The most common questions I've received about thought has been, "How do you know what the characters are really thinking?" This is a great question and important to the whole idea of narrative preaching. My answer is simple. If you place plot in the mind of the character by using thought, are you really adding to Scripture (a practice most would describe as being strictly prohibited by the New Testament)?[13] Others ask, "Isn't this doing eisegesis rather than exegesis?" While that sounds like a reasonable inference, upon further reflection, this concern may not be as strong as first impressions lead one to believe. Let me explain.

All preaching is based upon the interpretation of Scripture. Sermons explain what a text says. Through the use of exegetical principles and procedures, preachers interpret that meaning of a text and proclaim both what the text says and what the text means for you and me. This process is governed by both exegetical principles and hermeneutical approaches. In applying Aristotle's ideas to narrative preaching principles, there is no violation of Scripture as long as the preacher adheres to the idea that plot is key. If that principle is adhered to then you cannot change the direction of the plot in the story by putting into the thought of characters something that is not inherent in the text. The principle is simple: you cannot exegetically interpret the narrative by placing thought in conflict with plot. To put it in Aristotelian terms, thought cannot violate plot.

In the prodigal parable, you cannot put into the thought of the father what cannot be reasonable extrapolated from the plot of the story. An

---

13. "*I warn everyone who hears the words of the prophecy of this scroll: If anyone adds anything to them, God will add to that person the plagues described in this scroll.*" This is the most quoted text on this issue in my experience. It is from Rev 22:18 and appears to be directed specifically at the prophecy that constitutes the book of Revelation. It is frequently used to apply to any aspect of any biblical text that is not derived directly from a scriptural text, regardless if it is connected to Revelation or not. I would point out that it does not really apply to the issue of thought as we are using it, but it is the concern that is most applied to it.

eisegesis example of this would be to attribute to the father a whole new storyline not covered in the parable. For example, having the father be widowed or divorced may help explain one possibility for the prodigal's decision to leave, however, it adds to the plot in ways not warranted by the text itself. However, to put into the thought processes of the father a concern for what has become of his son would not violate the exegetical, plot-oriented process. To say, "The father went out to the fields every day and looked for his long, lost son to return" would be expressing motive for what eventually happens on the day he does see his son far off. The first one adds something to the story that is not there while the second expresses an action in the mind of one of the characters that is totally consistent to what eventually happens in the plot. Thought is designed not to change the story but to reveal thoughts, to reveal the effects and affects of characters, to unfold the plot, to reveal causation, and to show how twists and turns are experienced by turning plot into the revealing thoughts of the character. Fortunately, you don't have to always interpret what a character is thinking. Sometimes they actually tell you their innermost thoughts and struggles. Aristotle calls this diction.

ELEMENT #4: DICTION

If thought reveals what is going on inside the person's mind then diction is the way in which those thoughts are expressed in words and in dialogue with others. As with all stories, words matter; as with all conversations, words attempt to communicate meaning; as with all sermons, how one says what one says is crucial to understanding plot, thought and character.

How One Says What One Says

There is a sense in which how one says things can be more revealing than what one says. While diction in Aristotle means far more than just proper pronunciation, it should be noted that this is the area where such things as emphasis, pace, volume, and pitch can truly influence meaning. In the church today, too little emphasis is given to how Scripture is communicated, read, expressed and interpreted in the reading of it let alone in the preaching of it. Remember, how one says what one says is synonymous to what one means.[14]

While fulfilling a Postdoctoral Teaching position at Princeton Theological Seminary, I was asked to teach a course on Speech Communication. It was a labor-intensive course that required a huge commitment on the part of the seminary. Every incoming student was required to take this one-hour course for a whole year and classes were limited to about 8 students per section. Depending on the professor, the course could easily be turned into a course on the public reading of Scripture. I did that and found that it had rich rewards for both student and professor. Suddenly, students started to realize that the interpretation of Scripture is not just about what you thought a passage means but, more and more, about how you communicated the meaning that is inherent in the text itself. In Aristotelian terms, you had to be able to turn thought into diction; you had to realize how one says what one says affects meaning.

I once told one of the sections that I was teaching that, "I know this is not one of the most theologically challenging courses you are taking here at Princeton." One of the students, a bright theologically trained and focused student, thrust his hand up quickly.

He said, "I disagree, professor. I think this is the most challenging theological class I've taken."

I probably should have left it there and enjoyed the affirmation, but I pressed him as to why he thought that way.

He replied, "This class has forced me to think not just about how to say things when I'm reading Scripture but why I'm saying what I'm saying."

That is the meaning of diction. It had begun to dawn on him that even in the vocal reading of a scriptural text, how one says what one says is crucial for understanding. Remember, diction is not simply the effective pronunciation of words but the ability to communicate meaning in texts, especially when the passage is narrative in its approach. How do you give life to questions, conversations, exclamations, and pronouncements that are made by characters in stories? These and a myriad of other concerns require us to turn more deeply to an important subject in diction: the public reading of Scripture.

Preachers and worship leaders can relate to the importance of diction when dealing with things like the public reading of Scripture in

---

14. There are numerous resources to help with this idea. See n. 16 below for a list of possible resources.

worship services. All you have to do is sit in most any congregation on a Sunday morning and listen to how Scripture is being read. How often do you hear a slopy reading of the Scripture reading done in such a way that it makes you keenly aware that it has not been rehearsed, practiced, or prepared by the reader? Below are some principles that can positively affect how you use Aristotle's concept of diction to the reading and preaching of the Bible.

Principle #1: Reading as Interpretation

Every reading of a text is an interpretation of that text. If someone reads a text flat without any insight or inflection, they still have interpreted the text. Poorly for sure, but the way in which it is read communicates a great deal to the listener. If preachers are going to interpret the text in their sermons using words and explanations related to their exegesis, shouldn't they use diction to interpret the text in the same fashion? Can someone say that they have read Paul's intent in the following text if they read his statement without ascribing any emotion to it: *What then? Should we sin because we are not under law but under grace? By no means!* (Rom 6:15 NIV). How you read that verse interprets the meaning of Paul's statement to the Romans. The KJV gives even more weight to this when they end the verse with "God forbid." Surely Paul had emotion in the pen when he wrote that verse and if we preach that text wouldn't it be appropriate to communicate to the congregation that Paul uses the word μὴγένοιτο, which means that such a thing should never come to pass? If it's appropriate to preach such a point with inflection, wouldn't it be equally important to read that statement with the intent of Paul's meaning to be clear? Remember, every reading of a text is an interpretation of that text. Let your reading express the interpretation of it that you have come to realize through your exegesis of the text.

Principle #2: Vocal Insight

Preachers should capitalize on the wide availability of paraphrases and translations that give insight into biblical interpretation by vocal means. I have always advocated for using translations rather than paraphrases to do exegesis. At the same time, I firmly believe that paraphrases are vocal treasures for the church to incorporate into worship. In some ways, the very purpose of a paraphrase is to give vocal expressiveness to textual passages. Let me suggest two keys that I have found helpful over the years for giving vocal insight into biblical texts.

- *Reading from The Voice*

One of the most helpful ways to grasp diction in a text is to use The Voice translation. For those unfamiliar with this particular paraphrase, let it suffice to say that it is designed to be used in a "Reader's Theater" style of scriptural expression. For instance, since we have been using the Luke 15 passage about the Prodigal as an example throughout this chapter, here is an adaptation from The Voice that expresses the dialogical (diction) nature of the parable by giving vocal insight:

> **NARRATOR:** *Hear the Word of the Lord from Luke, chapter 15. "Once there was this man who had two sons. One day the younger son came to his father . . .*
>
> **PRODIGAL:** *Father, eventually I'm going to inherit my share of your estate. Rather than waiting until you die, I want you to give me my share now.*
>
> **NARRATOR:** *And so the father liquidated assets and divided them. A few days passed and this younger son gathered all his wealth and set off on a journey to a distant land. Once there he wasted everything he owned on wild living. He was broke, a terrible famine struck that land, and he felt desperately hungry and in need. He got a job with one of the locals, who sent him into the fields to feed the pigs. The young man felt so miserably hungry that he wished he could eat the slop the pigs were eating. Nobody gave him anything.*
>
> **PRODIGAL:** *What am I doing here? Back home, my father's hired servants have plenty of food. Why am I here starving to death? I'll get up and return to my father, and I'll say, 'Father, I have done wrong—wrong against God and against you. I have forfeited any right to be treated like your son, but I'm wondering if you'd treat me as one of your hired servants?'*
>
> **NARRATOR:** *So he got up and returned to his father. The father looked off in the distance and saw the young man returning. He felt compassion for his son and ran out to him, enfolded him in an embrace, and kissed him.*

PRODIGAL: *Father, I have done a terrible wrong in God's sight and in your sight too. I have forfeited any right to be treated as your son.*

FATHER: *Quick! Bring the best robe we have and put it on him. Put a ring on his finger and shoes on his feet. Go get the fattest calf and butcher it. Let's have a feast and celebrate because my son was dead and is alive again. He was lost and has been found.*

NARRATOR: *So they had this huge party. Now the man's older son was still out in the fields working. He came home at the end of the day and heard music and dancing. He called one of the servants and asked what was going on.*

SERVANTS: *Your brother has returned, and your father has butchered the fattest calf to celebrate his safe return.*

NARRATOR: *The older brother got really angry and refused to come inside, so his father came out and pleaded with him to join the celebration. But the Elder Brother would have none of it.*

ELDER BROTHER: *Listen, all these years I've worked hard for you. I've never disobeyed one of your orders. But how many times have you even given me a little goat to roast for a party with my friends? Not once! This is not fair! So this son of yours comes, this wasteful delinquent who has spent your hard-earned wealth on loose women, and what do you do? You butcher the fattest calf from our herd!*

FATHER: *My son, you are always with me, and all I have is yours. Isn't it right to join in the celebration and be happy? This is your brother we're talking about. He was dead and is alive again; he was lost and is found again!"*

ALL: *This is the Word of the Lord!*[15]

As you can see, by using The Voice as a guide, it is easy to see how the parable can be communicated in a style that connects with the importance of diction.

---

15. The main way in which I have adapted this reading is to assign the narrator parts to a single reader under the heading of Narrator. The Voice leaves this unassigned, choosing to only assign specific characters to be read. However, it is a simple process to cut and paste the passage and then "assign" the narrator(s) parts, splitting them up between multiple narrators if necessary. This can currently be done easily by going to Biblegateway.com and simply cutting and pasting the text to be read. You can add, as I have done, a speaking choir part to either the beginning or ending of the reading (or both) that gives an introduction and conclusion to the reading.

- *Combining Multiple Versions*

Once you get the hang of cutting and pasting and assigning narrators, you may want to move to a more creative process of developing a script for reading Scripture that provides vocal insight. Using the same resource, it is possible to view, review and cut and paste passages from multiple translations or paraphrases. Some of the more helpful paraphrases I have found are The Message, The Living Bible (or New Living Bible), The Voice, and The Amplified Bible. These four have unique phrasing and expanded expressions that can be delightful to use as ways of expressing vocal insight, giving the fullness of meaningthat biblical passages communicate. Combining paraphrases with translations (like the NIV, NRSV, NASB, or NKJV/KJV) can prove an engaging way of expressing vocal insight in the public reading of Scripture. Whereas translations give the specific translated meaning, paraphrases tend to give the emotional and interpretive reading of the text.[16]

Principle #2: Expressing Emotions

Effectively expressing emotions present in texts gives depth to any story. One of the reasons Aristotle is so effective as a guide for this area is that in character, thought, and diction expressing emotions present in stories help reveal meaning and understanding. Ferreting out what emotion is being expressed is often the role of diction. For instance, take a look at

---

16. There are numerous resources to help with this kind of process. While some have been cited already, I list them in full here for the benefit of the reader. For further study and research use the following as a general guide but not an exhaustive bibliography for resources in area of reading and expressing Scripture in worship: Jeffrey D. Arthurs, *Devote Yourself to the Public Reading of Scripture: The Transforming Power of the Well-Spoken Word* (Grand Rapids: Kregel, 2012); G. Robert Jacks, *Getting the Word Across: Speech Communication for Pastors and Lay Leaders* (Grand Rapids: Eerdmans, 1995); Charlotte I. Lee, *Oral Reading of the Scriptures* (Boston: Houghton Mifflin, 1974); Jack C. Rang and Charlotte I. Lee, *How to Read the Bible Aloud: Oral Interpretation of Scripture* (Paulist, 1994); Clayton J. Schmit, *Public Reading of Scripture: A Handbook* (Nashville: Abingdon, 2002); Charles L. Bartow, *The Preaching Moment: A Guide to Sermon Delivery* (Nashville: Abingdon, 1980); Charles L. Bartow, *Effective Speech Communication in Leading Worship* (Nashville: Abingdon Press, 1988); Charles L. Bartow, *God's Human Speech: A Practical Theology of Proclamation* (Grand Rapids: Eerdmans, 1997); Richard F. Ward and David Trobisch, *Bringing the Word to Life: Engaging the New Testament through Performing It* (Grand Rapids: Eerdmans, 2013); Jana Childers, *Performing the Word: Preaching as Theatre* (Nashville: Abingdon, 1998).

how the elements of diction affect both the reading and understanding of the Prodigal narrative:

Volume and Demeanor

- How does the prodigal say his confession to his father? Does the volume and demeanor of his confession have any bearing on how sincere it is or how it is received?
- With what attitude does the elder brother address his displeasure to his dad? Does his volume portray disdain or disappointment? Is he hurt or is he mad? What part does volume play in communicating attitude? What effect does your understanding of his demeanor have on the emphasis he places on his words to his father?

Emotional Content

- What are the emotions that the father is experiencing as he sees, greets and celebrates his sons return? How does you understanding of his emotions as a father affect the reading of that part of the parable?
- Does the servant who tells the elder brother that his younger sibling has returned do so with joy or with trepidation? Is he merely reporting facts to the elder brother or does he know this will not sit well with his employer?

Pace

- How quickly does the father tell his elder son about his views concerning the one who has returned? After all, he is quick to call for the robe, ring, and sandals—how quick is he to speak to his other son?
- When the father repeats his declaration of forgiveness this time to his eldest son (he was dead but is alive again), does he do it emphatically (emphasizing his joy at the prodigal's return) or with

sympathetic understanding toward his older son's faithfulness and hard work?

Emphasis

- In diction, the emphasizing of one word over another can radically alter the meaning of the text. Take this one line from the parable story. In the following sentence, which word would you emphasize? Does it change the perception of the intent of the elder brother? Does it affect the emotional content of what is said?
- Quoting Luke 15:28—*"I've never disobeyed one of your orders."*
- Reading #1: *I've <u>never</u> disobeyed one of your orders* (this would emphasize either the indignant nature of the elder brother—"I would never do that to you father!"or it may suggest a painful pleading feeling—"I never even considered doing what your other son has done to you").
- Reading #2: *I've never <u>disobeyed</u> one of your orders* (here you attribute honesty to the elder brother—"I may not be the perfect son; I've done some things wrong, I know; but I've never even considered going against your wishes.").
- Reading #3: *I've never disobeyed <u>one</u> of your orders* (here you emphasize his faithfulness vs. the prodigal's egotistical stubbornness—"He couldn't take your rules. Me? I've not disobeyed even a single request you've made of me.").

Typically, concerns about diction do not come up until the preacher or worship leader has to vocalize the narrative and give expression to the diction. That is why dialogue can be challenging to write and to express. Of course, the "problem" of preaching is, as Charles Bartow accurately notes, that it is a vocal art, an aural-oral experience.[17] As such, preaching and diction are inexorably intertwined. For the storyteller, diction can change the way in which the story is told, thoughts are disclosed, characters are viewed, and plot is revealed.

---

17. For further study on preaching as an oral-aural art see not only the cited works of Bartow, Ong, and Childers and Schmit, but Peterson, *Eat this Book*; Webb, *Divine Voice*.

ELEMENT #5: MELODY

The fifth element is melody. Anyone who has ever attended a movie in a theater has seen melody in action. Listening to John Williams haunting score for *Jaws* or his Imperial March for Darth Vader in *Star Wars* provide simple examples. In Aristotle's time, the choir was often incorporated into plays or epic poetry. He saw music, choirs, songs and harmonies as integral parts of the story. While the parable has no musical accompaniment to it (like the prescripts to many of the Psalms), stories are full of sounds. Like melody, sounds form an important part of understanding a story. While not nearly as crucial as the elements that precede it, melody is, nevertheless, revealing.

Looking for Sounds

Stories do not take place in an aural vacuum. Any capable preacher knows that context is an important part of understanding a text. Before preaching the story of the prodigal son, the preacher should know, understand, and be familiar with the whole of Luke 15—including a series of parables about lost things (sheep, coin, and son). But within stories, part of the context is to understand the sounds that take place in them. There are sounds that can express loose living, the hunger pains in famines, disgust in pig farming, rejoicing and celebrating at parties, eating and making merry with friends. These may not be sounded out when telling the story (though sometimes they are noted), but they are part of the atmosphere that the storyteller knows and communicates.

Sounds form their own melodies in narratives that help explain the tension that is so insightful when looking at the plot. Sounds are essential to know why a character says something one way or the other. Sounds can easily affect the thought experience of a character as they strive to make a decision. Sounds can be distracting, enhancing, or essential to what a character knows or how a scene develops. Sounds can form a kind of melody that brings rhythm to both the reading of a scene and to the experience of the actual story itself. It is incumbent on the preacher/reader to find the sounds in a text as well as the words of that text.

As an example, I've always suspected that part of the dynamic of the prodigal story is the contrast in sounds between the kind of parties he threw when he still had money and friends and the party celebration he received from his father at the homestead. I also wonder if the squealing of pigs sounds anything like the wailing of the brother's complaints. So many stories come to mind where sound is such a part of the whole experience: the bleating ram caught in the thicket with Abraham and Isaac; the wild behavior of the Israelites in front of the golden calf; the cheering for the one-man parade of Mordecai that Haman was forced to lead through the city streets; the purring of lions in Daniel's den during an uneventful night; the cock crowing three times; the stone being rolled away by the hand of God; the difference between how Stephen sounded in praise and the stones sounded in anger; how the heavenly choir sounds as they sing about the Lamb who was, and is, and is to come. The Bible is full of sounds that enhance and reveal what is happening in the story.

Rhythm in Stories

Stories are also rhythmic in nature. The effect of diction—volume, demeanor, emotional content, pace, emphasis—all bring to a narrative a certain kind of rhythm in stories that is distinguishable in the text. The more dynamic the plot, the quicker the pace of the complications and the more radical the inciting incident. These have serious effects and influence the entire story. In the same way, narrators can definitely impact both the listener and the story by either speeding up the pace of the story or by slowing down and becoming more deliberate. In teaching these vocal dynamics in class I often refer to these elements of speech as using the Vocal Orchestra. Your voice has a greater range than you might imagine. Rather than being a single note monotone or a single instrument with limited dynamic and range, your vocality has the opportunity to produce sound and rhythm that usually comes from a full orchestra rather than a single trumpeter.

In the story of the prodigal, one of the key ways to grasp the tension of the narrative is to pay attention to the pace and rhythm of the story. Jesus begins the story with some deliberation (after all, the inciting incident happens after the story begins). But soon after he begins to unfold the events of the familial breakup by using time sequences in the story.[18]

- "Rather than waiting until you die . . . " (v. 12, The Voice) *Can you hear the anxiousness of youth in his voice?*

---

18. These are quotes variously from both The Message and The Voice.

- "The father *liquidated assets and* divided them." (v. 12, The Voice) *The division of assets took time to accomplish. I wonder if the Father and Elder Brother used the time to try and talk him out of this fool hardy venture?*
- "A few days passed and this younger son gathered all his wealth and set off on a journey to a distant land." (v. 13, The Voice) *How long did this breakup take? How awkward was the time between the "rather than waiting until you die" and the final preparations for the journey to a foreign land?*
- "Once there he wasted everything he owned on wild living." (v. 13, The Voice) *How long did it take to lose it all?*[19]

These sequences are more than just time markers in an unfolding process, they are rhythmic indicators that affect how the story is to be read, portrayed, and interpreted.

Rhythm not only brings information to bear on a narrative, it is also a key component in the preaching event. One of the most common errors I hear in my preaching classes is a preacher who speaks too quickly. Everything seems to be spoken at breakneck speeds. There is no room for the listener to breathe or to catch up to the words being spoken. If preaching is supposed to be a dialogical event between the preacher and the listener, the preacher and the Trinity, the preacher and the Word, the listener and the Holy Spirit, and the listener and the Word, then the rhythm of preaching is essential to allow the melody of the narrative to be played out in fullness.

Melody has long been a recognized staple of black preaching. Evans Crawford coined the phrase "hum thoughts" to describe this melodic way of preaching. He calls it a kind of "homiletical musicality" that derives from the call and response traditions formed in West Africa and honed in the crucible of slavery.[20] In an African American setting, the congregation is looking for ways to create melody in preaching. Melody is not viewed solely as a cultural expression but as an interactive experience that fosters the dialogical nature of homiletical revelation.

In a related way, anyone who has ever preached with an interpreter in a multicultural setting knows how difficult it can be to find a rhythm

---

19. While I alluded to this issue earlier (see n. 15) Powell has a most intriguing discussion of the whole story of the prodigal son from a social location point of view. See Powell, *What Do They Hear?*, 21ff.

20. Crawford and Troeger, *Hum*.

when the sermon goes back and forth between two languages. The first time I ever heard a translated sermon what caught my attention was the way in which the interpreter (we could only hear him through headphones) and the preacher (live in front of us) created a powerful rhythm for the gospel proclamation. There was little pause except for effect. Each of the speakers appeared to seamlessly "step" on the final word of the other so there were no gaps in the sermon. Each used pace and pause for weight and force of communication. They sped up and slowed down with purpose, and they rushed through parts that caused the audience to rise up in their hearts and sing, while they slowed down at places that allowed us to take in the impact of the Word. It was powerful and thrilling because both preachers understood the importance of rhythm and cadence in creating melody. Sermons always utilize rhythm, it's what moves the story from a monotone to an orchestral symphony.

ELEMENT #6: SPECTACLE

Finally, there is the element of spectacle. Aristotle quickly notes that, "The Spectacle, though an attraction, is the least artistic of all the parts, and has least to do with the art of poetry." He goes on to say that this is usually left up to the "costumier rather than the poet."[21] It may not prove valuable to know what the prodigal was wearing, but as you view the story, it is likely that in your mind's eye you probably change his garb from the opening of the story to the farming scene. Also, the father calls for him to be re-wardrobed with "the best robe" and to put a ring on his finger and new shoes on his feet. It may be that what he is wearing at the end of the story is of some importance in order to catch the theme of the parable, which is redemption.

Settings

One of the influences that narrative preaching approaches have had on preaching is to elevate and incorporate spectacle through verbal expression of the physical setting. Geography, smells, architecture, scenes, and settings have often been relegated to the pastor's study where they are interesting for deep background but not really valuable for the actual sermon. While Aristotle recognizes that spectacle is not nearly as crucial

---

21. Aristotle, *Rhetoric and the Poetics of Aristotle* 1467–1470b.

as plot, he does note that it has a particular influence. This is certainly true in our example of the prodigal when it comes to the issue of physical setting:

- *Physical Setting:* Does the physical setting of the famine affect the whole issue of the prodigal's actions and priorities? How often have you thought about or communicated in a sermon the physical setting of a people suffering famine deprivation and how hunger and deprivation determines the actions and decisions of the prodigal and all the people in the story?

- *Cultural/Religious Setting:* What does the scene at the pig farm say about the lowly condition (both economically and spiritually) of the prodigal? Have you ever considered what it means for a boy raised in Jewish teachings and practices to be feeding pigs? What does his willingness to take the job at the pig farmer's ranch say about the spiritual condition of the prodigal?

- *Social Order Setting:* How much does the characterization of the servant affect the perception of the prodigal? Considering the setting of the elder brother and the sudden appearance of the prodigal, does the elder brother have an accurate picture of what the prodigal has gone through or only what he is told by the servants? Does that matter? Is the servant's description affected by the *social order* of the two of them?

CONCLUSION

Any effective telling of the story of the prodigal son requires the storyteller/preacher to incorporate the fullness of Aristotle's elements of *Poetics*. Ultimately, all storytelling is a movement toward what we have already defined as Haggadah. It uses the facts of the story to help imagine the fuller story that is in Jesus' mind as he relates the parable. It is not trying to limit the story to literalness but, as all sermons do, point the listener toward the truth. Narrative storytellers, like Haggadah preachers, believe that the story holds more information than the words of the narrative initially reveal.

Relating biblical stories is more than the employing of a "sanctified imagination," it is the hard work of exegeting not just part of the story but the whole story. It uses the Aristotelian elements of plot, character, thought, diction, melody, and spectacle to allow for a proper exegesis of the text, the full text. What is said, what is thought, what is done, what is heard, what is felt, and what it looks like are essential questions to a narrative preacher. This is why narrative-based biblical preaching is like Haggadah . . . it believes there is more truth in the story than a proposition can express.

5

Narrative Journey, Narrative Sense
Learning to Preach from Inside the Story

> *The only way to start an exploration of the gospel as storytelling is to learn to tell the stories. Until you have experienced the stories as stories, all arguments about the meaningfulness of "telling" the stories will be more or less meaningless abstractions.*[1]
>
> Thomas Boomershine

> *"Just the facts, ma'am, just the facts."*
>
> Joe Friday in Dragnet

Just before I graduated from Fuller Seminary, Princeton Theological Seminary invited me to interview for a postdoctoral preaching position. While I couldn't imagine getting the job, I was highly honored to be considered and to have made it to the interview stage. In spite of my assumption that I would not be the final candidate, I prepared for the interview as hard as I had for any interview in my life. I found out who the interviewers were and bought their books, read them, and prepared myself to converse with the authors about their scholarship. I took three days away from the rewriting of my dissertation to prepare for the interview. I sat down at my computer that morning for the Skype interview

1. Boomershine, *Story Journey*, 17.

and made up my mind that any question they asked relating to whether or not I could do something, I had a singular response: "Yes!"

As the interview went along, everything was going extremely well when the dean asked me if I would be willing to teach some electives on preaching. I, of course, replied, "Yes!" The dean referred to the fact that I had taught a course on Creativity in Preaching while at Fuller. Could I teach that at Princeton as an elective?

"Yes!"

I told them I already had a syllabus that I could adapt for the semester-based routine of Princeton and I had two semesters of teaching experience with it. That seemed to please them very much. I figured I was set. And then they asked if I had another class/elective I could teach. For the first time in the interview I was stuck, unprepared to answer a question. But, of course, I had already committed myself to answer every question in the affirmative. So, I blurted out:

"Yes."

Then the dean wanted to know what other course I could teach. I recovered as quickly as I could and told them, "I would love to teach a course on Narrative Preaching." Before I could say another word, the dean said, "That would be great. We would love to have you teach that class." And with that, I was committed to teach a course I had never taught before, but had spent my life preparing to teach.[2]

As I developed the course from scratch, I began by searching for required books to assign. I quickly gravitated to the books I've mentioned in previous chapters: Aristotle's *Poetics*, Fred Craddock's *As One Without Authority*, and Eugene Lowry's *The Homiletical Plot*. They seemed obvious choices. I was encouraged to use my first book as a text (*Preaching the Story*) and decided to assign that, too. Eventually, I added books by Tom Long (*From Memory to Hope*), Joel Green and Mike Pasquarello (*Narrative Reading, Narrative Preaching*), Jana Childers (*Preaching as Theater*) and Richard Eslinger (*The Web of Preaching*). They have all become familiar dialogue partners for me in my teaching about narrative. I have now been teaching that course for the last 10 years to hundreds of students in two different seminaries. It has proved a fruitful study for the students who have joined me on that quest.[3]

---

2. I did end up teaching the Creativity in Preaching course twice during my two years at Princeton and the Narrative Preaching course during May term both years.

3. For ease of the reader, here are the books I've used as textbooks (see bibliography): Aristotle, *Rhetoric and the Poetics of Aristotle*; Childers, *Performing the Word*;

While the previous chapters can rightly be described as a compilation of what I teach in that course, there is one more thing that is important to add. Most everything I teach about narrative has been cobbled together from the work of other scholars and practitioners who have written about the craft of narrative preaching and invested their scholarship in this vital area of learning and practice. As I reviewed my class notes for this book project, I realized there is really only one thing I teach in that class that is original with me. It is the most insightful piece I have and I hope to add to the scholarship on narrative preaching. I don't know if it will help you as much as it has helped me and my students, but I believe it is worth considering. To understand its import, it may be helpful to turn to the worlds of theater and television to make my case. But before we go there, let's explore what it means to have a *Narrative Sense* based upon a *Storytelling Lens*. It will be important to understand these concepts if you are to learn how to tell a story from the inside.

A NARRATIVE SENSE

In chapter 4, I contemplated what exegesis really does in preaching. The most important thing exegesis accomplishes is to give the preacher what I call a *Narrative Sense*. Narrative sense is the way in which we view all stories but, in particular, biblical stories. Living in the age of Hollywood "movie magic" and CGI capabilities that allow superheroes to fly around in iron suits has allowed us to forget that the mind is a better motion picture camera than anything Hollywood has invented. Our brains are an unlimited canvass filled with inexhaustible resources for painting pictures and creating movies needed to experience a story. After all, our minds are wired for stories!

What storytellers have developed that most non-narrative preachers have not is that narrative sense. It is the innate understanding that stories are powerful and can do far more than my words can do. It is a belief in the example of Jesus as a storytelling Messiah who refrained from using PowerPoint, blackboards, and whiteboards in order to tell stories about rebellious children, unprepared bridesmaids, and how Samaritans are sometimes heroes instead of second-class citizens. While human beings are natural born storytellers who both learn in story and communicate in

---

Eslinger, *Web of Preaching*; Frymire, *Preaching the Story*; Green and Pasquarello, *Narrative Reading, Narrative Preaching*; Lowry, *Homiletical Plot*; Lowry, *Homiletical Beat*.

stories, there are steps preachers must take to develop a deeper and more prolific narrative sense. The first key step in developing a narrative sense is to understand how to use the storytelling lens.

THE STORYTELLING LENS

While most of us take pictures today with our smartphones, professional photographers continue to use SLR or DSLR cameras.[4] These cameras are able to zoom in from great distances and make things that are faraway look up close and personal. A different telephoto lens can provide high quality pictures from great distances. Like photographers, good storytellers/narrative preachers have learned the value of having a telephoto lens attached to how they tell stories. Getting closer to the narrative is the key to helping you understand how to tell a story from the inside.

Flatlander

Too many preachers tell biblical narratives from a perch high above the story itself. Most preachers tend to do a flyover of the biblical text. They see the story like they are in an airplane 30,000 feet above the ground. Stories are told from the perspective of a flatlander, full of basic facts, general details, geographic generalities and a broad overview of social customs and cultural interactions and told in two dimensions. Maybe the best way to describe this kind of storytelling is to quote the iconic 1950s character Joe Friday from Dragnet. When he interviewed witnesses, he always told them, "Just the facts, Ma'am, just the facts." While facts are integral to storytelling, narratives are so much more than just the facts. Preachers stuck in flatlander mode have developed a rudimentary understanding of a narrative sense. But there is so much more to stories and storytelling.

Landscaper

The next class of preaching storytellers have increased their narrative sense by moving on from Joe Friday to something more intimate. These

---

4. SLR stands for Single Lens Reflex and DSLR stands for Digital Single Lens Reflex. Both related to cameras that have high quality resolution and have the ability to change lenses for close up or panoramic pictures.

preachers begin to see biblical narratives through an interpretive paradigm of understanding. Having spent time exegeting the text, Landscapers interject insights gleaned from the story. Instead of just bare facts, the landscaper begins to plant an arrangement of historical details, relational interactions, and implications found in the story. In other words, they begin the work of fleshing out the barebones of the flatlander approach by creating a stronger narrative sense. For example, instead of just noting in Exodus chapter 1 that there was a change in pharaohs, landscapers search out the historical understanding of that dynastic change and discover that the previous ruling house of Egypt were foreigners who hailed from the land of Canaan. A connection is made between Joseph and the previous rulers because they had a common ancestry. As a result, exploration is initiated into how that may have influenced the connection between Egyptian royalty and Joseph's descendants. As more interpretive detail is added to the story, the narrative begins to take on more depth and features and a deeper and richer narrative sense is formed as landscaping is done.

3-D Set Designers

Preachers with an eye toward the value of depth and detail find there is yet another dimension to storytelling that aids in the growth of one's narrative sense. The greater the storytelling acumen the more 3-dimensional the stories become. These 3-D set designers begin constructing stories rather than telling stories. Stories become living narratives rather than written novels. 3-D set designers don't simply add more detail, they add more insight and revelation. Emotions and feelings are not just mentioned in the story but are explored as a way of understanding the true dynamic of the narrative. 3-D set designers can't pass over the birth of Moses without exploring how the parents must have felt or the atmosphere in the slave camps of the oppressed Jews when it came to newborn male children. To the 3-D set designer these are not just additional facts, they influence the whole understanding of the story. They are not add-ons but get at the heart of what was really going on in the house where Moses was born. You can imagine how much deeper the *Narrative Sense* grows when one becomes a 3-D set designer.

Cinematographers

As the storytelling preacher moves from a flatlander to a 3-D set designer, they find that the dynamic nature of the story is enhanced by each step up the storytelling ladder. But there comes a time when the 3-D set designer yearns for an even more intimate experience with the text. The question becomes, "How can I get even closer to a biblical narrative?" Enter the cinematographer. Cinematographers tell stories as though they are unfolding before them and they are capturing the event with their movie camera. In literary terms, they take on the perspective of a third person narrator but in a narrative sense, they become an unnamed character that has a panoramic view of the whole story. While they are in the story, they are not seen by the other characters nor do they affect the scene. They see the story unfold through a panoramic view that is not merely "seeing the landscape" of the story. They are not simply noting the constructive elements of the events that influence the characters' lives and relationships. No, this kind of storytelling spans both time and space.

In a narrative sense, the panoramic view is not just to know the story setting. The cinematographer is able to see and experience all that has happened before the story (those elements that influence the story's plot development), as well as all the events that will come after the current narrative reaches its climax (the implications or applications of the story's meaning). A cinematographer might add the colors of God's silence while the Jews are enslaved and the shades and gradients of suffering at the hands of their oppressors while mixing that with the emotional agony of having to drown your own offspring in the very river that provides life to the whole community. The cinematographer is able to add understandings that not only colors the narrative but allows the listeners to relate their world to the world of the text. The cinematographer doesn't want you to know that the Jews were slaves forced to commit infanticide; she wants you to experience the pain and agony of placing your own baby in the Nile. That is what it means to increase your narrative sense.

The Insider

Finally, there is but one more step in the storytelling ladder that grows one's narrative sense. It is the accomplished storyteller/preacher that takes the rare step to tell stories from the inside. The insider completes the journey from what I call "Joe Friday to Break a Leg." This is the final and most important step for a narrative preacher to make. It completes the cycle of storytelling that begins with a flatlander approach and brings to a fully mature narrative sense. Let me explain what I mean by "Joe Friday to Break a Leg."

In theater parlance, "breaking a leg" is a common phrase when desiring to wish an actor good luck but few know its origin. When talking to my youngest son (who has his Masters in Theater) Joel helped me understand the meaning of this odd phrase. It seems that the curtains one typically finds on the stage have names. While we are all familiar with the Main Curtain, few of us know what the side curtains (the ones that prevent you from seeing backstage) are called. That's right. They're called "legs."

When you wish an actor good luck by "breaking a leg," you are encouraging them to part the curtain; get out on the stage; to become part of the story; to become an insider. Old school folks can think of Johnny Carson entering onto the stage after Ed McMahon says, "Here's Johnny!" Until Carson parted the curtain and walked out on stage nothing could happen. He had to enter the arena before the show could really start. From that moment forward, he parted the curtain and initiated a kind of breaking of the leg; Carson became an insider. He was in the story and, in some ways, even part of the story. He told his comedy from inside the story rather than from outside the story. There came a point when the audience stopped sensing that Carson was telling a monologue to them and realized he was having a conversation with them. When he did "break a leg" the audience became part of the story, joining Carson on stage as an insider. The audience related to what he said because we felt like we were included, a character in the unfolding commentary on life, news, politics, and the foibles of human beings. Not only had Carson entered the story but so had we, the listeners. If Carson was an insider, then so were we. We had entered the arena, too. The listeners were now creating a space to experience their own version of a narrative sense.

Something happens when you break the leg and enter a story. Things that seemed inconsequential to you in exegesis can take on added value and meaning when you are inside the story. The questions change when you break a leg and enter the narrative. For instance:

- What does the room smell like when the alabaster jar is broken and Jesus' feet are anointed?

- What emotions were experienced when the disciples were in the boat being tossed to and fro by the waves and the storm?
- What did Jesus look like when he came walking on the water?
- What did the commotion sound like during the Palm Sunday parade?
- What did it feel like to see Jesus hanging on a cross in a public place, being ridiculed by passersby on the way to Jerusalem?
- What did it smell, taste, and look like in the temple on any given day when animals were being sacrificed?

This kind of immersion happens all the time when we go to a theater production or to the cinema to experience a movie. While actors want us to imagine them as someone other than who they are (i.e., Tom Hanks as a grownup juvenile in *Big* or Keala Settle as a bearded woman in *The Greatest Showman*), that is not the goal of the preacher. Storytelling preachers seek for the listeners to enter the story with them and see it unfold from inside the narrative. One doesn't tell a story from the grandstands to create a narrative sense. The storyteller stands in the middle of all that takes place and relates what it is like to be on the inside.

BEYOND JOE FRIDAY

Preachers begin to get to this stage when they realize that distance is the enemy of good storytelling. Like so much of preaching in whatever genre presented, sharing a sermon is an intimate act with a congregation. The preacher bares her soul and exposes her faith and struggles to anyone who enters the sanctuary on Sunday. In other words, you have to leave Joe Friday behind. All Friday wanted was the basic story; the unvarnished nuts and bolts of what happened. He didn't want any unnecessary detail or embellishment of what took place. He didn't want them to tell him a story, he wanted them to recite just the facts and nothing more. That might make for a good police interview but it makes for terrible storytelling.

Stories are about the details (at least, the relevant ones) and how those details are strung together.

First Approach: You can say, "David looked over and saw Bathsheba bathing, naked on the roof" and you get the gist of the story. Joe Friday would be proud. But when you move from Joe Friday to break a leg and enter the story, fresh details, emotions, and realities enter the picture.

Second Approach: Now it's, "David shouldn't have been there that day. He was a warrior king and it was the season for armies to venture out onto the battlefield. But he had disobeyed his calling and stayed behind. And when he looked over and saw Bathsheba naked, innocently bathing on a rooftop where she thought no one could see her, all the warrior instincts David expressed in the arena of combat now were focused on the conquering of a woman he had no right to subdue. The wife of one of his most loyal and fierce fighting men. That day, David lost the battle by not going to war."

Which approach engages you more? Which one do you want to hear more from? Telling a story from the perspective of an insider allows the storyteller to cross the bridge from intimacy in front of a congregation (Bathsheba was naked and David lusted for her) to intimacy with a congregation (it's not just David who lost his way, I have made the same mistake of not being faithful to God in what I knew to do). When you enter the story and tell it from the inside, listeners enter it with you and carve out their own place in the narrative. What happens is that the congregational members develop their own narrative sense and enter the story with you.

CROSSING THE STORYTELLING BRIDGE

When Fred Craddock suggested back in the 1970s that the secret to good preaching was to build a "homiletical bridge" from the pulpit back to the pastors' study, he had in mind the idea of allowing the listeners to become dialogue partners in the journey of discovery with the text. As we pass the 50-year anniversary of Craddock's seminal work, maybe it's time to further expand his metaphor. Narrative preachers who preach a text as an insider not only invite the listeners to cross the homiletical bridge back to the study but they invite the listeners to cross a second bridge—the "storytelling bridge" that takes them back and forth in time with the biblical text. This storytelling bridge is the gateway that allows listeners to develop their own narrative sense.

One of the natural experiences of storytelling (and *"storylistening"* if I could coin a term) is how time collapses during the telling of a good story. Television watchers have no problem watching an episode of

M.A.S.H. followed by an episode of *Star Trek: Next Generation*. In one they have to imagine themselves in Korea during the early 1950s, while in the other they are transported into space during the twenty-fourth century. Because both series are based on the idea of storytelling and take advantage of storylistening, we have no problem spanning time and space in stories. The technical term for this phenomenon is analepsis and prolepsis.

ANALEPSIS

Analepsis refers to where the storyteller and listeners recall what has already been as though it was happening now, in the moment. What occurs is that biblical stories are brought forward into the present by the very act of storytelling. Who brings the story forward? In most ways it is the listeners as they develop and experience their own version of a narrative sense. That is why the preacher doesn't have to contemporize the story, all they have to do is tell the story as if it were happening in this moment. Preachers don't have to create a narrative sense for the listeners as much as the listeners experience their own narrative sense. Congregations naturally fall into this because that is how we experience stories. Let me give you an example.

My last opportunity to preach in the Princeton Seminary Chapel came during my final semester of my postdoctoral position. I made the mistake of asking some students what they thought I should do for the sermon. Because they had been a part of my narrative preaching and creativity in preaching courses, they urged me to do a first-person narrative using the storytelling principles I've outlined here. I thought it was a good idea and determined there and then to do a first-person narrative sermon. Then one of them suggested that I do the narrative from the perspective of a female character. Before I could respond, they all chimed in on what a good idea that was. I felt trapped in my own teaching!

I began looking for a text and settled on an Old Testament story. I proceeded to do my exegetical work and started looking at the possible narrative perspective I could use as an approach. Eventually, I shared what I was going to do with the chapel leadership team. One of the professors was particularly excited and supportive because he had just finished a project which required their editorial board to struggle with how to do true biblical lament in a sermon. I had told them that I would be preaching from Exod 1:21—2:41 and doing it from the perspective of Moses' mother in the days and weeks following Moses' birth. It seemed like an opportunity to explore the power of lament. The professor seemed neither shocked nor surprised at the idea that I would be preaching from the perspective of a woman. As a matter of fact, his only comment was to encourage me to incorporate phrases from the Psalms into the sermon as an authentic way of expressing the Jewish practice of lament before God. His suggestion cemented my thoughts on the sermon.

When it came time to preach, I eschewed the pulpit and spoke from the center aisle. I wore no special costume but was dressed in a suit with a stole hung around my neck. I gave no indication that I was going to be a woman or that I was about to share a first-person sermon. I simply placed the stole in the crook of my arm as though I were holding a newborn and began the story. It took but a few moments before I knew that the analepsis miracle had taken place. No one moved or shifted in their seats; nobody got up and left; no one even coughed. They were mesmerized by the story (not the storyteller, mind you, but the story). Without any preparation, they had been transported from the stained-glass chapel to a humble slave quarters in ancient Egypt. A pulpit stole cradled in the crook of my arm was a baby. They had "suspended their disbelief" and entered the story with me.[5]

This ability to suspend disbelief is why we feel we are part of the M.A.S.H. 4077th unit or hanging out on the bridge of the Enterprise with Captain Picard or Commander Riker. We don't argue with the absurdity of it, we just go with it in the hopes that the story is worth the journey. As I stood there portraying a mother imaginatively holding a newborn Moses, the absurdity of that picture faded away as the congregation suspended disbelief and entered into the grief, anguish, and lament of a young mother forced to kill her own child. I didn't create the narrative sense in the chapel. It was the listeners who brought it with them to the storytelling.

PROLEPSIS

While analepsis transports us back in time, prolepsis is the ability to anticipate an event yet to come. I have experienced many moments of

---

5. Chapter 6 contains the manuscript for this sermon entitled, "The Journey into Grief: Moses' Mother Mourns."

prolepsis during the sermon. As the congregation entered the story and time collapsed between ancient Egypt and modern times, the listeners also held in abeyance their knowledge of how the story would conclude. Instead of saying to themselves, "This isn't real. I know how it all ends. Moses gets pulled out of the Nile and raised in Pharaoh's house," the listeners experienced the tension and struggle of Moses' mother who, at the time of Moses' birth, had no assurance that he would outlive the Nile execution ceremony. They anticipated her anxiety, grief, and lament as if they were walking through the painful story with her. By the time I concluded my lament with the fervent cry of "You alone are my hope, God" and the soloist rose to sing the old Negro spiritual, "Sometimes I Feel Like a Motherless Child," the congregation was still lingering in the aftermath of the ancient story. No one wondered any more why an old white guy spoke like the mother of a newborn—they had entered the story and time had collapsed backward in analepsis and forward in prolepsis.[6]

Preachers and congregations know this miracle all too well. We constantly tell the story of Jesus' birth during Advent and Christmastide; we tell the story of Jesus on the cross during the Lenten season and host Good Friday services that go over, once again, the seven last words of Jesus; we rejoice in the story of the resurrection not just on Easter Sunday but throughout the season of Eastertide and beyond. Congregations don't sigh with frustration when the sermon text is announced and the message is based on the Exodus story of the birth of Moses. While they have heard the story many times and sat through countless sermons on Moses and his birth, they are willing to once again enter the familiar territory of a known story and expand their narrative sense.

In its heyday the movie *Titanic*[7] was a blockbuster hit. Have you ever asked yourself, "Why?" Did people throng to the cinema thinking, "I hope the ship doesn't sink this time." Hardly. We watched the movie because the story was intriguing, the characters were interesting, and we weren't sure what happened to all of them during the journey. And we didn't care that the ship shown on the movie screen was built and filmed on a soundstage. We enjoyed the story. We experienced it afresh and new on the screen. We tapped into this wonderful narrative sense that we all seem to possess and went along for the ride.

---

6. The sermon has been recreated in chapter 6. Now that you know the story of how it came about and what occurred during the preaching, I hope it will make more sense as to why I've included it in this volume.

7. Dir. James Cameron, Paramount, 1997.

An even more stark example is the movie *Groundhog Day*[8] (one of my personal favorites). I've seen it numerous times and still tend to pause while flipping channels when I see that it is being broadcast. Imagine, watching over and over again a movie about a man who lives a day over and over again. It only goes to show that experiencing what we already know can be just as satisfying as experiencing something we do not know. Such is the beauty of storytelling. Such is the joy of narrative preaching. Such is the miracle of having a narrative sense, a storytelling lens, and knowing how to take the journey from Joe Friday to break a leg.

CONCLUSION

As you reach the end of Section One, it is time to focus on what we do with these principles. Preaching from inside the story requires you to actually tell the story and preach the sermon. Now that you are armed with an understanding of narrative principles and have begun to explore your narrative sense and storytelling lens, how do you put these principles into the pulpit experience?

Rather than simply give you sermons to read, Section Two will spend a lot of time applying what you've discovered in Section One. In many ways you are not finished with the journey begun in this section. In reality, you're not really done with this section. You'll see what I mean when you look at the next chapter.

---

8. Dir. Harold Ramis, Columbia, 1993.

SECTION TWO

Journeys in Narrative Preaching

An Introduction
to the Practice of Narrative Preaching

INTRODUCTION

This section is about the practical application of the principles expressed in Section One. The praxis that is related in these sermons conveys the way in which I teach narrative preaching at the seminary level.[1] In my class on Narrative Preaching each student is required to preach two sermons. The first must be a third-person narrative and the second must be a first-person narrative. I choose those two versions of the narrative approach because they afford students the greatest opportunity to engage with the realities of the narrative/storytelling approach. These examples are not to suggest that narrative/storytelling sermons are limited to these types. On the contrary, I have sought to examine the nuances of the Lowry Loop and I encourage the use of Paul Scott Wilson's *Four Pages of the Sermon*.[2] Both are highly valuable for narrative preaching and teach structures every preacher should know and use. However, those two structures are much more in line with a traditional mode of inductive preaching while the examples I start with here are significantly different than those more traditional approaches. I have included an example of one of my Lowry Loop sermons because I have spent so much time

---

1. Don't be intimidated by the seminary level expression. In my preaching classes at three different institutions, I have learned that about 30–70 percent of the students have not preached at all or have preached less than 2–3 times. Like many of you, they are starting from scratch. And if you are an experienced preacher (like the other 30 percent of my students) the challenge will be your willingness to unlearn the things that may have prevented you from preaching in a narrative vein.
2. Wilson, *Four Pages of the Sermon*.

discussing his method. But this section has multiple sermons told in either the first or third-person mode.

The reason I have chosen examples of this unusual mode of preaching is because I tend to see the Aristotelian principles of story and an application of the philosophy of stories most dramatically presented in these two structures. I realize that these are "off the beaten track" approaches for most preachers with the exception of an occasional Christmas event or Holy Week service. I do not suggest that these are the only or even the primary approach to narrative/storytelling sermons, but they are great examples of what I have been sharing in Section One. Before launching into them, let me share with you a few of the principles I use in teaching these two structures.

THIRD-PERSON NARRATORS

Third-person narratives require the preacher to decide what kind of narrator they want to be. There are several choices and each one has its strengths and weaknesses. (1) The *All-Knowing Narrator* is one who knows all of history, from before the story to the present day. They can make allusions to things that cannot be known in the period of the text. For instance, in Exod 1 when describing the enslavement of the Jews in Egypt under a new Pharaoh, the all-knowing narrator can say, "Like a Nazi SS officer with his boot on the neck of a Jewish prisoner, so the Egyptian soldiers mistreated the Jewish laborers." Time and space mean nothing to the all-knowing narrator. They know everything. (2) The *In-Story Narrator* knows everything that is happening in the story. They know what has happened before but not what is about to happen. They know what everyone is thinking and feeling and can relate the conflicting interpretations of the characters who are seeing the story unfold from differing perspectives. The in-story narrator must follow the unfolding plot of the story because that is all they know. In the story of David and Goliath, the in-story narrator does not know that David defeats Goliath until he actually kills him. He experiences David's victory and Goliath's defeat as it happens. (3) The *Reflective Narrator* has already experienced the story and, from a time in the near future, is reflecting back on the events that took place. As a result, the reflective narrator knows not only what is happening in the story but knows the results of the narrative. They can only know things up to the point of their telling, but they can know more than just the unfolding nature of the story to which the in-story narrator is limited.

THIRD-PERSON PERSPECTIVES

While third-person narrative perspectives allow the preacher at least three options of how to form the sermon, how does one choose which one to use? Each perspective provides a different level of knowledge and understanding of the story. There is no definitive matrix by which the choice should be made. It really comes down to the comfortability of the storyteller and the way in which the storyteller is most comfortable in unfolding the biblical narrative. The biggest rule of thumb is to make a choice and stick with the limitations of that choice.

There are inherent limitations in each perspective. (1) For instance, if you choose the all-knowing narrator then you can't be surprised by what happens in the story or feign ignorance of what is about to happen. You already know! (2) Nor can you determine to be the in-story narrator and speak as if you know how it will end. It unfolds for you in the same way it unfolds for the characters in the story. (3) The reflective narrator knows what has happened and is looking back upon it. They have the advantage of both knowing the ending and still being able to tell it as though it is unfolding. In other words, the reflective narrator is experiencing the story once again as it is being told even though they know how it concludes. This approach can be very helpful in allowing the preacher to make application of the story. For instance, telling the story of Pentecost from the reflective narrator approach allows the preacher to talk about Pentecost and apply what needs to happen to us now that "we" have been filled with the Holy Spirit. The limit is that the reflective narrator can't go too far into the future or they lose credibility. They also have the added burden of trying to help the congregation know who they are in the story. More on that later.

FINAL THOUGHTS

Some final thoughts about these perspectives: First, the all-knowing narrator doesn't have to worry about anachronisms, they are a built-in reality of the approach. However, the in-story and reflective narrator must make sure they don't use language or expressions that take the listener out of the suspension of disbelief.[3] With them, the preacher should avoid language and expressions that are so contemporary that they cannot be reconciled with the story. To say that David was "cool" or that Bathsheba was "hot" uses terms familiar to a twenty-first century audience but not to the biblical setting of the story. At the same time, the in-story and reflective narrator do not require us to use King James or Shakespearean language either. That may appear to some ears to be the "holy language" of the Scriptures but it does not reflect how those in the Bible spoke English.[4] Just tell the story in your own words and allow the story to be front and center.

Second, it can be very helpful for the listener to know who they are in the story. This is especially true with the reflective narrator (and, at times, the in-story narrator). It is quite a challenge to situate the audience in some way while maintaining the "campfire" nature of storytelling. But if you can identify to whom you are telling the story you answer the profound question of, "Why is this person telling this story to us?" Answering the "Who are we?" question allows the entirety of Coleridge's "suspension of disbelief" to have full effect. After all, if the reflective narrator is looking back on the story, then the audience is still situated in the time frame of the story. At some point the reflective narrator has to let the congregation know who they are in the time limits of the story. For instance, at the end of an in-story narrator approach to the Garden of Gethsemane event, the narrator could say, "As they march Jesus off to face a trial before the Sanhedrin, what will the disciples do next? What will you do next?" In a reflective narrator approach (where they are looking back on the scene from some time in the near future) the narrator could say, "Remember, none of them knew what would happen when they

---

3. Samuel Taylor Coleridge is the first one to have coined this phrase and defined its meaning. He believed this principle made the very concept of imagination possible (and that without imagination learning was not really possible). For Coleridge, the concept implied that human beings had both the capacity and inclination to "suspend" the reality of what we could see with the rational mind and interject into that the ability to see beyond the immediate and limited view of reality in front of us. It is this principle that makes all literary work possible. While we know that Sherlock Holmes did not really exist nor did Oedipus kill his father and marry his mother we read or see these portrayals and agree to imagine with the author the *possibility* that such a thing could be. The human ability to imagine a Field of Dreams or to "see" the confrontation between David and Goliath lies at the heart of all storytelling, story-making and learning. It is so ingrained in the human psyche that we don't even have to tell the listener to do it—it is how our minds are wired for stories (see ch. 3).

4. There is a pun there I hope the reader gets.

carted Jesus off that night. They didn't know, as you and I do, that Jesus would be crucified and resurrected within three days." The congregation sees themselves as one of the disciples watching Jesus being arrested and lead away. They even have a more visceral connection to the story.

Finally, it may be helpful to know that the narrator does not have to be a dispassionate observer. Whether the story is unfolding as they tell it or they are looking back upon it, the narrator has an emotional connection to the story. It is true of all humans that when telling a story, they are really reliving the story. My parents died decades ago but I can still get choked up or laugh out loud at a story from my childhood.[5] Human beings not only hear a narrative but they are invited to participate in the story. As a result, it is not necessary for the narrator to check their emotions as a storyteller. In fact, it is quite the opposite. The emotion of the storyteller both gives permission for the listener to feel the story but it also gives the storyteller the responsibility of reacting to the emotion that is already in the story. This makes the telling of the story even more real to the listener and the storyteller. Narrators are invested into what happens in the story.

This is not suggesting that you "make up" emotion but it does suggest that you can genuinely express the emotion that is inherent in the story itself. When you break a leg and enter the story it is likely that you will come to feel the tensions and struggles of the story. My suggestion is that you don't fight that any more than I would suggest you make it up. If the emotion is felt in the telling then it is germane to the reality of the story.

FIRST-PERSON CHOICES

When preaching a first-person sermon, preachers have several perspectives from which they can tell the story. Basically, there are three choices:

(1) Main Character—this is the most popular approach. If you want to tell the story of the prodigal son you can choose between the father, the prodigal, or the elder brother. All three form the main characters of the parable. However, in a first-person sermon it is best to choose one

---

5. This is the essence of Paul Zak's work on oxytocin in the brain. When telling a story or seeing a video (story) being played human beings release oxytocin as an emotional reaction to what is being told or shown. This explains part of the power of stories to engage listeners and make them feel as if they are part of the story. For more on this see chapter 3 of Zak, "Why Your Brain Loves Good Storytelling."

character and not several. While it is possible to do multiple characters, it is a highly developed skill that will require more than most can do.

(2) Minor Character—this is also a very popular approach. Think of all the minor characters that make an interesting perspective for preaching. How about telling the story of the wise men from the perspective of Herod? Or maybe telling the prodigal son parable from the perspective of the servant who speaks to the elder brother? Minor characters can be rich sources of insight in every story, from telling the rape of Bathsheba from her perspective rather than David's to Isaac's view of what his father is doing on that fateful day they went up the mountain. Not every story depends on the main character. Some are enriched by the lesser, more minimal characters.

(3) Implied Characters—this is perhaps the most unusual approach, but it has merits. An implied character is one who has to be there but never speaks in the text. For instance, in the feeding of the 5,000 the boy with the lunch never speaks but he certainly is there. What did he think happened to his meal? Also, those who were fed are rich sources to tell the story. What does that miracle look like when told by those who experienced it as it happened? While Andrew would be a minor character in that same story, what does that miracle look like through the eyes of Peter or Judas? They were there. What did they think?

In each case the use of narrators or characters require that the preacher be a good exegete of the text and context. Simply imagining and implying what you want to say is not textual preaching from a narrative/storytelling point of view. These kinds of approaches require even more emphasis on exegesis to ensure that the story that unfolds comes from the text and not simply the fertile mind of the preacher. If you think about it, there are depths of information that can aid you in this quest that might not be highly valued in a typical approach to a sermon. Geography would influence things about the feeding of the 5,000. So would the weather, time of day, animals in the wilderness, and the approaching darkness. Knowing the textual background of how Peter and Judas approached Jesus' unorthodox methods would provide fertile ground for understanding how they processed the miracle of the loaves and fishes. Doing these kinds of sermons drives the preacher deeper into their study not farther from the text. There are more details in the narratives of Scripture than you may imagine. Study them, use them, stick with them, and research them. If you do, the text will be deeper and more detailed than you can possibly imagine with just your own mind.[6]

Over the course of the next five chapters, you will be introduced to a variety of different narrative approaches that may whet your appetite for a more creative approach to narrative possibilities in the storytelling tradition. Below is a brief synopsis of the storytelling approach to each sermon. They vary and are sermons that I have preached in various places from seminary chapel to local congregations.

- Chapter 6: The Journey into Grief—Moses' Mother Mourns. This is a first-person sermon that takes on the perspective of an implied character, that of Moses' mother and her expressions of grief at the birth of Moses.
- Chapter 7: The Journey Toward Assurance—Mary and Joseph Wonder. This is a two person, "tag team" approach to a sermon. The sermon goes back and forth between the thinking and musings of Mary and Joseph about the birth of Christ. It is a two-person, first-person sermon.
- Chapter 8: The Journey from Tishbe—Elijah, the Man from Nowhere. This is a third-person narrative sermon that describes the development of Elijah's prophetic calling and mission. It utilizes the all-knowing narrator approach.
- Chapter 9: The Journey at the Altar—What Was Zechariah Expecting? This is an example of the Lowry Loop and my approach to this type of storytelling sermon. It was the first sermon I shared in Princeton Chapel and it reflects what I have tried to say about the application of the Lowry Loop.
- Chapter 10: The Journey of a Storytelling Savior—Jesus and His Teaching Method. The final example is another third-person narrative example that concludes the section with an understanding of how Jesus set the storytelling example. You can determine on your own which kind of narrator approach is used.

The reader is free to skip around in this part of the journey. The sermons are not built upon one another but give differing examples of how a first-person, third-person, or Lowry Loop approach to preaching can aid the

---

6. For a more detailed treatise of these principles, see my first book, *Preaching the Story*.

variety needed in our pulpit oration. You may want to see what principles from Section One are being applied in each sermon. Individual sermons reflect an understanding of a specific application of one of the opening chapters. Have fun with them (if that is not too much of a preaching heresy). I know I did.

6

The Journey into Grief
Moses' Mother Mourns

NOTE: You are encouraged to read this first-person narrative sermon and allow it to be experienced on its own storytelling merits. After the sermon there are questions and insights about the sermon to explain its context and implications. Each chapter in Section Two will follow this process.

> *Then Pharaoh gave this order to all his people: "Every Hebrew boy that is born you must throw into the Nile, but let every girl live." Now a man of the tribe of Levi married a Levite woman, and she became pregnant and gave birth to a son. When she saw that he was a fine child, she hid him for three months. But when she could hide him no longer, she got a papyrus basket for him and coated it with tar and pitch. Then she placed the child in it and put it among the reeds along the bank of the Nile. His sister stood at a distance to see what would happen to him.*
>
> EXODUS 1:22—2:4 (NIV)

HUSBAND FOCUS

What do I tell him?

My husband is a good man, a great father, a righteous and faithful believer in God. He is strong and protective of his family. How do I tell him that there is nothing that he can do to prevent this newborn son of ours from being killed, from being drowned in the Nile?

We have tried to protect him. I hid my pregnancy for as long as I could. We told no one that our son had been born. But the walls have ears. You cannot stop an infant from sobbing during the night or piercing the silence of the night with their cries. There are those in this village that would sell out their own family members if it meant an easier work detail, a larger ration of food, or better treatment by the Egyptian guards. How can we refuse to drown our son in the Nile as Pharaoh has decreed? What will that accomplish? They will simply kill me, kill my husband, kill my daughter, and then kill my newborn son anyway. How do I tell my husband that there is nothing that he can do to save this child?

DAUGHTER FOCUSED

How do I tell my daughter that we must drown her brother? Can someone so young really grasp the enormity of what that means? Will she know we do it without wanting to? That we only do it under threat of death ourselves? Of her dying? Will she realize how evil men can be and hate them forever? Will she be so damaged by the horror of us murdering her only brother that she will turn against her father and me? Against God and her faith? Will she look at me from now on with eyes that accuse and with a coldness of heart that hates? Will I cease to be her mother and become no better than the Egyptian guards that threaten her with torture and death when she gets out of line? How do I tell my daughter that her parents are not monsters?

CHILD FOCUSED

What do I tell my son, this precious gift given by God but condemned by man? All he knows to do is cling to me and feel comfort in my arms; to suckle at my breast and feed his needs through me; to have his fears calmed by me holding and rocking him to sleep. How can I betray this complete trust he has in me by tossing him into the deep? How do I explain that though God has blessed us with you, we are all cursed by your presence and must do an unthinkable thing? He is such a beautiful child, a precious gift of life, a loving baby—how do I explain that he must die so that others can live? How do I tell him about things he cannot possibly comprehend... but I can?

SELF-FOCUSED

How do I live with myself? How can I go on once I have destroyed this life that has lived inside my womb, touched the deepest parts of my body, been birthed from my loins and suckled at my breast? How do I live with myself? I have been created by God to be the bearer of new life, to birth and nurture life. How do I suddenly become the reaper of death and the taker of life? It is against everything that I am and all that I have been taught about who we are as a people and who God is as a god. How do I live with myself once I have denied everything that I am and know myself to be by putting away who I am and becoming who our Egyptian suppressors tell me I must become? How do I live with that? Will I ever be the same? How do I learn to live with myself?

Will I ever be the same? No, I will never be the same. I will be changed forever if I kill my own flesh and blood, if I murder the fruit of my womb. But, what am I supposed to do? Do I try and tell myself I am a good person in the dark reaches of the night when my nightmares will surely hound me? I have not slept since this baby arrived. Will I ever find rest again? Will I ever sleep through the night again without waking up in terror, screaming to protect a baby that no longer lives?

I cannot help but wonder that if I do this terrible deed, will I ever become a mother again? Would God, the God of Abraham, Isaac, and Jacob allow such an unworthy vehicle to become filled with a child and face this same agonizing decision again? What will I tell myself if I follow through with Pharaoh's edict? What will I tell my husband? What will I tell my daughter? What will I tell my newborn son?

GOD FOCUSED

Where are you God? Do not hide your face from me when I am in distress. Turn your ear to me; when I call, answer me quickly.[1] Why do you

---

1. I have tried to incorporate some phrases from Psalms of Lament in this section. Preachers often find it difficult to do lament in preaching. This sermon lends itself to such an expression. And since the book of Psalms is composed over many generations, who is to say that the phrases used in many of them are not taken from

not reach down from your heavens and pour thunder over those who destroy our lives? You know how we are surrounded by foes, soldiers who will just as soon run you through with a spear as look at you. And now that you have given me this child, my enemies are all around me. There are fellow Jews in this village who have doubted your very existence and who have cursed your name because you are silent in the face of such evil. Many believe that even our God cannot deliver us from this oppression let alone free us from captivity. Many are asking, who will bring us out of this terrible place? Are you even there God? Do you hear the cries of your people? Help us . . . we need you . . . you are our only hope! Deliver us from evil.

You alone, God, are my shield; when I lie down, you are there. When I rise up, you are there. When I cry out, you are there. When I weep with sadness or rejoice with gladness, you are there. Deliver us, O God. Deliver us from this evil decree and from this sinful system of slavery. There is nowhere else for me to turn but to you, O God. You alone have the power of life and death. You alone created this world and everything that is in it. Answer me when I call to you; give me relief from this terrible situation, from this horrible distress.

I have nowhere else to turn, God. Without you, there truly is no hope for me, for my husband, for my daughter, for my newborn son. So, I will go to the Nile and place my son in the waters. I will build him a small life boat from the bulrushes that surround the shore. I will cast him away from the shore and out into the Nile. But I will be crying out to you, O God. I will be praying for a miracle of redemption from your hand, O God. I will trust in you for there is no other hope. The gods of the Egyptians are made of wood and stone and offer nothing but death and hopelessness. I will trust in the God of Abraham, Isaac, Jacob, and Joseph. I will put my belief in the God of my forefathers and pray that you will deliver us all out of the grasp of the evil one. Help me, my Lord, help me. I put all my trust in you, God. All I know to do is believe and depend on You. This child is yours. He came from you and now, I give him back to you.

---

expressions of lament that were uttered during times of great distress—even in the Egyptian enslavement period. It would be a great touch for this sermon if the preacher would incorporate numerous phrases from psalms of lament to express her thoughts.

THE JOURNEY INTO GRIEF   121

QUESTIONS AND APPLICATIONS FOR PREACHERS: A NARRATIVE SENSE AND A STORYTELLING LENS

1. How does one develop a *Narrative Sense*?
2. How does one develop a *Storytelling Lens*?

A NARRATIVE SENSE #1:

As noted in the last chapter, the germination of this sermon occurred while I was in a postdoctoral teaching position at Princeton Theological Seminary. I gave some cursory details there. Now let me give you some additional background.

I received a call about preaching in chapel just before going into a classroom of seniors to discuss various aspects of preaching. To open the class, I told them I had just been asked to preach in chapel and did they have any suggestions about what I should do. The first thing they all agreed on was that I should preach a first-person narrative sermon. Most of the students had taken my Narrative Preaching Class and were interested in seeing me do one in a "real" setting. In that class I taught the principles of how to do both first-person narrative sermons and third-person narrative sermons. It did not surprise me that they would quickly embrace the idea that I should put into practice what I had taught in the classroom. As a matter of fact, I felt that if I didn't agree I would be betraying what I had taught them in the classroom. I quickly agreed. It seemed like a reasonable challenge and one that I was most willing to accept.

But then, the discussion took an unexpected turn. One of the women in the group said, "You should do a first-person narrative sermon as a woman." The group quickly agreed, much like an eager firing squad loads their weapons. I felt hoisted on my own petard, as Shakespeare would say. You see, in the Narrative Class I would always get a question during the first-person narrative section of the course about whether women could only do female characters in first person sermons. My reply was always, "No!"

After all, first-person narrative sermons are based on "the suspension of disbelief." Whenever someone attends a movie, play, or theater production the ability of the actors to accomplish the task at hand requires that the audience play along. The patron has to accept the fact that what they are seeing is not real life while at the same time believing that what they are experiencing on stage or screen is real. The good news is that listeners are always willing to suspend their disbelief and follow along even when they know that Tom Hanks has not really become "Big" on the outside while remaining a 12-year-old on the inside. Nor is there really a character with the powers of Captain America, Iron Man, Wonder Woman, or Black Panther (though I secretly wish there were . . . Wakanda!). And Hugh Jackman does not have claws made out of Adamantium nor is Patrick Stewart really like Jean-Luc Picard . . . yet, we easily go with them when they transform into the characters they portray.[2]

If this was true for those in the world of movies and television then why would it not be available for preachers in the pulpit? The question is, are congregations are willing to suspend disbelief when preachers take on the task of first-person preaching? As you might suspect, my resounding answer to such a query is "Yes!" and I have the experience to back that up. I have preached numerous first-person narratives in churches where I was the senior pastor, in seminary chapels, at youth retreats, senior adult conventions, and as a guest speaker at a local congregation. So, if that is true that congregational members have the same ability to suspend disbelief if I portray David, Paul, or John the Baptist, then why couldn't a woman portray Elijah on Mt. Carmel or Daniel in the lion's den? If the congregation has already suspended disbelief that they are hearing from Daniel or Elijah, how much of a stretch is it to suspend gender when portraying a character?

Of course, as I stood before my students, the shoe was on the other foot, so to speak. If the above was true then why couldn't a man (me) portray a woman? So, I accepted the challenge and began to prepare the sermon, looking for a narrative wherein I could take on the voice of a woman. As I began to pray and consider the challenge, I ended up concentrating on the Book of Exodus and the dynamics of being a new mother having to execute her own child at the orders of Pharaoh. The story appeared rich in the human-divine dynamics that can make a biblical story come alive in fresh ways. Having settled on the story, I began my exegetical work. My exegesis was not any different from any text that I sought to mine for truths and insights. The only difference here was that I paid special attention to the emotional realities that were in the

2. I know this was covered before, but it bears repeating here as background for why this sermon was developed the way it was.

text and context but not fully expressed in detailed terms. What, exactly, were those emotional realities that help explain Exodus 2 and the story of Moses? It was this question that took me on a journey to discover the *Narrative Sense* of the passage.

The first thing that helped me form a *Narrative Sense* of the passage was the brutality of the Egyptian slave masters in 1:11–14. This social reality was instructive of the depth of the brutality that the Jews lived under after being enslaved. What they experienced was more than oppression; it was a ruthlessness that we rarely detail in our preaching because it is too horrific. To counter this inhumaneness, the text speaks of the heroism of the Jewish midwives, portrayed through the stories of Puah and Shiphrah. This represents the spirit of opposition that must have been present in both the enslaved community and the Egyptian culture.[3]

But that is not where the story ends. The same text that exalts the Jewish midwives also relates the increasing brutality of Pharaoh and his regime. By the time chapter 1 ends and Moses is born at the beginning of chapter 2, Pharaoh has abandoned the idea that enslaved work and cruel living conditions will thin the Hebrew herd or that using midwives as abortion agents will lower the birth rates of male children. Now he has placed the burden on the Jewish parents themselves—*they must drown their own newborn male babies!* I tried to let that reality sink in for a while and explore what questions arise from such a horrendous situation.

- What does it do to a society when forced infanticide is the law of the land?
- How does a mother or father recover from that kind of psychological devastation?
- What happens to a social structure when children are killed before being weaned?

I'm not sure PTSD even begins to try and diagnose the kind of holocaust that Jewish mothers, fathers, and families endured during this horrific period. The only parallels I could think of was the callousness of slavery, the oppression of blacks on the plantation and the Nazis'

---

3. There are various traditions surrounding the identity of the Hebrew midwives. One Rabbinic tradition identifies them as non-Hebrews who were either secret converts to the faith or opposers of Pharaoh's edict. For a more detailed examination of this issue see Kadari, "Shiphrah: Midrash and Aggadah."

systematic destruction of Jews in Europe during WWII. People lost not just their lives but their identity as human beings. They became chattel rather than persons of worth. The brutality of that reality is the *Narrative Sense* of Exod 1 and 2.

Exegetically, you cannot read Exod 2 without understanding it through the *Narrative Sense* that is formed in Exod 1. These two chapters are intertwined; they are not separate stories but an extension of the same atmosphere of callousness that existed during this time. The fact that the opening verses of Exod 2 are told so flatly, so matter-of-factly seems to confirm that the pain and anguish of killing their own children had already dulled the communal outrage of both Jews and Egyptians. Like prisoners in the German concentration camps in WWII, they seemed to resign themselves to existing in a place where they could not control their own destinies, let alone the fate of their children. The only sense you have of real humanity in the midst of such harshness is the papyrus basket into which Moses' mother places her three-month old child. I can imagine that the lining of pitch and tar was cured by her tears. How do you get to the place where you can make such a boat let alone put your baby adrift in it? How damaged, depressed, oppressed, and despondent do you have to be to kill your own child in such a brutal fashion?

The absolute cruelty and sense of hopelessness becomes the real context of the story, the true *Narrative Sense*. Knowing it is crucial to really knowing the narrative, experiencing the story. *Narrative Sense* is more than the general context. It includes the psychological, emotional and relational dynamics that are part of all human interaction and social struggle. To explore these realities is how you develop a *Narrative Sense* of a story. Sensing that the real story is "in-between the lines" of what the text says outright, *Narrative Sense* creates an exegetical model wherein the story begins to unfold in storytelling terms rather than propositional facts.

A STORYTELLING LENS #2:

Once you have found a *Narrative Sense* in the passage, you must now turn toward a *Storytelling Lens*. In the case of this sermon, the decision about the *Storytelling Lens* had already been made in part by my students. They had suggested that whatever passage I would choose it would have to be told in the first person from the perspective of a woman. While there were possible choices (Moses' sister is mentioned in 2:7; one of the Jewish women living in the neighborhood could become an "implied character";[4] or even Shiphrah or Puah or a midwife noted in chapter 1), the one that was most obvious to me was Moses' mother. Once I had settled on her, the challenge was to filter all the things I had discovered and explored in my search for a *Narrative Sense* and funnel it through Moses' mother as my *Storytelling Lens*. In other words, the experience of cruelty and barbarism had to be connected to how she would see the story unfold. Not only see the story but feel the story. This is where the crucial move took place—the move to inside the story; from Joe Friday (just the facts) to break a leg (enter the story and tell it from the inside).

As I began to funnel the context through her eyes, I found myself concentrating on how a wife would try and help her husband deal with the tragic consequences of not being able to protect his family. Once there, it was a short excursion around the room so that Moses' mother would have to try and find a way to explain it to her daughter, her baby boy, and, ultimately, to herself. While this was the easy part, the hard part was finding a way to preach this story with hope. It is one thing to spend an entire message on lament, but it is quite another to find hope in the midst of despair. It was at this point that the testimony and witness of the Hebrew midwives came into play. As they lived out their faith in spite of human sinfulness and governmental oppression, they found a way to allow their trust in God to shine in spite of the overwhelming darkness. If Shiphrah and Puah could manage to find that kind of hope and meaning—placing their trust and belief in God in such devastating circumstances—why could that not also be true of Moses' mother? After all, the making of a papyrus vessel and the care with which she lined it with tar and pitch bespoke a faith that remained even when the waters were lapping up the side of the makeshift arc. How would a woman, a mother of faith express her hope in the midst of her tears and the seeming certainty of death? Once I had that as my conclusion, the sermon was complete. I had a *Storytelling Lens*.

---

4. For more information on what is meant by an implied character see my book, Frymire, *Preaching the Story*.

A NARRATIVE SENSE AND A STORYTELLING LENS #3:

I know the question on your mind must be, "Did it work?" Well, as noted in chapter 5 the congregation's silence was telling. The immediate feedback from students and faculty would also confirm the success of the task. However, it was most interesting to me when I was talking to another faculty member some weeks after the chapel service and he commented to me about the sermon. He was frank in saying that when I began the sermon he thought, "This is going to be a train wreck." But he related how in short order he became lost in the story, mesmerized by the text placed in a *Storytelling Lens*, engrossed in the lament turned to hope that the sermon expressed. Rather than a train wreck, it contained an insight and emotional connectivity he had not considered before.

It has been my experience that if a preacher will commit to the storytelling process and allow the story to have the central role in the sermon by using a narrative sense and a storytelling lens, then the sermon will have an effective impression upon the listener. If you can move away from the narrowness of "just the facts" and lean into the reality that these are real people, living real lives, doing real things, in a real way. Once you break that leg, the story has the power and weight it had as it originally unfolded. At least it did that day in Princeton Chapel.

7

The Journey Toward Assurance
Mary and Joseph Wonder

> *Around the time of Elizabeth's amazing pregnancy and John's birth, the emperor in Rome, Caesar Augustus, required everyone in the Roman Empire to participate in a massive census— the first census since Quirinius had become governor of Syria. Each person had to go to his or her ancestral city to be counted. Mary's fiancé Joseph, from Nazareth in Galilee, had to participate in the census in the same way everyone else did. Because he was a descendant of King David, his ancestral city was Bethlehem, David's birthplace. Mary, who was now late in her pregnancy that the messenger Gabriel had predicted, accompanied Joseph. While in Bethlehem, she went into labor and gave birth to her firstborn son. She wrapped the baby in a blanket and laid Him in a feeding trough because the inn had no room for them.*
>
> LUKE 2:1-7 (THE MESSAGE)

PART ONE: MARY MEETS AN ANGEL AND A LEAPING CHILD

MARY

It was just a normal, usual, regular day—just like any other day. I was at home going about my daily chores. You know, baking bread, washing dishes, sweeping the floor, those normal everyday things we do. Then, out of nowhere, this stranger appeared and before I could say anything, he said, "Greetings, you who are highly favored! The Lord is with you."

Highly favored? The Lord is with me? What in the world was this? I was truly frightened and confused. What was he doing here? What had he to do with me? Then he called me by my name and told me "Don't be afraid."

Don't be afraid? Found favor with God? What had I done to find favor with God—at least the kind of favor that warrants a visit from a messenger of God, an angel? I just knew this was an angel from God. Who else could it have been? An angel of the Lord telling me that I was not to be afraid? He kept on talking, so I didn't really have time to think about it. He said that I was going to conceive a child, a son, and his name was to be Jesus. "He will be great," he said. "He will be called Son of the Most High. The Lord God will give him the throne of his father David, and he will reign over Jacob's descendants forever, his kingdom will never end." It was almost too much to comprehend.

Then I asked "How can this be happening? I am a virgin. I have never even been with a man." The angel told me that the Holy Spirit would come upon me and the power of the Most High will overshadow me. So the holy one to be born will be called the Son of God.

Then the angel told me that my cousin, Elizabeth, was six months pregnant! She and Zachariah had given up trying to have a child for they were well beyond the childbearing years. "Nothing is impossible with God," the angel said.

In the face of such startling news, what was I to say? If God could open the womb of my barren cousin; if he could send an angel to speak to me; if nothing is truly impossible where God is concerned, then could God not also open my womb and plant a baby inside of me? Was it so fantastic, so implausible? Overwhelmed by God's presence I found myself blurting out, "I am the Lord's servant. May your word to me be fulfilled." And with that he left as quickly as he had come. He was . . . just . . . gone.

It was hard trying to take it all in—all that he had said . . . it was so much to try to fully understand. Out of all the women in the world . . . God has chosen me to be the mother of his son. Did I really hear the angel correctly? Did I misunderstand what he had said? I am going to become pregnant by the Holy Spirit of God? I know that I am to live according to God's will. That my life is his to use, to lead and guide. That's what I told the angel . . . that I am the Lord's servant and am willing to be used as God has chosen.

I'm still not sure I even understand all this. Who wakes up in the morning and expects to be spoken to by an angel of the Lord? But I thought that if my cousin, Elizabeth, was six months pregnant as the angel said . . . what a miracle that is. I knew I had to go and see her. It may not have been the smartest thing to do. She lives in the hills of Judea, south of Jerusalem—a good four-day journey from Nazareth. But I had to go to her. It certainly gave me time to process all that was transpiring.

I was pregnant with God's Son. It took me a whole day's journey just to try and comprehend that thought. What were people going think? I am not even married yet. What about my parents? Will they believe me when I tell them what happened? Who is going to believe that an angel appeared to me and told me that I would become pregnant by the Holy Spirit? Will they think this a joke? What about Joseph? Will he still want to marry me? I don't even want to think about telling him. But . . . maybe it's not too much harder than believing that Elizabeth is pregnant. The angel did say that with God all things are possible. As the end of the long journey came into sight I found myself confessing, "God, I believe you. I trust you, even if this whole thing is a bit much to take in."

When I walked in the door, I greeted Elizabeth and before I could tell her my miraculous news, Elizabeth's baby leaped in her womb and Elizabeth was filled with the Holy Spirit. She was so excited that I was with child—before I could even tell her I was pregnant or how it came to be. Yet, she knew. She not only knew I was pregnant but that the child within me was God's Son. The first thing she said was, "Blessed are you among women, and blessed is the child you will bear! But why am I so favored, that the mother of my Lord should come to me?" When Elizabeth's baby leaped inside of her it was as though the baby recognized the truth of what was going on in my body, that I was bearing the Son of God.

God was providing some needed affirmation here. This whole thing was just too big for me to be the only one to know and work through. Being with Elizabeth was really good for me . . . .and for her, too. To be able to share the changes that one's body goes through while being pregnant. She helped me process all that the angel had told me and to remind me how important this baby was and what an honor it was to be the chosen one to carry this child. She, too, carried a miracle infant inside her. Elizabeth was so encouraging and affirming. I stayed with her for about three months. She was going to be giving birth soon and I needed to go home. It was going to be an even longer walk home, now that I was beginning to show. I needed to face all the people at home and deal with whatever they would think or believe. The walk was not going to be easier the more the baby grew inside me.

Once I started my journey home, the questions continued to wrack my brain:

- What kind of mother was I going to be?
- How do you parent the Son of God?
- How do I continue to find favor in God's eyes and continue to be worthy of being his son's mother?
- How was I going to tell my parents and family and . . . and . . . and Joseph?
- How was I going to tell Joseph?
- Will he still want to marry me?
- What were people going to think?
- God, what is your plan from here?[1]

PART TWO: JOSEPH AND THE DREAM OF REVELATION

JOSEPH

I needed assurances. Considering all that had taken place over these last few months, can you blame me? It all started out so normal. My parents had arranged my marriage to Mary. It was done in all the traditional ways. Our families met together and had a public ceremony where our fathers signed the marriage contract. The bride price was agreed upon and Mary and I were officially betrothed, married in the eyes of God. Mary immediately returned to her parents' house for a year in order to prepare herself to be a wife and manage our household. I returned to my parents' house and earnestly worked to complete my carpenter's apprenticeship. I was determined to provide for my wife and, should God bless us, our children.

It was all so normal, so good, so idyllic . . . until it wasn't. I guess I should have suspected something when, a few months after the ceremony, Mary left her parents' home to travel to Judea to see her cousin Elizabeth. Everyone had heard the great news that Elizabeth, who was

---

1. When my wife and I originally preached this sermon, she sang the song, "Breath of Heaven" at this point. It was very, very effective. If you have that kind of musical ability, I would highly encourage that to be part of the sermon.

thought to be barren, miraculously conceived in her old age. It was something we rejoiced about throughout the village. I could understand why Mary might want to go and celebrate with her older cousin but . . . for three months? I was working hard to provide for us and there were many decisions and actions to be made so we might finally come together as husband and wife. It was awkward not having her here to consult about those things. Little did I know that the time she spent away was the least of our problems.

When Mary finally returned, she carried with her a story too wild, too fantastic to be believed. She told her parents the story who then, doing what is prescribed by the Law, set up a meeting to tell my parents. My parents then sat me down and told me that my betrothed, my Mary, was pregnant. I was devastated. Had she been unfaithful with someone in the village? Did this occur when she was with Elizabeth? Was there someone else? What my parents told me next was too much to grasp.

We were told that Mary claimed she had not been unfaithful to her vows; that she had not committed adultery with another man; that she had been visited by an Angel of the Lord who told her she would become pregnant by divine means. When asked if she could somehow confirm this visitation, she said she could not. But she did say that this message had been confirmed by Elizabeth in a prophetic pronouncement when Mary first arrived in Judea through some kind of baby movement in Elizabeth. The only thing my parents could tell me was that Mary was adamant about her story and clung convincingly to the angel visitation.

Angels? The Holy Spirit? Babies leaping in the womb? Prophetic pronouncements? It was all too much for me to comprehend. Neither I, nor any of my family or friends, had ever seen or heard a prophet. There hadn't been one in Israel in centuries. What was I to think? What were we to do? We were nearing the end of the betrothal year, before we had ever lived together as husband and wife or had come together as one flesh, and now I have to deal with the news that Mary is pregnant? What am I to do? I am no Hosea to her Gomer, that's for sure! The only thing I knew to do was to divorce her quietly in order to avoid the inevitable scandal this will cause. She will face the scorn of the village, she and her parents both. For that, I cannot help her. It was the worst day of my life.

(*Change of mood*)

Even if her story were true, and I'm not saying it is, I would need more proof, more assurance than just a fantastic tale about angel visitations or an old woman's pregnancy pronouncement. Besides, Mary is as unlikely a candidate to be the mother of the Messiah as I am to marry a pregnant woman. I don't mean that Mary is not special. She is, but just to me. She is not royalty and neither am I. Our only claim to fame is that we are both of the house and lineage of David, but that doesn't make us royalty, does it? Certainly, we are not the only ones walking around with some drops of blood in us passed down from King David's reign? Do you think that being in David's line and lineage is enough to qualify us as parents of a special, divinely ordered birth? I'm a carpenter not a king.

As I went to bed that night, I could hardly sleep. The questions in my mind would not be silent. All night long I tossed and turned, prayed and wept. Toward the dawn of that fateful night something incredible happened to me. I can only describe what I experienced as a kind of waking dream. In that moment between dreaming and being awake I received an angelic visitation from God, different than what Mary had experienced but surely just as real. In the dream, God told me in no uncertain terms, that Mary's story was true and that I was to take her as my wife without hesitation or reservation. The angel explained that what was growing inside Mary was, indeed, from the Holy Spirit.

When I awoke from the dream I sprang out of bed. I knew I had to speak to Mary. I know that going to her house early in the morning was breaking with tradition and that, should anyone find out we were together, alone, we would be in violation of the Law. But I had to see her; speak to her; tell her the good news. I ran to her parents' home and roused her to come to the window. We spoke for the first time as husband and wife. I told her my dream. She told me hers. It was the first time we had talked about the visitations. We compared the angelic messages and we knew that God had spoken to both of us. I asked her what name she was to give to the child and together we blurted out at the same time, "Jesus!" It was a sign from God. It was the assurance I needed.

After the early morning meeting, we decided to move in together immediately. Since the year of betrothal was nearly up, it caused no stir in the village. The tradition was up to a year so we were well within our rights. I took Mary to our house to live as husband and wife. The village celebrated the consummation of our marriage. For all appearances' sake, we looked like the perfect couple. We announced almost immediately that Mary was pregnant since we feared she would be showing soon. Our families and friends rejoiced at the good news, but we could tell no one that we had never lain together, even after she moved into the house. If she had conceived as a virgin, she would birth the baby as a virgin as well. We both believed this to be the will of God.

Our first order of priority was to try and figure out where to go and what to do about the birth. It wouldn't take much for people in the village to add up the dates and realize that she was pregnant long before the year of betrothal was up. Scandal still lurked at our doorstep. But we came to realize that when God has a plan he has already worked out all the fine points of that plan. All we had to do was trust that God would make a way for us. It was during this time that Nazareth was informed that the Roman occupiers were ordering that a census be taken that included all of Israel. In addition, the method of the census was that all households were required to return to their ancestral homes in order to be enrolled in the census.

Well, you can imagine the stir this caused in our village. Everyone complained about this forced trip. Everyone grumbled about the imposition of the Romans and the expense of having to leave your home for weeks not to mention your business, your farms, your crops; we had to leave everything behind or take with us what we could. No one liked the news . . . except me and Mary. To us this was a gift from God, another assurance that amazed both of us. Imagine, God was using the ruler of the most powerful nation in the world to give us the opportunity to leave our village, travel to Bethlehem and have our baby without the prying eyes of those who could claim something impure in this divine birth.

And so it was that we packed everything we could and traveled to Bethlehem. The journey was hard on Mary, but we traveled with the knowledge and assurance that God was with us and that God would protect us. During our journey, Mary and I talked together about all that had taken place already. We had received angels, messengers of God to give us understanding. I had been given a dream to assure us of God's will in this time. Mary had been the recipient of a prophecy, uttered by a woman who, herself, was the recipient of a miracle child. And now, here we were about to enter Bethlehem and experience the birth of this child, this holy child and name him Jesus. What more assurance would anyone need?

PART THREE: MARY AND THE SHEPHERDS' ASSURANCE

MARY

What a relief it was when Joseph told me about the angel appearing to him in his dream! The Lord already had a plan. The Lord is sooo good! God will make a way.

Why do I keep questioning what is going on? I told the angel "Let it be with me as you said." What it is about being human that makes us question everything that God says he will do? I couldn't help but rejoice with how God had worked out so many details. His miracles never cease!

As the days counted down, Joseph and I were hit with another challenge to overcome. The Roman government had ordered that a census be required with each person traveling to the town of their family's origin. It meant that we had to go to Bethlehem. Though it wasn't as far to Bethlehem as it was to Elizabeth's, it was still over a three day journey when you were in good health. While I had already made that journey once when pregnant, now I had to do it again . . . this time even more pregnant.

We did not make great time. I kept needing to stop and rest. At least I wasn't alone this time. Joseph was very caring and patient with me. When we finally arrived in Bethlehem, there were so many people everywhere. I was in the beginnings of labor when we arrived in the city. It was obvious the baby was on its way. Joseph finally found a place for us to have some privacy. He made a comfortable make-shift bed for me out of straw. Not a place where one would expect to give birth to any baby, let alone God's Son.

It was there, in a feeding trough that we laid Jesus after he was born. God's Son had entered the world. No one else was there. Just Joseph, me and the baby. We were resting; the baby was finally asleep. I was contemplating what our next step was to be. What were we to do now? We weren't sure we wanted to go back to Nazareth at this time.

I thought about how Hannah, after giving birth to Samuel, took him to the temple to be raised there as she had promised God she would do. Is that what we should do with Jesus? Take him to be raised in the temple? Joseph and I were certainly not special people, not special parents. But to take him to the temple, this precious little helpless baby? How could I do that? If that's what God really wanted, wouldn't the angel have told me that raising him in the temple was God's plan?

Amidst the straw and animals, I wondered aloud why he wasn't delivered in a royal household. If he is to be given the throne of David and reign over the house of Jacob, shouldn't he be with royalty? But I kept coming back to the words of the angel—God had found favor with me. What I had done that God found favor with me above all other women was still a mystery to me. I do not know why but I do know that he chose me as the mother of His son. He is Jehovah Jireh, "The Lord will provide."

We heard some commotion outside and there came some shepherds-shepherds who had been out on the hillside watching their sheep. They were dirty, smelly shepherds, but they came right into our humble little abode. They said they were looking for a baby. A baby lying in a manger and dressed in the most common garb. Joseph and I looked at each other in surprise. They were talking about our newborn baby. We showed them where he was lying in the manger and dressed in the most basic of materials. Now it was their turn to look at one another in amazement.

They told us an amazing story of how an angel appeared to them and a glorious light had shone around them. When they told us that an angel told them not to be afraid, Joseph and I were thrilled. I wondered if the same angel that spoke to me and that revealed God's plan in a dream to Joseph was the same one that spoke to the shepherds on the hillside?

But their angel was not just a single messenger but was joined by a whole army of angels who began to proclaim the good news—the wonderful, joyous news about a savior being born in David's city, Bethlehem. Like my angel had said to me, this baby was to be the Christ, the Lord, the Messiah. This sign was that they would find a newborn baby wrapped snugly and lying in a manger. And, as if to put an exclamation point on their pronouncement, there was suddenly a multitude of angels in the night sky singing and praising God, "Glory to God in the highest and peace on earth and goodwill to men." The angels had told the shepherds about us here in this place in Bethlehem.

Like Elizabeth's unborn child leaping inside her womb, God gave me another miraculous affirmation of his goodness and grace when he told these shepherds about this child that I gave birth to on that night. After the angels left them, the shepherds decided to come see what the Lord had made known to them. The shepherds came, found the baby, and bowed down in front of my newborn baby. They worshipped him and gave honor to him, Jesus. This child, this freshly minted infant, this small little person was, once again, affirmed that he was the long-awaited Son of God. What a miraculous thing to happen! The baby Jesus, whom the angel promised to me those many months ago, is indeed here to change the world. In spite of all my back and forth between praising God for what he was doing and yet questioning so much out of my own uncertainty . . . I realized at that moment that I had, indeed, been a part of God's almighty plan.

God has used me to bring about a miracle. God has always had a plan and I was included in that plan. Every time I doubted, he gave me assurances that I needn't worry. It has been many months since the angel first appeared to me to tell me that I would conceive this child by the Holy Spirit. He first gave me affirmation and assurance when I visited Elizabeth and the baby inside her leaped and she blessed me as the mother of the Lord. I received assurance again when Joseph told me that he was visited by the angel in his dream. Once again, this night, the shepherds have provided me with yet another assurance that what God said would come to pass has indeed happened.

When the shepherds went away from us, they left proclaiming to all they met what they had heard and seen about this miraculous child. And all who heard it were amazed at what the shepherds told them. The shepherds were another important assurance to me that God has fulfilled his promises to me and to all of Israel. I will treasure all these words and I will ponder all these things in my heart for the rest of my life.

PART FOUR: JOSEPH AND THE WISE MEN'S VISITATION

JOSEPH

You would think that it was enough to have all the assurances that we shared together. That we would need nothing more to assure us of God's will in our lives. But we are human beings, frail and often afraid. In spite of all that had taken place I found myself once again asking for God to give us some assurances of his will for our lives. And, as he always does, God spoke to us in a dramatic way.

After Jesus was born, Mary and I decided to stay in Bethlehem— at least for a while. We wanted our son to grow up enough so that no one back home would be able to tell the difference in his age and our marriage. Once the census was over, the overflow crowds in Bethlehem dissipated quickly and there were plenty of places to live. It wasn't hard for a carpenter like myself, to find a house that needed some work and establish a home for the three of us. I found work in the town pretty quickly and word got around that I was a pretty good carpenter. I even got a few jobs in Jerusalem since the capital was just a few miles down the road. Between the tourist traffic on their way to and from Jerusalem and the residents of Bethlehem, we managed to establish a modest but comfortable life together.

The problem with a comfortable life is that questions, doubts, and fears can easily creep into your mind and thoughts. What were we to do now? Jesus didn't appear to be anything other than a normal, beautiful baby boy. Had we misread the signs? Was he really the Messiah? Is this how God comes into the world? One by one the questions would arise and day by day doubts would surface. It wasn't long after all of this that I found myself asking God once again for a sign, for some kind of assurance of his will in our lives. Little could I have known the lengths God would go to give us that assurance.

I remember that it began with concerned talk in the town. It seems as if Jerusalem was in quite the upheaval because of unexpected visitors from the East. Word was that these foreigners, astrologers from somewhere far away from here, had come to Jerusalem seeking to find the King of the Jews. Naturally, they were directed to King Herod, but word was that he was not the one they were looking for. That made everyone nervous. Surely Herod would not be pleased to hear about another king of the Jews. He was not a man to be trifled with at all. He could be brutal, vengeful, hateful and he had the power to enforce his anger. Like I said, it put everyone on edge.

Late one evening Mary and I were trying to get Jesus down for the night without success. He wasn't fussy at all, but nothing we did could get him to sleep. It was as if he was expecting something to happen and, sure enough, it did. It was unusual to receive visitors at night, especially in Bethlehem. But the rapping on our door was the unmistakable sound of visitors at our home. Nothing I had imagined could have prepared me for what Mary and I saw when we opened the door.

There before us stood a whole caravan of men, animals and supplies. Lavishly dressed and adorned, the strangers at our house could only have been one group. This must be the wise men that the town was all buzzing about. I'm sure my eyes were pretty wide open even though my mouth was sealed shut. For their part these strangers were filled with an excitement I had rarely seen on anyone's face. They started babbling in their thick accents about a star they had been following. I wasn't sure I understood, but one of them motioned for me to come outside and he pointed up at the sky. And, sure enough, there seemingly perched above our home was the brightest star I had ever seen. It was as though it had been plucked out of the sky and place right over our home. I was dumbfounded.

They quickly told me that this was the star that had first appeared in the sky months and months ago. When they told me when they had first seen it, I realized that it was the exact time we had been crowded into an empty cave to experience the birth of Jesus. They were emphatic that the star had led them to Jerusalem before it disappeared and had only reappeared this night to lead them to Bethlehem, to our home. Once again, I was trying to comprehend all of this and understand its meaning when Mary arrived at the door with Jesus in her arms. Suddenly, everything seemed to stop. The light of the star shone down on her and the baby. Immediately, the travelers fell at her feet and began to worship.

Mary and I stood there looking at this amazing scene and trying to figure out its meaning. Before we could even ask a question, the men began to pull out gifts for our child. And not just the typical gifts parents receive when a child is born. These were expensive gifts, more wealth than I had never seen in one place before. Gold, frankincense, and myrrh—the most expensive substances in any culture. They were worth a fortune, more money than I would ever amass as a carpenter. The only place I knew that trafficked in gold, frankincense, and myrrh was the temple where the Holy of Holies was inlaid with gold; and the priests burned frankincense on the altar of incense; and the temple priests used myrrh to anoint other priests or kings when they were crowned and prophets when they stood in place of God and spoke his words. But for a carpenter's kid? Never. What was God trying to tell us? What were we supposed to do with this king's ransom?

By the time the gift giving was completed and the wise men had shared the totality of their story, it was nearly dawn. Jesus was fast asleep in his mother's arms as we talked the night away. They left before sunrise to situate themselves outside the city and rest for the day before heading home. Mary and I went to bed and fell fast asleep, not even talking about the events of the evening. We were too tired. And yet, during that sleep I had another waking dream. A dream so real that I thought it was really happening. The same angel that had spoken to me about marrying Mary had returned with an ominous warning. He told me that we had to leave our home in Bethlehem and flee our homeland entirely. The angel told me to escape to Egypt with my family and wait there until I was called to come home.

When I awoke, I told Mary about the dream and said that we had to leave and leave quickly. There had been an urgency about the angelic message. There was no time to waste. As we packed our meager goods, I started to wonder where we would get the money for the trip or the funds needed to set up a home in a strange and foreign land? I said it out loud one time and Mary heard me. She turned and said to me, "God has already provided for us." I started to ask her what she meant when it hit me. We had been given a king's ransom for our son by the wise men. It was more than enough for whatever we might need for the trip and for years to come. Once again I was flooded with the knowledge that God had not only provided sustenance for our family but he had provided assurance for me. What an incredible God we serve! He gives us everything we need exactly when we need it.

CONCLUSION: MARY

MARY

When I visited Elizabeth I said, "My soul magnifies the Lord and my spirit rejoices in God my Savior, for he has looked with favor on the lowliness of his servant. Surely, from now on all generations will call me blessed. Not because of what I have done, but because of what God has done. My God is faithful; my God has a plan; my God will make a way. If only we stay in his will. God sent angels to proclaim what God is going to do. God gave me assurances of his continued guidance and faithfulness as I visited Elizabeth who was filled with the Holy Spirit and her baby leaping inside her, as Joseph is visited by an angel to confirm what happened to me and to carry on our with our plans to marry, as the shepherds saw the angels that night who sent them to find the baby Jesus—the savior of the world. When we took Jesus to the temple to be presented to the Lord for purification, there were further assurances to us of God's continued guidance. We met Simeon. He was an old man to whom it had been revealed that he would not die before seeing the Lord's Messiah. He entered the temple guided by the Holy Spirit. He took the baby Jesus in his arms declaring that now he had seen the salvation of the Lord, prepared in the presence of the people, a light for the revelation to the Gentiles and for glory to the people of Israel. And the prophetess, Anna, who worshipped in the temple every day. She came and praised God for the child and told all there he was the redemption of Jerusalem. There continued to be assurances to me all along the way. God is faithful. God will make a way and will fulfill his plan. We can trust him.

CONCLUSION: JOSEPH

JOSEPH

(*taking Mary's hand*) God has provided all that we need for our journey to Egypt. He has given us substance for our journey; protection for our travels; grace for our doubts; wisdom beyond our understanding; and assurance for all our wonderings and questions. As we leave Bethlehem and make our way to Egypt, we will be retracing the steps of Moses and the Jewish people as they came from Egypt to the Holy Land. One day, when the Lord calls us again, we will make our own exodus back to Israel. This is the story of our journey. It is not complete yet. Who knows what our son will really become when he is grown? Who knows how he will sense his calling and take up the mantle God has placed upon him? Who knows whether his mother and I shall live to see his mission and ministry fulfilled? But those are questions for the future. As for now, it is enough to know that God has affirmed, confirmed, and assured us of his presence and protection over us.

What I believe is that whatever journey you are on with God, I know that God will provide a way, provide assurances along that way and give you everything you need to follow the way. Do not be afraid, my friends, and do not be dismayed. For this God who has done so much for our family and for yours will lead you into his holy and righteous will. All you have to do is follow him.

(*Mary and Joseph walk down the center aisle and out the door. The Worship Leader/Team comes up and closes the service.*)

QUESTIONS AND APPLICATIONS FOR PREACHERS: NEUROSCIENCE AND NARRATIVE

1. Having experienced a first-person narrative that is singular, what are the challenges and pitfalls that can be experienced when more than one person is doing a narrative character?

2. How does this sermon help affirm the issues of neuroscience raised in chapter 3?

Neuroscience and Narrative Interaction #1: Focus

It may be obvious, but the most pressing challenge for a two-person narrative is to have strong coordination between both preachers when it comes to transitions, connections, and, especially, the focus of the sermon. A dual first-person narrative can easily fall apart if the two preachers fail to make sure that all they do coordinates with the other preacher. The goal is that the sermon flow should be seamless between them—in this case between the ending of Mary and the beginning of Joseph. To that end, both preachers must first agree on an overarching theme that can be the focus of both characters.

Tom Long speaks about every sermon having a Focus Statement and a Function Statement.[2] A first person sermon (or any narrative sermon) requires this as much as any other kind of sermonic form needs a focus and a function. Here is how Long describes these two kinds of statements:

> **Focus statement:** "a concise description of the central, controlling, and unifying theme of the sermon. In short, this is what the sermon will be about."
>
> **Function statement:** "a description of what the preacher hopes the sermon will create or cause to happen for the hearers."

Can you see the common theme that both characters are exploring? What is their common concern, difficulty, or problem? This focus must arise out of your study of the text and what you see happening to the characters in the story. As a way of practicing this discipline, see if you can write out in one sentence the central, controlling, and unifying theme of the sermon about Mary and Joseph. Then come back to this section, and I'll tell you what our Focus Statement was when we first preached this text.

Now that you've written down your idea, let me share what the Focus Statement for the sermon was in our minds.

Focus Statement: *There is a need for assurance when following the Will of God.*

The rationale for this was that both Mary and Joseph are faced with supernatural realities that no one is prepared to face. Simply hearing an

---

2. Long, *Witness of Preaching*. See especially chapter 4 on "The Focus and Function" of the sermon, 78–91.

angelic pronouncement or the testimony of shepherds and wise men does not lessen the difficulty anyone would have with these kinds of miraculous actions. Since both characters must be struggling with need for assurance during this time, it seemed a natural fit for each character to be able to explore the difficulty of wanting to believe the angel and still finding themselves in need of assurance from God.

In the case of Mary, the need for assurance is answered during her visit to Elizabeth and the baby leaping in Elizabeth's womb. In the story of Joseph, he needs to be assured that this pregnancy really is from God and that Mary's story is true and, as with Mary, that God is the true author of this miracle. Even when given a powerful insight through a waking dream, Joseph remains in need of further assurance as the story unfolds. Being given assurance once does not end their need or desire for assurance again and again.

As each character moves forward in the story, they face internal questions about what God is really doing. How should they react? What should they do next? The questions come at them continually:

#1: They question.
#2: God replies.
#3: They have more questions.
#4: God, in his great grace, gives further assurance to them both.

The underlying point is that the revelation of who Jesus is and what that means is an ongoing experience for both of them and, by extension, for all of us. And, just as they both continue to seek assurance from God so we, too, are in continuous need of having the Spirit of God provide for us reassurances along the journeys we travel. This is the focus of the sermon.

Since we brought up the Focus of the Sermon, it might do well to let you in on the Function of the Sermon. What do you think it might have been? Why not try again to write down the Function as you see it play out in the sermon? Then come back and I'll let you in on what we thought it might be.

> Function Statement: *To help the hearers understand that seeking assurances from God is not doubting him because God is gracious in giving us many reassurances along the journey.*

As you can see the Function arises out of the Focus. In some ways, it is the answer to whatever the dilemma is in the text. If Mary and Joseph seek assurances along the way, then God is gracious in providing them over and over to his children. This is a new understanding of the interpretive story of Mary and Joseph. As such, the Function Statement provides an example of Goldberg's neuroscientific research discussed in chapter 3. Every sermon tries, in some way, to provide a new way of looking at the text through proper exegesis and application of God's word. In this specific example, the listeners are challenged to use the executive functions of the brain to see the text in a new way but to do so through new eyes. The medium is a way of changing how we hear new information. This change in our hearing allows the listeners to experience vicariously the kind of change Mary and Joseph are needing in order to fulfill the will of God. The reason for including this particular sermon is not just to see how a two-person narrative might go but to reinforce Goldberg's research that neuroscience and narrative have strong and vital connections.

Neuroscience and Narrative Interaction #2: Transitions

Transitions are always important in preaching. Many sermons struggle because they create "whiplash" transitions for the hearers. The movement from one point to another is often done so haphazardly that the listeners stop hearing the sermon and try to make connections between what was said before and where the sermon appears to be going now. The lack of a strong yet simple transition can provide a place for listeners to stop hearing the sermon and let their minds drift toward other things. While transitions can be very brief and simple, they are still important and often determine the overall effectiveness of the sermon.

If you look back over the Mary and Joseph sermon, you will see that each concluding thought from Mary provides an opportunity for Joseph to explore his concern about assurances. At the end of the first monologue, Mary asks a series of questions that are her pleas for assurance. When Joseph steps up for his first soliloquy, he begins by allowing the congregation to know that he has the exact same problem that Mary is struggling with—assurance. By connecting the two sections through a common transitional theme, the listeners never experience the kind of whiplash that such a stark transition from Mary to Joseph could engender.

Now if you look at the footnote at the end of Mary's first section, you will notice that when this sermon was originally done my wife transitioned from the questions into the song, "Breath of Heaven." Our concern was how to transition from the song to the character Joseph and his first monologue. We felt that some kind of transition was necessary to ease the transition to Joseph but that going back into a longer section for Mary would be more difficult to follow. So when the song was completed, she simply said, "I must go and tell Joseph what has happened." Even that simple sentence provided a good segue into the concerns of Joseph about assurance. It neither distracted from the power of the song nor did it make the movement from her sitting down to Joseph coming up awkward. As the congregation reveled in the experience of the song and its meaning, Joseph simply walked up and began speaking about the very thing Mary had been dealing with—assurance.

Either way the transition is done, it must allow the listeners to follow the change in focus from one character to another. What a transition cannot do is introduce an entirely new focus into the situation. The listeners must adapt to a new character coming to speak, so it is better to allow that to be the only transition they have to make. If both characters are struggling with the same issue, then the only change the listeners need to make is to hear the same ideas coming from the perspective of another character.

The neuroscientific principle at work here is a further development of Cron's work on the importance of first sentences in preaching. The challenge of this sermon is that every time you transition from Mary to Joseph and back again you are faced with the same crisis of how to craft a first sentence. While Mary must find a way to set up Joseph who is coming to speak, Joseph is challenged with coming up with an opening sentence that establishes his identity and struggles while at the same time affirming the Focus Statement for the whole sermon. Every time the characters change, the challenge is to find a way to "hook" the listeners again from the very first sentence of this new monologue. The *assurance* we have in this is that, since our brains are wired for stories, we are eager to hear the next chapter in the unfolding story of Mary and Joseph. While it is a change in the way most people have experienced preaching from the pulpit (a single speaker addressing a congregation), a dialogically-based first person narrative is the way we experience most stories in novels, plays, or movies. We easily move from one character's perspective on the story to another. We see the parable of the prodigal son do this as it shifts from the prodigal's point of view to the father's point of reference to the elder brother's take on the return. No whiplash effects are experienced because, neurologically, we move easily through a single narrative being told from multiple points of view. This is one of those stories/sermons where neuroscience and narrative are easily integrated together.

8

The Journey from Tishbe
Elijah, the Man from Nowhere

> *Now Elijah the Tishbite, of Tishbe in Gilead, said to Ahab, "As the Lord the God of Israel lives, before whom I stand, there shall be neither dew nor rain these years, except by my word." The word of the Lord came to him, saying, "Go from here and turn eastward, and hide yourself by the Wadi Cherith, which is east of the Jordan. You shall drink from the wadi, and I have commanded the ravens to feed you there." So he went and did according to the word of the Lord.*
>
> I KINGS 17:1–5A (NRSV)

He came from nowhere, at least as close to nowhere as you're ever going to find. The greatest prophet in the history of Israel begins his initial foray into the political-religious world of the northern kingdom as a no one from nowhere. The fact that he hailed from Tishbe didn't help. Tishbe just wasn't that important a place. It was small, on the wrong side of the Jordan River, out in the desert, away from everything. It had no natural wonders to attract tourists, no hanging gardens and no picturesque waterfalls. It was a dry, arid and desolate place. No Jewish father ever gathered his family together to announce, "This year we will celebrate the Passover in Jerusalem!" Only to have one of his children ask, "Daddy, if we're going to Jerusalem, can we go by Tishbe, too?" Tishbe was not attractive. It held no interest from the outside world; it had no importance. It was a place people were *from* but not a place people went *to*. It was about as close to nowhere as you're ever going to find.

No one famous ever hailed from Tishbe. No prince or king or royal official reigned in this remote and deserted place. No military strategist looked over the terrain of the Middle East and said, "If we're going to conquer Israel, we must first capture Tishbe." Tishbe wasn't tactical; it wasn't the key to an invasion It just wasn't that important. It lacked any real value or significance geographically, aesthetically, or politically. It was as close to nowhere as you're ever going to find.

To complicate matters, this nowhere place on the back side of the desert was originally founded by nomadic tribesmen. Periodically, these desert wanderers would do what nomads always did—they picked up Tishbe and moved it. The ironic truth is you could know where Tishbe was and still not find it. It was the textbook definition of a nowhere town in a nowhere place. Tishbe was less of a place and more of a "state of mind." Why? Because Tishbe was about as close to nowhere as you're ever going to find.

So when Elijah, this unknown, unheard of, newly branded prophet of God—this unfamiliar mystic from a mysterious, mobile, wilderness community—trekked some 50 miles from nowhere to the somewhere of Israel's capital city, it was a significantly longer journey than the miles would suggest. Samaria, the newly built capital city of the northern kingdom was a bustling cosmopolitan center of commerce, trade, politics, and religion. Built by Omri, king of Israel, to rival the southern kingdom's grand capital Jerusalem, this new city set on a hill quickly grew in splendor and majesty. After Omri heavily fortified his freshly minted capital city, he ruled in it for six years before his death. After Omri's son buried his father in Samaria, Ahab ascended to the throne, committed to adding grandeur to his father's legacy by building great religious temples of worship to foreign gods like Baal and Asherah. Samaria was in scope and culture unlike any city the Jews had ever built in the promised land. When Elijah entered the metropolis of Samaria, it must have seemed like he had entered into another world. In fact, for all intents and purposes, this no one from nowhere, this country bumpkin of a prophet, had left the old world behind and entered a brand-new arena.

So, as Elijah the Tishbite, this nomad from the province of Gilead, met the big city folks in the marketplace of Samaria, some residents naturally inquired where he was from. When he announced, proudly I'm sure, that he was from Tishbe in Gilead, he received two different kinds of reaction. One was polite and courteous and must have gone something like, "Oh, so you're from Tishbe. How . . . ah . . . interesting." The other was more pointed and reflected what all the refined folks were really thinking but not saying. I'm certain the reaction came from some old, crotchety guy shoving his way to the front of the pack to eye this stranger. Unlike the politically correct response of the more sophisticated crowd, the old man, having lost his social "filter" a long time ago, looked Elijah in the face and cried out, "Tishbe? You say you're from Tishbe? I've been alive a long time, sonny, longer than your pappy and his pappy before him. I've been a lot of places and traveled all over the kingdom, but I ain't never heard of any place called Tishbe. You sure you're telling us the truth? Where's Tishbe?"

Poor Elijah. How do you explain to those who live in the big city that you come from a place that is as close to nowhere as you're ever going to find? How do you tell those who accept and worship idols as gods that you are on a mission for the only true God, the God of Abraham, Isaac and Jacob, the God of Israel as well as Judah? To a group of unbelievers, it can be a treacherous thing to believe in a God that they don't know and they don't serve. I'm sure he tried, but to no avail. And if that wasn't enough of a barrier to overcome, things got worse for Elijah when he was asked what his business was in the capital. When he announced to them matter-of-factly that he was seeking an audience with the king, the questions, undoubtedly, came fast and furious. Someone asked, "Do you have papers of introduction to King Ahab from the leader of your community or the governor of your province?" Another one spoke up saying, "Have you some tribute from a satrap, prince or political leader in your area?" Still another questioned, "Do you come from a family of wealth and influence?"

When Elijah could only shake his head and answer "No" to all of these questions, the crowd shook the dust off their collective feet and told Elijah that he had as much chance of meeting the king as they had of ever going to Tishbe. It was depressing, defeating, and deflating for Elijah to hear their skepticism and not to have a good answer. But, you see, here's the thing—Elijah had one source and one source alone that would provide him access to King Ahab. Elijah—this no one from nowhere, this reluctant prophet from the wilderness, this non-idol worshiping commoner from the wrong side of the tracks—had divine authority and a message from God to deliver. And if God gives you a message, then he will find a way to get you to the one who needs to hear it.

The text gives us no clue as to how God solved the dilemma of Elijah's lack of credentials and put the Tishbite in front of Israel's King Ahab, but in spite of all the odds against him and the crowd's sure verdict, Elijah, the Tishbite, from Tishbe found himself in the great hall of the king's palace. Standing in front of the court and surrounded by the palace guards, Elijah may have looked overwhelming out of place. His lack of standing, his poor clothing, his lack of any formal education, his obvious lack of sophistication disqualified him from a royal audience. He looked out of place. He was out of place. But looking out of place or being in over your head does not disqualify you from divine service. Elijah remained true to his calling and prepared to deliver the message God had given to him. It was then that Elijah did something that no prophet ever did, that no preacher ever does and that no professor ever teaches—he preached a one-sentence sermon.

Instead of couching God's message in a story, as Nathan had done when confronting King David about his murderous affair with Bathsheba; instead of spending time in a great fish before walking through the city and proclaiming God's judgment as Jonah would do; instead of meandering around naked for three years as Isaiah did, foreshadowing the march into captivity that Israel would be forced to do; instead of marrying a prostitute as Hosea would do as a way of showing how Israel had prostituted themselves with foreign gods, Elijah simply delivered a one-sentence sermon. One sentence! How does one go about preaching a one-sentence sermon? Do you begin with an illustration? Do you close with a heart-wrenching story about someone dying? Do you conclude with a poem? How can you effectively preach a sermon without points? How can a preacher preach an entire message in one sentence? Where is the beginning, middle, and end? You can't do Four Pages of the Sermon—it's only one sentence! You can't try a Lowry Loop with an Oops, Ugh, Aha, Yeah and Whee—there's only one sentence! How do you deliver a one-sentence sermon?

The answer is . . . I have no idea. But Elijah did. Gathering himself in unfamiliar and intimidating surroundings, Elijah communicated God's simple, direct message to King Ahab: "As the Lord the God of Israel lives, before whom I stand, there shall be neither dew nor rain these years, except by my word." The room was silent as though they expected this to be the opening salvo in some prophetic rant against the king. Ahab was not well liked by the prophets nor well respected by the southern kingdom residents. His own people regarded him more out of fear than appreciation. It was not usual to find anyone who would talk to the king so directly and forcefully. What else did the prophet have to say? What other words would he deliver? They craned their necks forward to hear the next pronouncement from Elijah but behold, nothing more was to come forth. Elijah was finished with his sermon and Ahab was finished with such divine foolishness. When Elijah was done, so was King Ahab; he just didn't know it yet.

With his task completed, Elijah the proverbial no one from nowhere; the wandering wise man from the desert; the uncivilized nomad from an unknown place, turned away from the king and left the Great Hall without saying another word. Can you imagine the awkwardness of that moment? Do you think Elijah even knew the proper protocol for leaving the king's presence? Did he bow as required? Did he back out as prescribed by law? Did he wait for the king to dismiss him from the court as the rules of diplomacy stated? It's doubtful that this humble drifter knew any of the protocols that surround how commoners behave around royalty. After all, Elijah was no from nowhere, an unsophisticated sheepherder from a town that was as close to nowhere as you're ever going to find. The surprised court eyed him silently and cautiously as they watched him leave. The king began digesting this new and unwelcome development. Stunned and surprised by Elijah's audacity or boldness, the guards did not detain him or, more properly, run him through with a spear for acting so brashly in front of the king. Elijah, the Tishbite from Tishbe, left the court, went down the palace stairs, and walked out into the great city of Samaria having delivered the message God had given him.

What now? Where was he to go? What do you do next after preaching your first sermon, in one sentence to boot? Was his mission complete? Was there more to be done? Did God have further use of his time and abilities? Was this the end of the calling?

It must have never dawned on this freshly minted prophet that he was about to become the most wanted man in all of Israel. He was simply delivering a message to the king as God had directed him. His task was over, or so he thought. But when the heavens closed down and the wells dried up; when the people of Israel could not find so much as dew on the ground, everyone, from the loftiest royal member to the average family farmer, sought the man of God hoping he would unlock the divine judgment upon the land and relieve their suffering. But Elijah was nowhere to be found. He was sent away from Samaria for a time. It seems that when you are faithful to speak God's word, even when it is hard to do, the God who speaks (Jehovah Dabar) is also the God who protects (Jehovah Jireh). So as Elijah stood in the street that fateful day wondering what to do next, God spoke to him directly for a second time. Elijah exited the great city of Samaria under the explicit directions of the God that had brought him from nowhere to the court of the king. Where was Elijah going? He was sent to where God would send any good Tishbite from Tishbe. God sent him back to nowhere.

God commanded Elijah to cross back over the River Jordan and go to a wadi named Cherith. There he was to remain during the drought while the Jewish world searched for him. Every morning the ravens brought him bread and meat for breakfast, and every evening they came back with a supper of the same. Elijah would camp out by himself at Cherith Ravine and be sustained by the water from the wadi. It sounds so idyllic, peaceful, restful, vacation-like doesn't it? Except a wadi is not a brook or a meandering river and Cherith was no resort. The wadi at Cherith was a dry riverbed that flooded during the rainy season. And in case you've forgotten, this was not going to be a rainy season! This was not going to be a comfortable place during a drought, but there might be enough muddy water left over from the previous rains to sustain the prophet, but there would be no flowing streams. And the ravens might transport enough partially chewed meat and half-digested bread to keep him going. It was evident, though, that Elijah was not going to be hiding out in the lap of luxury. Like the nation that suffered under the drought, so the man of God was provided for but not sustained in some plush retreat. He survived on little, but little is much when God is in it. He endured in a place of paucity, but the desert is an oasis when you are being sustained by a miracle from the hand of God. God suffers for his people when they disobey him, and God's prophets suffer along with the people they are sent to redeem. The weeks grew long and the food grew scarcer and the water got dirtier. Such is the calling of those who deliver truth to power.

And what of all those soldiers and citizens that looked for Elijah so that he might reverse the curse? None of them ever found him. They turned Samaria upside down and inside out. The searched the surrounding countryside looking for this nobody turned suddenly somebody special. They considered sending troops to search Tishbe, but nobody knew where it was. Why were they unsuccessful in their manhunt? Because no one ever thought that someone with the kind of power and miraculous might that could shut up the heavens and turn off even the dew from falling to the ground would ever go somewhere as remote as the Wadi Cherith. They never found Elijah because the Wadi Cherith was nowhere close to Samaria, nowhere inside the important places in Israel. It was nowhere on the east of the Jordan River. It was not near the Sea of Galilee or even close to the banks of the Jordan. No, the Wadi Cherith was exactly where you would expect it to be. It was right next to Tishbe. You can find it on a map as long as you can find a map that has Tishbe on it. And since no from Samaria knew where Tishbe was, nor could they find it even if they knew where it was, it was the ideal place to live unseen from the world. And that's what Elijah did. He lived unseen by people but seen by God. God's provision and care are not limited to the places of the rich and powerful. God's concern is not confined to the wealthy or the politically well connected. God's reach went all the way to the west side of the Jordan; all the way to the desert places where no one really lives and thrives; all the way to the Wadi Cherith were no one would camp and hide from the world . . . God's love reached all the way to Tishbe, a place that was as close to nowhere as you're ever going to find.

QUESTIONS AND APPLICATIONS FOR PREACHERS: TISHBE AND A NARRATIVE HERMENEUTIC

1. If Tishbe is an example of an Old Testament Haggadic interpretation of a text, what aspects of Haggadah can be extrapolated from this narrative?

2. What are the concepts, narratively speaking, that one can draw from this story?

3. The following insights are designed to allow the reader to explore both the nature of narrative and the approach of Haggadah.

The Narrative Hermeneutic of Tishbe

Since Haggadah concentrates on taking the narrative seriously and "filling in the details" that may not be readily seen, this narrative incorporates the hermeneutical idea that *narratives are about more than what is written.* In Haggadah there is a great deal of information that can be gained from what appears, at first glance, to be shallow wells of possibility. The quest of Tishbe was to find out those details and allow them to give life and meaning to the brief snapshot provided by the text in 1 Kgs 17:1–5. Below are some of the ways in which that was attempted. See if these insights give you help in how to construct a narrative story in the Haggadic tradition.

Narrative Hermeneutical Principle #1

As all preachers know, exegesis can provide important details for a sermon as well as give the preacher a perspective on the text. This is especially true with biblical stories that thrive on details. Principle #1 is this: *The greater the detail, the more compelling the story will be.* But details without connection to both the story and real life can be less insightful and more like travelogue. When you find an interesting detail, make sure that you are able to connect it to something that is meaningful. This principle goes hand in hand with the next idea. In some ways, they are two sides of the same coin since details provide not only perspective on a text, but they also create the compelling nature of narratives that grab our attention.

Narrative Hermeneutical Principle #2

The second principle is that the more relevant the material the more insightful the story. In the "Tishbe" story, the exegetical information about the nomads that founded the village and periodically moved the town, the fact that Tishbe was an arid, desert place that was devoid of natural, scenic wonders, the location of Tishbe on the relatively deserted east side of the Jordan River are all helpful details that add to the development of a compelling narrative. Adding detail that most listeners do not know or have not heard before creates a renewed interest in a most important biblical character. This helps the narrative to fulfill Principle #1 while at the same time developing a more insightful and fuller story that is crucial to Principle #2.

When you are preaching, you will undoubtedly have congregants in the listening audience who, like Elijah, hail from someplace insignificant ("A man from nowhere"). There are also people who feel like they are insignificant or less than valuable. They may be working at a menial job that provides little stimulation or hopes of a career that is fulfilling. Hearing Elijah's story of being from nowhere can provide hope for those in a dead end job or living a less than exciting life. This helps to fulfill Principle #2.

Narrative Hermeneutical Principle #3

In traditional sermon preparation, the information about Tishbe might be overlooked, go unused, or never even be considered as relevant for preaching. Too often we as preachers skip over details in a story that can help to open up and expand the meaning of the narrative. Narrative Principle #3 is to find interesting ways to use background material on a text in the narrative telling of the text. Intuitively, preachers know the importance of background materials. For instance, when telling the story of Jesus on the Cross, preachers know how powerful it can be to give the details of how he was nailed and how he suffered. In truth, the same thing is true about any biblical story (even Tishbe). The greater the detail about things like the Wadi Cherith, the capital city of Samaria, and the protocols of court behavior, the better the mental picture the listeners create in their mind's eye. Such background material breathes new life into even well-known stories.[1]

Narrative Hermeneutical Principle #4

Good storytellers (and good preachers) know that repetition is your friend. In telling a story, it is important to be repetitive. In writing, you have the advantage of using tools that help to organize thoughts and ideas. Writers use numbers, italics, paragraph divisions, parentheses, section headings, exclamation points, punctuation, quotation marks, and a myriad of tools to create emphasis, organize thoughts, and show breaks in the flow of the writing. Storytellers cannot bring these things out effectively by using the same cues that a writer employs. Instead, the

---

1. Resources that can be extremely helpful for gathering this type of information are Bible dictionaries, commentaries (both in the introductory notes as well as the commentary section), Intro to the Bible textbooks (often referred to as Survey books) such as Strege, *Bible Backgrounds*; La Sor et al., *Old Testament Survey*; Green and McDonald, *World of the New Testament*. In addition, students of the Bible may want to look into books that provide quality background material on aspects of culture that directly affect our understanding of biblical texts. One good example of this kind of material is deSilva, *Honor, Patronage, Kinship and Purity*.

cues in storytelling (and in preaching in general) are oriented toward the performative process. Cues, changes, and emphasis must come from the body and the voice. The voice must utilize volume, tone, inflection, variety, and pace. The body has to find a way to use gestures, body language, eye contact, and visual cues. Together, the voice and the body combine to produce a storyteller that has conviction, produces energy, speaks with passion and projects authenticity.[2] This is why this narrative principle is so important in good storytelling. Repetition acts like an exclamation point or quotation marks. It provides an oral/aural marker to the listeners that reminds them of three very important concepts:

- Repetition orally emphasizes the overall thrust of the story (i.e., "a no one from nowhere").
- Repetition allows the hearer to know that the storyteller is concluding one thought and moving to another idea (i.e., "But, you see, here's the thing. . .").
- Repetition drives home a single, focused idea designed to bring life to the whole narrative by building intensity (i.e., "Tishbe was about as close to nowhere as you're ever going to find.").

Narrative Hermeneutical Principle #5

When building a story/sermon, you must always answer the "So What?" test. Principle #5 is that stories must have a point to them; they must have meaning, focus, and significance. Think of stories like a piece of pie: if you eat the point of the pie there is no point in eating the pie. If your story doesn't have a point then there is no point in telling the story. Stories that meander through a long line of unnecessary detail or travelogue become tedious to the listeners. Have a point and make sure everything in the story helps the listeners understand the point. Make sure that the point has an impact and place those things into the story that help the listeners experience the impact of the story's main point.

---

2. For further discussion of these concepts, it may be helpful to look at the following materials. Some of these have been cited before but are listed here in full for the reader's convenience: Childers and Schmit, *Performance in Preaching*; Bartow, *God's Human Speech*; Childers, *Performing the Word*; Schmit, *Too Deep for Words*; Ward and Trobisch, *Bringing the Word to Life*.

Storytelling Pitfalls

To that end, here are some pitfalls in telling stories. Not all stories, even biblical stories, should be told without making sure that you avoid the following problems in storytelling. By avoiding them I mean to avoid them at all costs. These pitfalls can ruin and good story.

Pitfall #1: Travelogue

Have you ever heard someone tell a story like this? "I was on my way to church one Sunday. No, wait a minute, it was Wednesday night. Or was it Sunday afternoon? I'm not really sure, but . . . No, wait a minute. It was Tuesday. That's right, it was the night before I cooked that lasagna for the Senior Adults. You remember that lasagna, don't you?" After all that, you still have no idea what the story is about because the teller never got to the point. While details make a story, don't get bogged down in dates, times, how you know when something happened or where. Tell the story—not your long road to the point of the story.

In Tishbe, the point of the story is that even those who come from insignificant places or backgrounds can be used by God to do great things. While it takes a little while to get to that revelation, it becomes obvious early on that there is a meaningful connection between someone so famous and historic as Elijah and the humble beginnings from which he sprung. Rather than getting caught up in what road he took from Tishbe to Samaria, time is spent painting the picture of Elijah's humble beginnings as a way to understand God's greatness.

Pitfall #2: Hopscotch

Storytellers have a tendency to take shortcuts to ideas that are obvious to them but unfamiliar to the listeners—leaving them going around in circles or lost on the side of the road. While the storyteller knows the whole story and has developed the main point, it's a good idea to remember that the listeners are hearing the story for the first time. More than that, they are hearing your perspective on the story for the first time. Even if you are retelling a familiar story, the congregation is still hearing your interpretive understanding of the story for the first time. Therefore, make sure you make the main point clear to them. It may be clear to you, but you must make sure it is clear to the listeners. Therefore, don't hopscotch over things that help the listeners follow the thrust of the story.

In Tishbe the single, main point of the story is that God will make a way. He makes a way for a nobody from nowhere to be a prophet, to speak the word of God to a king, to be cared for during a drought and a famine, and to be led every step of the way. While the repetitive nature of "a no one from nowhere" emphasizes the inability of Elijah to accomplish anything on his own, it also sets up the antithesis of that statement, which is the main point of the story.

Pitfall #3: Missing the Point

The main point in Tishbe can be summed up in one simple phrase: Elijah can't, but God can. In Haggadah, it is always important to follow the principle that the main thing should remain the main thing. Too often storytellers miss the main point of the story. The solution for narrative preachers is to make sure the sermon is single-mindedly concentrating on the point of the story, the purpose of the story, and the focus of the story. In other words, let the main thing remain the main thing. Haggadah helps the preacher stay on point and avoid falling into the pit of losing the true focus of the scriptural text.

9

The Journey at the Altar

What Was Zechariah Expecting?

(NOTE: Since this sermon is in the form of the Lowry Loop, I've included the main titles of the movement of the Loop in the manuscript below. They are here for reference and I would not include them in the sermon itself.)

> *In the time of Herod king of Judea there was a priest named Zechariah, who belonged to the priestly division of Abijah; his wife Elizabeth was also a descendant of Aaron. Both of them were righteous in the sight of God, observing all the Lord's commands and decrees blamelessly. But they were childless because Elizabeth was not able to conceive, and they were both very old. Once when Zechariah's division was on duty and he was serving as priest before God, he was chosen by lot, according to the custom of the priesthood, to go into the temple of the Lord and burn incense. And when the time for the burning of incense came, all the assembled worshipers were praying outside. Then an angel of the Lord appeared to him, standing at the right side of the altar of incense. When Zechariah saw him, he was startled and was gripped with fear.*
>
> LUKE 1:5–11 (NIV)

UPSETTING THE EQUILIBRIUM: THE OOPS!

So, what was Zechariah expecting anyway?

After all, he's a few feet away from the Holy of Holies; a stone's throw from the place where God's Spirit and presence dwell above the ark; he's a first down yard marker away from the curtain that separates him from the Ten Commandments, the rod of Aaron, manna from the wilderness. If you're that close to where God dwells why would it surprise you that he peeks out from behind the curtain and speaks to you? Zechariah has gone as far into the temple as he will ever go; as far as anyone except the high priest will ever step; as far into the bowels of the mystery of the temple as anyone dead or alive will ever be. What should he be anticipating? What should Zechariah have been expecting? It's obvious from his reaction that he wasn't expecting and angel to appear—to be fair, who amongst us would? But for someone so heaped in the practices and rituals of the priesthood, shouldn't he have been expecting, I don't know, something? What was Zechariah expecting?

ANALYZE THE DISCREPANCY: THE UGH!

It's not like Zechariah is unprepared for this task. Like all Levites, Zechariah has been identified and called to be a priest from the moment he was conceived. Unlike those of us who received a calling to become a preacher, Zechariah was born into the priesthood. He was a priest from birth and a Levite by birth. His household was made up of all priests (at least the men). Then, as if this wasn't enough of a heritage and background, he marries a woman named Elizabeth who is a descendant of Aaron. As a result, this couple can both trace their lineage back to the progenitor of the priesthood—Aaron himself. They are a pure bread, Aaronic priesthood family in the Levitical line.

Can you imagine the backyard BBQs at Zechariah and Elizabeth's house? "John, so glad you could come. Let me introduce you to everyone. This is my father, the priest. Here are my two brothers—priests. This is my uncle . . . he's a priest. Oh, and here comes my father-in-law. He's, you know, a priest. And finally, here's my brother-in-law and yes, you got it, he's a priest."

From the time he could first walk and talk Zechariah has been taught, trained, primed, and practiced to be a priest in the temple. There were so many priests by this time in Israel that they divided them into groups—families of priests. Zechariah's division, called Abijah, were scheduled for two weeks every year to minister as priests in the temple.

For years, every year, for decade upon decade, Zechariah prepared and became proficient in the rites and rituals that are the work of priests in the temple in Jerusalem. He studied every aspect of the routines he might be called on to perform—including ministering at the altar of incense. He was prepped, prepared, and primed for this performative priesthood practice. Every detail had been rehearsed. So, the question remains, what was he expecting?

As a matter of fact, since the most prestigious task during those two weeks was to minister at the altar of incense; and since there were so many priests in the division of Abijah; and since there were only two opportunities per year for this special task to be performed by the division, once you were chosen for this duty your name never again was entered into the lottery drawing. Once you ministered at the altar, you would never be asked to do it again. By the time Zechariah's name is chosen for this special duty, he is, by his own admission, an old man. Decades have passed since he first prepared for this sacred duty. There is nothing about this ritual that Zechariah doesn't know, hasn't prepared, didn't practice, couldn't do in his sleep. He knows the routine inside out, upside down, thoroughly and completely. So, what was he expecting?

And on top of that, if he has waited so long for this duty and, once chosen, will never again repeat this honor, Zechariah is about to do a once in a lifetime event, a priestly function he has prepared his whole lifetime to perform, this will be the pinnacle of his career and calling as a priest. If you've spent your whole life waiting for this moment, if you've thought to yourself that this may never happen and you will die before being chosen by the Lord to do this work, if you have done everything in your power to be ready for this moment, this once in a lifetime opportunity, this divinely ordered ritual . . . shouldn't you be expecting something to happen? Anything? But Zechariah seems befuddled by the angelic appearance. He is startled. Gripped with fear, according to Luke's text. He appears before the angel disquieted, anxious, restless at the interruption. Inwardly he is experiencing turmoil, his mind is perplexed, his calm has been taken away and his spirit is wracked with questions and doubts. What was Zechariah expecting, anyway?

Considering his age, experience, maturity in the faith, preparation for this moment and divine calling to minister at the altar of incense shouldn't Zechariah have been expecting something? Anything?

THE KEY TO RESOLUTION: THE AHA!

I'll tell you what Zechariah was expecting. He was expecting the exact same thing that we expect whenever we enter into worship on a Sunday morning . . . absolutely nothing! Zechariah was expecting routine, ritual, a tried and true practice that had been done for years with little to no divine interaction. He was expecting the "same old same old" of worship. Just like our modern expectations in worship Zechariah expected God to behave, sit quietly like some aging senior in a nursing home and be grateful for how polished and professional Zechariah would do the ritual. Any one of us could find ourselves in Zechariah's shoes if an angel showed up on Sunday morning in the middle of our singing, praying or, God forbid, in the sermon!

God is not supposed to do anything outside of our expectations. God does not really show up at a worship service. No, he observes our worship from a gentle distance so as not to upset our performance of worship. Like the presence of God in the temple, God is to be nicely tucked away behind a curtain no one can part and no human being can survive if it did. If a priest dared to overstep his bounds and enter the Holy of Holies without the proper preparation and authority God would strike him dead! Hence the reason that the high priest, on the Day of Atonement, when he was allowed to enter the Holy of Holies to offer sacrifice on the part of the people, would be tied around the waist with a rope so he could be removed from the room should he displease God and die in the Holy of Holies. God wasn't supposed to leave the room where he was shut up and dwelt. There was nothing in Zechariah's theological training that prepared him for the outrageous idea that God might peep out from behind the curtain and speak to him.

EXPERIENCING THE GOSPEL: WHEE!

What Zechariah could not know, was about to find out, and could not have anticipated is that God was doing a new thing in preparation for sending his son, Jesus Christ, into the world. No longer confined to a temple or a room, God was giving full expression to his presence in the lives of people. The experience of Zechariah is the beginning of the Pentecost experience of the unleashing of the Holy Spirit into people's lives and experience.

Worship can no longer be about the mere ritual of performance; the routine of the liturgy; the comfort of knowing that everything will be done by our definition of "decency and order." God is breaking into the human condition in ways only experienced by the Wilderness Generation of the prophets of old. God is now Emmanuel, "God with us!" Whenever we enter into worship God is present; he is not hidden; he does not reside in a box nor is he shut up in a place. God is unleashed in worship and his Spirit is speaking, acting, calling, healing, saving, sanctifying, and empowering his children. No longer can we merely enter worship and be content that we are in proximity to God. Now we must wrestle with the reality that when we enter worship, that as we approach the altar this unseen God manifests himself in our midst and engages each of us and all of us with his presence. He is not a god of stained-glass windows or gold platted crosses. He is not mere ritual or remembrance. God is a real person, revealing himself to his children as they worship, sing his praise, hear his word, respond to his Spirit, and bring an offering of praise.

The church must learn that we do not worship a god who is far off but a God who is transcendent yet present. God is living and moving in our every presence and in our daily existence. He is always present in our lives and always peeking out from behind whatever curtains we put up between us. The story of Zechariah in the temple ushers in the age of God's immanence with us. He is no longer "out there" but it is now possible for God to be "in here." As a result, we no longer have the luxury of approaching worship in the same way that Zechariah did. We can no longer enter the sanctuary and believe that our mere presence or our acquiescence to those who lead worship is enough to experience the presence of God. No, God is in our midst and we must respond to God being with us!

ANTICIPATING THE CONSEQUENCES: YEAH!

Now that we are living in the shadow of Zechariah's experience in the temple, how should we approach worship? What are the lessons to be learned from Zechariah's revelation at the altar of incense?

We must enter worship with the expectation that God will present himself. No longer can the popular phrase, "Wow! God really showed up today in worship!" be used as something that describes something unusual. The truth is that God always shows up; God is always present and active in our midst; God is not just the prompter of worship nor the audience for our worship—God is the prime mover in worship and he is always active when we gather. The age of Zechariah is gone when we can come to the sanctuary and observe worship. Worship is not an observational sport. It is intended to be a participative experience where God manifest himself and we respond to the power of being in the presence of God.

Today, may this common call to worship take on the reality of what it means to know that God is present and active in our lives and in our worship service today. "Come, let us worship the Lord, together!"

QUESTIONS AND APPLICATIONS FOR PREACHERS: THE LOWRY LOOP

1. How does the Lowry Loop fit the narrative/storytelling nature of preaching?
2. What are the keys to understanding how the Lowry Loop functions?

THE LOWRY LOOP AS NARRATIVE STRUCTURE

One of the most important aspects of the Lowry Loop is how it demands that the preacher keep her foot firmly planted in the biblical narrative. Much of narrative preaching today violates this simple axiom. Narrative is often viewed as a convenient way to leave the biblical text and substitute stories and illustrations for in-depth exegesis. The genius of Lowry's approach is that the narrative is the key to the entire structure. Like Aristotle's admonitions about drama, the Loop gives the preacher a structure by which the plot and characters of the story are preeminent.

You may notice that the opening section (the Oops!) is rather short, especially compared to the second section (the Ugh!). This is one of the keys to the Lowry Loop that is often overlooked. In some ways the Loop is founded upon the length of the Ugh! To be truly exegetical, the sermon must delve deeply into the meat of the narrative text. It should produce strong exegetical insights based on solid research. The second move of the Loop requires the preacher to mine the text for more than just the surface of the story. For instance, in this sermon the exegetical insights that were gained from the actions of the division of Abijah were crucial. It was a key piece to understanding Zechariah's experience, anticipation and preparation for his service.

In addition, the teasing out of the Ugh! section provides a key element to the Loop. The entire structure is built upon the "reveal" of section three—the key to resolution. The inclination of most preachers heaped in a more didactic, three-point structure is to quickly move to the solution/answer portion of the sermon and spend considerable time on the application of that solution. While this has merits it also gives short shrift to the power of story to create tension and tease out solutions. Like other forms of communication (movies, plays, television, etc.) the listener enjoys the tension created by trying to figure out "who done it." We don't jump to the end of the novel to see how it resolves the difficulties presented at the beginning. We enjoy the journey toward discovery upon which all drama is based. I was told once that this ability to maintain the tension of the discrepancy was vital to the Loop. I fully agree. I tell my students that when you think you have held that tension as long as you possible can in the sermon and that you can't hold it any longer—go five minutes more. People love tension that leads to resolution that provides understanding. Every mystery writer worth his or her salt has found that to be true. Biblical stories are no different. Hold the tension. Nurture the anticipated consequences. Uncover the story of the text like you would peel back the layers of an onion.

Finally, the Lowry Loop is an antidote for the heavy doses of application that have become the norm in the pulpit. Preaching today rushes from the text to application and spends the majority of its time there. It is important to notice that the Loop has five movements to it and only one is about application. It's also important to note that the application portion is short and does not require the bulk of the message. This highlights one of the more important truths about the power of story. Stories are vehicles for application rather than being a conduit to get to application. When people hear stories, they begin to formulate how this narrative may be able to apply to their lives. This occurs long before the preacher even gets to application and allows the application to be shorter and, in many ways, less specific. While the concluding section of the sermon helps to bring home the point about our role in worship and how it must be participative rather than observational, it leaves room for the hearer to insert the "how?" into the message. Too much of our preaching devolves theologically into a sort of works righteousness whereby we tell the congregation to do this or that in order to be saved and holy. The Lowry Loop mutes our tendency to do that and allows for the leading of the Holy Spirit to be predominant in how to apply the biblical insights.

KEYS TO UNDERSTANDING THE FUNCTION

I once had a congregant who had heard me preach a couple of Lowry Loop sermons say to me, "You like to live dangerously, don't you?" I asked what he meant by that and he told me, "You like to call the text into question and make us think that there's something wrong with it before you finally resolve the meaning." I think his evaluation of the Lowry Loop is correct. The opening of the Loop requires that the preacher explore questions, inconsistencies, even doubts about the text without resolving them immediately. Stories are journeys not solution conduits. We enter into stories without knowing the solution or if they even will be resolved. The Loop requires the preacher to focus more on the power of the story than the importance of my application.

More often than not the opening line of a Lowry Loop can be couched in question form. While questions imply answers, they also create tension. For instance, in a sermon about Jesus being crucified between two thieves it is appropriate to open the sermon by saying, "Jesus died between two thieves and only one of them went with him to Paradise." This opening is true to the text but it fails to engage the audience or create an Oops! I would think that a better opening would be, "What happened to the other guy? One thief goes to Paradise but what happens to the other one?" This opening does not resolve or affirm something but brings into question one aspect of the text that we often ignore—what did happen to the so-called "impenitent thief?" That's why the opening of a Lowry Loop is more dangerous. It asks questions and calls into question things in the biblical writ. And then, it spends a lot of additional time proving the problem (the Ugh!).

I must confess that part of me is drawn to the Lowry Loop because I love irony and its cousin, sarcasm. Irony points out the incongruity of something in a story and gives credence to the possibility that what I think I know might not be true. The implication of the above opening is to bring into question our widely held but not thoroughly thought-out idea that one thief went to heaven and the other went to hell (or one went to Paradise and the other to Sheol). The sermon explores whether or not this is what happened to the other thief by delving into both what was said by Jesus on the cross and what was not said. Intriguing idea? That's what makes the use of the Lowry Loop so engaging. It uses irony (maybe we don't know what this narrative really says) to invite the listener into a discovery process (which is an active posture) rather than inviting the listener into an information dump (which is a passive posture). My rule of thumb about the Oops! is a simple one: the more outrageous the claim (within exegetical reason) the more intrigued the congregation is.

More preachers would be helped by remembering that most laypeople have more questions about Scripture than they do answers. By acknowledging their right to ask questions of the text the preacher gives credence to a kind of Socratic method of biblical exploration. By providing solutions and resolutions to those questions the preacher gives affirmation to the congregation that questioning God's word can lead to divine insight and understanding. This may seem heretical to those who see preaching as indoctrination of thought and regurgitation of principles but this idea melds well with Jesus' approach to teaching which often involved parables and stories that required discovery. The Lowry Loop lends itself well to the principles of narrative storytelling.

10

The Journey of a Storytelling Savior
Jesus and His Teaching Method

> *The disciples came up and asked, "Why do you tell stories?"*
> *Jesus replied, "You've been given insight into God's kingdom. You know how it works. Not everybody has this gift, this insight; it hasn't been given to them. Whenever someone has a ready heart for this, the insights and understandings flow freely. But if there is no readiness, any trace of receptivity soon disappears. That's why I tell stories: to create readiness, to nudge the people toward receptive insight . . . "*
>
> *All Jesus did that day was tell stories—a long storytelling afternoon. His storytelling fulfilled the prophecy: "I will open my mouth and tell stories."*
>
> MATTHEW 13:10-13, 34-35 (THE MESSAGE)

Jesus stepped out of the house and looked at the crowds. "Something has to change," he thought.

The crowds were large and enthusiastic to be sure. But they came with all kinds of baggage . . . they came full of needs, questions, concerns. Their bodies wracked by disease; their minds confused by the Law. If Jesus only wanted to be a healer, he would have been busy from sun up to sun down touching, laying on hands, anointing and healing all manner of diseases. But what concerned Jesus the most that day was their hearts.

As Jesus peered out over the gathered throngs, he instinctively knew he was in a war; he understood at the visceral level that he was in a fight for the soul of humanity. Intuitively he realized the human heart would be the battleground for this war that would take place. And he was standing on the front lines.

As he emerged from Peter's house by the Sea of Galilee, Jesus contemplated a change of strategy. His current approach was not producing needed results. He thought through his evaluation carefully. He had some time as they walked along the seashore looking for a place to hold a teaching session. Today would be a good day to introduce this new strategy for ministry and discipleship. Today would be a great day... but he was still formulating the plan.

He had been trying to *convince* their minds of the truth about his Father.

He had *quoted* Scriptures from Isaiah and Jonah, *explaining* how they should apply to the present day and age.

He had walked through a field plucking grain on the Sabbath to *show* the multitudes the *difference* between adherence to the Law (as interpreted by the Pharisees) and doing God's will (as urged by the Holy Spirit).

He had *confronted* misunderstandings about the nature of his mission and ministry when it was attributed to Beelzebub.

He had *responded* with affirmations when John the Baptist questioned his once unequivocal stance about Jesus' messiahship.

He had *taught* them a different way when challenged by those who thought his ministry should bring peace without conflict.

He had *instructed* the crowd by analogies, giving strong connections between what comprises a "true" family and what happens to an "unclean spirit."

He had *healed* withered hands and broken bodies.

But *nothing, nothing* was effective ... at least not as effective as Jesus wanted and needed it to be. A change in approach was warranted and as Jesus exited Peter's house and walked along the Sea of Galilee, he determined that today was the day. From this day forward he would try a different tactic. Instead of appealing exclusively to the head, he would now be vying for the heart as well. But the question he struggled with now was this: How do you engage head and heart in such a way that you can contend for the soul as well?

Jesus contemplated the details of such a change. How could he pivot his public ministry to reach out to head, heart, body, mind and soul? What he needed was a strategy that was all encompassing in its scope and all-inclusive in its function. What should he do?

Should he step up his healing ministry? After all, there was an abundance of sickness, disease, paralysis, leprosy, and people dying from unknown maladies. Nothing had confounded the Pharisees or engaged the masses as much as had his healing ministry. Was that the answer?

Or, should he be even more confrontational with the Pharisees and Sadducees? After all, it was often their well-intentioned, traditionally-based teachings that were leading people away from God rather than into his arms.

Or further still, did he need to require more hands-on ministry from those who sought to follow him? He had already sent the Twelve on mission. Should he send them on another? Should he expand the leadership base to include a larger inner circle? Should he turn the crowds into a massive army of spiritual soldiers that could flood the countryside with healings and miracles?

Stepping into the boat to speak to the growing crowds on the seashore, Jesus thought about the water beneath him. It ebbed and flowed; it washed in and out; it provided a natural resonance that would bring everyone together in order to hear whatever Jesus proclaimed. It inspired him in his deliberations. He determined in his heart the new strategy that would define his ministry from this point forward.

He would continue to use all the tools at his disposal to reach the crowds—healing, analogies, confrontation, Scripture explanation, and personal example. But now Jesus would use opportunities like this one to speak to the crowd in the most effective teaching method he could find. He looked at the people gathered on the beach and began this new approach.

What was this new approach? Simple. He told them stories.

Telling stories brought a satisfaction to Jesus that none of the other methodologies had done. It was difficult to get across complex, spiritual ideas in merely logical argument. Stories gave the opportunity for depth of meaning without losing the simplest and least educated among the throngs. It gave Jesus a warm feeling that he was connecting to his roots—to the roots of the crowd. His approach sounded more like the synagogue in Nazareth than the high-handedness of the temple. His voice grew even more confident as he spoke to the crowd in the familiar currency of everyday life—stories.

The change in approach was almost instantaneously discernable. Stories brought the crowd satisfaction rather than information. While the crowd was often untrained in the intricacies of the Pharisees' theology as they rattled on and on about every jot and tittle of the Law, the approach of Jesus was simpler, more direct. He told them stories . . . stories about fishing, farming and daily living . . . stories that struck a familiar chord within them. The masses resonated with these stories and, by virtue of that, they resonated with Jesus.

To the growing crowds, stories were more authoritative than pronouncements from the Talmud. While they couldn't articulate it in a technical way, it was clear that stories had a greater impact than the Law. They turned their ear to Jesus and, maybe for the first time in his public ministry, they really listened to what he was saying.

Why the change in attention span?

Why did the crowd respond differently?

Because Jesus' stories had the luxury of being open-ended while at the same time sharply pointed. His stories actively included the crowd in interpreting the meaning rather than passively having them sit and memorize the Law.

The stories Jesus told engaged the crowd in the same way that Jesus had been engaged so often in the synagogue; they didn't load up the listener with evidentiary material like they did in the tedious addresses at the temple. Instead, Jesus' plots and mysteries welcomed his listeners into an event they could relate to on a conscious level. Stories were interesting, especially in the hands of a master storyteller like Jesus.

At first, it seemed like Jesus had solved his problem. He had finally landed on the perfect strategy. But after his storytelling session was completed, Jesus found that his new strategy raised more questions with the disciples than it answered.

After the crowd had dissipated, Jesus and the Twelve took time to process this dramatic change. They were anxious to know why the Master had made such a drastic adjustment in his approach. They quizzed him.

"Why stories, Master? Why limit your wisdom to tales and legends, fables and yarns?"

It was a good question. Many of them, like Andrew, had followed John the Baptist. The Baptist told it straight. He had an economy of speech. "You brood of vipers" was a favorite phrase of his. He had neither time nor inclination to waste his precious ministry on fanciful sagas of seeds, sowers, sons or Samaritans. For followers of John who were raised on asceticism and austerity; who were fascinated by listening to a man clothed in animal skins and eating locusts; this storytelling approach was too simple, too juvenile, too beneath the life-altering mission of the Messiah.

"Why do you tell stories?" The disciples pressed their concerns.

It was more than a question. If you think about it objectively, it was an accusation. It had an attitude included in it that Jesus instantly recognized. He'd heard that tone every time one of the teachers of the Law was in the crowd and openly challenged his teachings.

It wasn't so much the question as it was the tenor of the voice—it was tinged with negativity and dripping with disagreement. They asked respectfully, as though they wanted to know. In some way all those who questioned Jesus' approach were searching for answers and understanding, but Jesus knew very well that such inquiries were often set in the concrete foundation of disbelief. Jesus shifted in his seat. These questions weren't coming from frustrated Pharisees or smug Sadducees. They were coming from his most trusted and faithful followers. He had to answer well. He knew what they were really asking.

It should not be surprising then that Jesus heard a different question than merely, "Why do you tell stories?" What Jesus heard was . . .

"Stories aren't an effective way to present the Gospel."

"Stories are too simple, too fanciful to communicate the complicated theology of the nature of God."

"Stories are fine for children or campfires but they're unworthy of a ministry of someone like you."

"All you're doing by telling stories is entertaining people. You may get a crowd to hear it, but you'll never change the minds and hearts of stiff-necked people by telling them about weeds and mustard seeds; about treasures in fields, pearls of great price or nets for fishing."

"Wouldn't it be better to just lay it out to the crowd in plain and forceful teaching like you've been doing?"

"This will never work!"

Jesus heard all the negative feelings tucked away in the disciples halting question. It didn't faze him, though. Not one bit. After all, he had an answer—a good one. And he didn't mind letting them know what it was.

Jesus began gently by explaining to the disciples that the crowd needed something very different than they did. The Twelve were ready to hear the deeper things of God. They had dedicated themselves to becoming students of Jesus, learners who would sit at his feet and imbibe his teachings.

But the crowd came for different reasons. They came with all kinds of barriers, hesitations, and resistance to the message that Jesus proclaimed. They had hidden agendas, open agendas, political influences, familial prejudices. They had been influenced by those who wanted to argue with Jesus about how he interpreted the Law. They were skeptics.

They came to get what they could from Jesus before returning to their own lives. They wanted bread for their stomachs, healing for their bodies, reassurances for their actions and hope that tomorrow would be a better day.

Jesus put it as succinctly and clearly to his disciples as he could:

"They aren't ready."

Jesus tried to explain to the disciples his quandary: how do you make someone ready to hear what they did not come prepared to accept? How do you engage those who already have their minds made up as to what they want from this encounter? How do your create readiness to really hear the gospel?

Again, Jesus' answer was simple, yet profound.

"Tell them stories. Nudge them forward toward the Gospel; don't drive them to it with a whip." It seemed like such a simple solution—too simple, it seems, for the disciples to grasp. So, Jesus made it more complex for the men who were following him everywhere. He quoted Scripture as the basis of what he was doing. That really caught them off guard.

"I'm doing this because I don't want a repeat of what happened in the time of Isaiah the Prophet. So far, all I see from the crowd is the same thing that God told Isaiah—they listen hard, but they don't get it; they look intently, but they don't catch on."

There was an urgency in Jesus' voice that stopped the disciples from asking any follow up questions. Some of them knew the words of Isaiah the Prophet by heart:

"Make these people blockheads, with fingers in their ears and blindfolds on their eyes, so they won't see a thing, won't hear a word, so they won't have a clue about what's going on and, yes, so they won't turn around and be made whole."

The disciples had the dawning realization that Jesus was convinced that, in spite of the size of the crowds, his approach had allowed the people to stick their fingers in their ears and had allowed them to listen with blindfolds over their eyes. He needed something more effective, more insightful to those who had stopped seeing with their eyes. He needed something that would smooth out the rough edges of the crowds and saw off the parts that turned them from blockheads into seekers. They needed to listen; they needed to hear; they needed to be engaged in the message. They needed something old that could be turned into something new.

They needed stories.

Jesus realized, as had Isaiah, that the crowds could be like a tree stump—stuck in the ground, unmovable, firmly planted in their ways, grounded in what they wanted by strong roots that had to be pulled up with great effort. But Jesus also believed what God told Isaiah about the insides of those seekers. They may be tree stumps, but inside? Inside "there's a holy seed in those stumps!"

So, Jesus declared he was finished trying to pull up stumps. Instead, he was aiming for the holy seed inside the stump. He would bypass the roots and go for the heart of the tree. He would seek to reach that part of God's image that dwelt in each of them—the part of themselves that had been created in God's image. He would tell them stories and watch the stumps come back to life, seedlings arising from the sawed off stubs, burgeoning trees that could grow some new wood. Stories, Jesus reasoned, had the potential to make a dead trunk grow into a great oak.

This was the answer he had been looking for over these days and months. This was the way to get at the insides and not just the outsides. Jesus knew exactly what to do to reach the multitudes. Jesus told them stories. Why? Because stories are powerful. And Jesus was a storyteller.

QUESTIONS AND APPLICATIONS FOR PREACHERS: JESUS AND ARISTOTLE

1. If this story is an example of a New Testament Haggadic interpretation of a text, what aspects of Haggadah can be extrapolated from this narrative?

2. What are the concepts, narratively speaking, that one can draw from this story?

The following insights are designed to allow the reader to explore both the nature of narrative and how Aristotelian principles can be incorporated into narrative preaching.

Aristotelian Principle #1: Thought

This story highlights the ability of narrative-based preaching to explore two very important aspects of dialogue. First, narrative preaching can explore the thought processes of characters that are in dialogue with one another. In exegesis, preachers are trying to interpret the meaning of what is being said when two or more folks are in a conversation. Narrative exegesis is very similar except that it interprets the thought process that gets you to the answer rather than simply exploring the meaning of the answer by itself. Since we rarely think in "answers" but are more likely to think in "process," this fits the shape of our thinking more clearly than giving pronouncements and explaining why they should be followed. Using thought processes allows for the preacher to lead the listeners through the progression of how one gets to the answer.

In the story, Jesus is contemplating changing his approach. What he has been doing so far has not worked. This is implied in the disciples question about "Why stories?" By engaging in the thought process that Jesus uses, it allows the preacher to bring in the greater context of Jesus' ministry. Rather than having to leave the text in order to explain his answer, following his thought process allows the preacher to bring the greater gospel story into the event without leaving the moment. It enables the listeners to "wander" through the gospel rather than merely catch a snapshot of the moment.

Aristotelian Principle #2: Diction

The second principle is that narrative preaching allows the preacher to explore the emotions that are inherent in dialogue, what Aristotle refers to as Diction. Rarely do conversations of any significance occur without being accompanied by emotion, oftentimes strong emotions. Some examples that we readily recognize are Jesus praying drops of blood at Gethsemane or weeping at the tomb of Lazarus. You cannot effectively deal with Jesus turning over the tables of the moneychangers without acknowledging Jesus' significant emotional engagement. While these examples are easily seen, the emotions of a typical narrative dialogue are often overlooked. They shouldn't be. They are essential to the scene and to the understanding of the moment. Express them but do so in a manner that is true to the point and context of the narrative.

In the story, the disciples are being passive-aggressive in their approach. They are asking for clarification and making an accusation at the same time. When people do not want to directly confront someone of authority, they often resort to such tactics. You know how this goes: "Honey, that dress looks fine, but have you thought about the red one?" "You know, honey, I love the blue tie with that suit more than the green one." Behind each statement lies the truth that neither the dress nor the tie works. Therefore, what is really being suggested is that you change the dress. You need to change the tie. So, the disciples say the same thing to Jesus. They try to communicate, "Stories don't work, so change your approach!" But they say it so nicely that it is easy to ignore it and it's possible to miss the heart of the question.

A good example of this can be seen in 2 Sam 12:7. I often use this passage in teaching the importance of oral interpretation in scriptural interpretation and exegesis. Nathan the Prophet is confronting David about his sin with Bathsheba. There is so much emotion in the story. David is outraged at the story that Nathan tells; Nathan is disappointed in the sinfulness of his hero, the king; God is bringing judgment to a man that he has described as someone "after God's own heart." So, considering the emotional cauldron of the event, how would you read v. 7—"You are the man"? Does Nathan say it triumphantly as though he has caught a thief with his hand in the till? Does he say it firmly with the conviction of the prophet from on high? Does he say it sadly, revealing his grief along with his outrage? Does he whisper it in the ear of the king so as to not embarrass him in front of the court? What emotions does Nathan have? It is the emotion you interpret in the text that should drive not only how you read it but also how you explain the moment. A whispering, grieving prophet sounds differently than a triumphalist, confrontational one. The moment is different depending on the emotion you understand to be involved. Dialogue requires that you investigate not just the words said but the emotions conveyed, even those that are beneath the surface. You have to revisit Aristotle's concerns about Thought and Diction.

Epilogue: The Journey Commences
Storytelling as Interactive Drama

> *Technically, the term narrative means a "story" and a "teller." Which is quite appropriate...*
>
> EUGENE LOWRY[1]

I love stories. I love telling stories. I love reading stories, watching stories, listening to others tell stories. I'm guessing, if you've gotten this far, you do to. I have just one more thing to add to what I've already said...

If the premise of this book is true—that Jesus was a storyteller and that our brains are wired for stories—then *preachers must excel at storytelling*. How does one become a better storyteller? I would refer you to the old Carnegie Hall joke. You know the one. Some guy yells at a cabbie in New York City, "How do you get to Carnegie Hall?" And the cabbie, without missing a beat, yells back, "Practice, man, practice." While storytellers are informed by books like this one, they are formed through the practice of storytelling.

When I was a local pastor, I almost always had a children's sermon that I did. While it was designed for young kids it was always a favorite of the adults, too. While they liked it because everybody loves a good story, I liked it because it gave me a chance to practice doing stories. Telling my children bedtime stories helped prepare me for telling children's sermon stories... and children's sermon stories helped prepare me for telling illustrations in sermons... and illustrations in sermons helped prepare me

---

1. Lowry, *Sermon*, 23.

to be a narrative/storytelling preacher. The formula is simple . . . practice, man, practice.

"Once upon a time" invites the listener into a world they can both anticipate and help form. Saying to a congregation, "David looked up and saw the giant Goliath cursing God" invited them into the heart of the biblical story. If our brains are wired for stories then every beginning of a story in a sermon offers a promise to the listener. Preachers invite their congregations on a journey into the life of Christ, David, Moses, Paul or hundreds of other characters and events. People are eager to take the journey. They are looking for a good story and a good storyteller to take them on the journey. Preachers have the greatest storybook of all time. All you have to do now is refine your storytelling gifts and invite others to take the voyage.

One of the major critique's others level at this kind of preaching is that it turns the preacher into a "dramatic performer." Homiletician David Buttrick was concerned with the difficulty of telling stories with a theological meaning. His critique has merit.[2] There is one saving grace, however, that relieves the preacher of having to become a dramatic performer in the sense that Buttrick warns about. Simply put:

The drama is in the story not the performer.

In the same way the expository preacher proclaims that the message is in the text (and in the Holy Spirit's leading) and not in the preacher's intellectual brilliance, narrative preaching proclaims a similar truth. The truth and the drama that conveys it are present in the story. All the preacher has to do is let it out. If three-point preachers need to get better at preaching didactic sermons, then narrative/storytelling preachers need to improve their game as well. Both must be wedded to the preaching of the text. Didactic preaching distills the truth in the text. Narrative preaching displays the truth of the text.

It's not that the preacher cannot improve or should not work at improving her storytelling, it's the recognition that the narrative drama of the sermon is located in the kerygma, the gospel, the story of Scripture, and not centered in the dramatic chops of the preacher. That's why the admonition to improve your preaching is not merely true of narrative preaching, it is true of all preaching. We strive to be better as preachers not so we will be hailed as great orators but that we will be less conspicuous when preaching. When we preach for our own gratification or

---

2. Buttrick, *Homiletic*, 11–20.

popularity then we sin by seeking to be in the spotlight instead of shining a light on the gospel text and story. That's why folks pray for the preacher to be "hidden behind the cross" and that "the preacher must decrease and God might increase" or "hide the speaker behind the sacred desk and let us see Jesus only." As we've argued here, preachers are performers in the true meaning of performance theory. We bring the story of Scripture to completion when we preach it out loud from the pulpit. The drama is in the text, the Word, the Scripture itself. We, as performers of the Word, merely bring it to completion. Preachers should preach well so that they are less of the focus of the sermon. Narrative preachers should practice narrative skills in order to become better storytellers so that they might become less prominent when telling his Story.[3]

The other point is what Buttrick fails to mention in his critique. While his concern about preachers having to become dramatic performers has merit there is another value that occurs in telling stories that we have only slightly mentioned.

Narrative preaching turns people into interactive listeners.

Stories have to be entered into in order to be truly heard, in order to be experienced. Like Buttrick, Lowry does not fully embrace the fact that a narrative sermon requires not just a story and a teller but also requires interactive listening. When narrative/storytelling preaching turns congregations into listeners it turns the church into active participants in the storytelling process. It forms them so strongly that, eventually, interactive listeners become storytellers too. Let me illustrate (OK, let me tell you a story).

One Easter Sunday when I was pastoring, our youth minister was scheduled to do the children's sermon. Our process at that point required the children to participate each week through the use of a special bag. Every week it was handed to one of the children with the instruction to bring it back the next Sunday with something of theirs in it. The person doing the children's sermon would ask for the bag, pull out the object, ask the child to describe the object and what it was used for, and then the preacher would have to use the child's object as an object lesson or at least a springboard toward a spiritual application. It was a great way

---

3. Even Buttrick admits that, when it comes to biblical narratives, "preachers will be imitating a language of immediacy in which the movement of a plot structures consciousness and draws out what we have termed 'analogies of experience.' Of course, all narrative sermons will be moving toward the formation of reflective consciousness." Buttrick, *Homiletic*, 335.

to train parents to use ordinary, everyday objects for spiritual insights and lessons. The other benefit was that church folks love to watch their preacher get stumped by the kids and have to work their way out of the conundrum! It gave us a chance to do two sermons for the adults and, sometimes, the children's sermon hit home better than the one delivered from the pulpit!

On this particular Easter morning the youth pastor was already nervous about the children's sermon because the parent of the child with the bag had told them prior to the service, "I want you to know that my wife and I had nothing to do with what's in the bag. This was our daughter's idea and hers alone." Tough spot, especially on Easter Sunday with a full house. So, trying not to show his trepidation, he called for the kids to come forward and asked for the bag. Speaking to the children as he searched for this child-inspired object, he made small talk as he rummaged around in the bag. Finally, he paused, looked into the bag, and with genuine perplexity looked at the six-year-old who had brought the bag and said, "I think something has gone wrong. There's nothing in the bag." To which the prescient young girl replied, "That's the point. It's Easter. He's not in the tomb. He's risen." The gasps were audible in the sanctuary as folks realized that the six-year-old had moved from the listener and focus of the children's sermon to the storyteller and preacher that morning. To his credit the youth pastor realized that the children's sermon had already been given. He merely replied, "You're right. He has risen. And that's better than any children's sermon I could have done." And with that, he dismissed the children to children's church where they could continue to experience the real meaning of Easter. I was very proud of the parents and the youth pastor that day because as storytellers they had turned a six-year-old into a listener and the story had turned her into a storyteller. Easter was no longer an abstract thought. She had come to understand the meaning and power of the greatest story ever told. Intuitively, a six-year-old told a better narrative/storytelling sermon than her pastor did or could have. My sermon that morning paled in comparison to hers. I simply rejoiced that the gospel had been preached that day in an unforgettable way. That's why I want to encourage you to tell stories, to tell stories from the inside, because it turns passive sermon spectators into active/interactive storylisteners who contribute to the ministry of the Word and the power of the biblical story.

So, I urge you to practice this narrative/storytelling approach to preaching. Don't give up if the first volley misses the mark. And don't assume that it will fall flat, either. My experience tells me that parishioners are so hungry for the powerful, unfettered stories of the Bible that even imperfect storytelling will bring great rewards. After all, it's not like your other sermons all hit the mark every Sunday, right? Take a chance; be creative; let the Holy Spirit work in another form and structure for your preaching. After all, to be a good preacher, a good narrative/storyteller all you really have to do is "practice, man, practice" while telling the greatest stories ever told. You can do that. I know you can. Start the journey!

Bibliography

Alcántara, Jared E. *Crossover Preaching: Intercultural Improvisational Homiletics in Conversation with Gardner C. Taylor.* Strategic Initiatives in Evangelical Theology. Downers Grove, IL: InterVarsity, 2015.
Allen, Ronald J. *Patterns of Preaching: A Sermon Sampler.* St. Louis: Chalice, 1998.
Anderson, Kenton C. *Choosing to Preach: A Comprehensive Introduction to Sermon Options and Structures.* Grand Rapids: Zondervan, 2006.
Anderson, Ray Sherman. *The Shape of Practical Theology: Empowering Ministry with Theological Praxis.* Downers Grove, IL.: InterVarsity, 2001.
Aristotle. *The Rhetoric and the Poetics of Aristotle.* Translated by Rhys Roberts and Ingram Bywater. New York: McGraw-Hill, 1984.
Atwood, Margaret. *Alias Grace.* 1st ed. New York: Nan A. Talese, 1996.
Bacher, Wilhelm, and Lewis N. Dembitz. "Synagogue." https://www.jewishencyclopedia.com/articles/14160-synagogue.
Barron, Frank, et al. *Creators on Creating: Awakening and Cultivating the Imaginative Mind.* A New Consciousness Reader. New York: Putnam, 1997.
Barth, Karl. *Homiletics.* 1st ed. Louisville, KY: Westminster/J. Knox, 1991.
Bartow, Charles L. *Effective Speech Communication in Leading Worship.* Nashville: Abingdon, 1988.
———. *God's Human Speech: A Practical Theology of Proclamation.* Grand Rapids: Eerdmans, 1997.
———. *The Preaching Moment: A Guide to Sermon Delivery.* Abingdon Preacher's Library. Nashville: Abingdon, 1980.
Beardslee, William. "Uses of the Proverbs in the Synoptic Gospels." *Interpretation* 24 (1970) 65.
Beecher, Henry Ward. *Yale Lectures on Preaching.* New York: J.B. Ford, 1872.
Benware, Paul N. *Survey of the New Testament.* Everyman's Bible Commentary. Rev. ed. Chicago: Moody, 2001.
Boleslavsky, Richard. *Acting, the First Six Lessons.* London: D. Dobson, 1949.
Boomershine, Thomas E. *Story Journey: An Invitation to the Gospel as Storytelling.* Nashville: Abingdon, 1988.
Branson, Robert. *Judges.* New Beacon Bible Commentary. Kansas City, MO: Beacon Hill Press of Kansas City, 2009.
Branson, Robert, et al. *Discovering the Old Testament: Story and Faith.* Kansas City, MO: Beacon Hill Press of Kansas City, 2003.
Broadus, John Albert, and J. B. Weatherspoon. *On the Preparation and Delivery of Sermons.* New York: Harper & Brothers, 1944.

Brooks, Phillips. *Lectures on Preaching Delivered before the Divinity School of Yale College in January and February, 1877*. New York: Knickerbocker, 1877.
Brueggemann, Walter. *The Prophetic Imagination*. Philadelphia: Fortress, 1978.
———. *Texts under Negotiation: The Bible and Postmodern Imagination*. Minneapolis: Fortress, 1993.
Buttrick, David. *Homiletic: Moves and Structures*. Philadelphia: Fortress, 1987.
Childers, Jana. *Birthing the Sermon: Women Preachers on the Creative Process*. St. Louis: Chalice Press, 2001.
———. *Performing the Word: Preaching as Theater*. Nashville, Tenn.: Abingdon, 1998.
Childers, Jana, and Clayton J. Schmit. *Performance in Preaching: Bringing the Sermon to Life*. Engaging Worship. Grand Rapids: Baker Academic, 2008.
Cicero, Marcus Tullius, et al. *Cicero. De Oratore*. The Loeb Classical Library. 2 vols. Cambridge, MA: Harvard University Press, 1942.
Cocker, B. F. *Christianity and Greek Philosophy*. New York: Harper & Brothers, 1870. http://hdl.loc.gov/loc.gdc/scd0001.0020198919A.
Coleridge, Samuel Taylor, and J. Shawcross. *Biographia Literaria*. 2 vols. Oxford: Clarendon, 1907.
Craddock, Fred B. *As One without Authority*. 3d ed. Nashville: Abingdon, 1979.
———. *The Collected Sermons of Fred B. Craddock*. 1st ed. Louisville, KY: Westminster John Knox, 2011.
———. *Preaching*. Nashville: Abingdon, 1985.
Crawford, Evans E., and Thomas H. Troeger. *The Hum: Call and Response in African American Preaching*. Nashville: Abingdon, 1995.
Cron, Lisa. *Wired for Story: The Writer's Guide to Using Brain Science to Hook Readers from the Very First Sentence*. 1st ed. New York: Ten Speed, 2012.
Currie, Gregory. *Narratives and Narrators: A Philosophy of Stories*. New York: Oxford University Press, 2010.
Curry, Samuel Silas. *Foundations of Expression*. Boston: Expression, 1907.
Dargan, Edwin Charles, and Ralph G. Turnbull. *A History of Preaching*. 3 vols. Grand Rapids: Baker, 1954.
Davis, Henry Grady. *Design for Preaching*. Philadelphia: Muhlenberg, 1958.
Deeg, Alexander. "Imagination and Meticulousness: Haggadah and Halakhah in Judaism and Christian Preaching." Academy of Homiletics Paper, Boston University School of Theology, 2008.
Demaray, Donald E. *An Introduction to Homiletics*. Grand Rapids: Baker, 1974.
deSilva, David A. *Honor, Patronage, Kinship and Purity: Unlocking New Testament Culture*. Downers Grove, IL: InterVarsity, 2000.
Dillard, Annie. *The Writing Life*. 1st ed. New York: Harper & Row, 1989.
Edwards, O. C. *A History of Preaching*. Nashville: Abingdon, 2004.
Eisenberg, Joyce, et al. *Dictionary of Jewish Words*. Rev. ed. Philadelphia: Jewish Publication Society, 2006.
Ellul, Jacques. *The Humiliation of the Word*. Grand Rapids: Eerdmans, 1985.
Eslinger, Richard L. *Narrative and Imagination: Preaching the Worlds That Shape Us*. Minneapolis: Fortress, 1995.
———. *The Web of Preaching: New Options in Homiletical Method*. Nashville: Abingdon, 2002.
Fant, Clyde E., and William M. Pinson. *20 Centuries of Great Preaching: An Encyclopedia of Preaching*. Waco, TX: Word, 1971.

Field, Syd. *Four Screenplays: Studies in the American Screenplay*. New York: Dell, 1994.
Finney, Charles Grandison. *Charles G. Finney: An Autobiography*. London: Salvation Army, 1903.
———. *Finney's Systematic Theology*. Minneapolis: Bethany Fellowship, 1976.
———. *Revivals of Religion*. Virginia Beach, VA: CBN University Press, 1978.
Finney, Charles G., and Charles G. Finney. *Lectures*. The Complete Biblical Library Christian Classic Series. Springfield, MO: World Library Press, 1998.
Florence, Anna Carter. *Preaching as Testimony*. Louisville, KY: Westminster John Knox, 2007.
Frei, Hans W. *The Eclipse of Biblical Narrative: A Study in Eighteenth and Nineteenth Century Hermeneutics*. New Haven, CT: Yale University Press, 1974.
Freytag, Gustav, and Elias J. MacEwan. *Freytag's Technique of the Drama; an Exposition of Dramatic Composition and Art*. 2d ed. St. Clair Shores, MI: Scholarly, 1969.
Frymire, Jeffrey W. *Creating Interesting Sermons: The Role of Originality, Creativity, and Novelty in Preaching*. PhD diss., Fuller Theological Seminary, 2010.
———. *Preaching the Story: How to Communicate God's Word through Narrative Sermons*. Anderson, IN: Warner, 2006.
Garner, Stephen Chapin. *Getting into Character: The Art of First-Person Narrative Preaching*. Grand Rapids: Brazos, 2008.
Garrison, Webb B. *Creative Imagination in Preaching*. New York: Abingdon, 1960.
Gladwell, Malcolm. *Blink: The Power of Thinking without Thinking*. New York: Back Bay, 2007.
Goldberg, Elkhonon. *The Executive Brain: Frontal Lobes and the Civilized Mind*. Oxford: Oxford University Press, 2001.
Graves, Mike, et al. *What's the Shape of Narrative Preaching? Essays in Honor of Eugene L. Lowry*. St. Louis: Chalice, 2008.
Green, Joel B., ed. *Hearing the New Testament: Strategies for Interpretation*. Grand Rapids: Eerdmans, 1995.
———. *Seized by Truth: Reading the Bible as Scripture*. Nashville: Abingdon, 2007.
Green, Joel B., and Lee Martin McDonald. *The World of the New Testament: Cultural, Social, and Historical Contexts*. Grand Rapids: Baker Academic, 2013.
Green, Joel B., and Michael Pasquarello. *Narrative Reading, Narrative Preaching: Reuniting New Testament Interpretation and Proclamation*. Grand Rapids: Baker Academic, 2003.
Groome, Thomas H. *Sharing Faith: A Comprehensive Approach to Religious Education and Pastoral Ministry: The Way of Shared Praxis*. 1st ed. San Francisco: Harper, 1991.
Guber, Peter. "The Four Truths of the Storyteller." *Harvard Business Review*, December 2007. https://hbr.org/2007/12/the-four-truths-of-the-storyteller.
———. "The Inside Story." *Psychology Today*, March 2011. https://www.psychologytoday.com/us/articles/201103/the-inside-story.
Guilford, J. P. "Creativity: A Quarter Century of Progress." In *Perspectives in Creativity*, edited by Irving A. Taylor and Jacob W. Getzels, xiv. Chicago: Aldine, 1975.
Hancock, Angela Dienhart. *Karl Barth's Emergency Homiletic, 1932-1933: A Summons to Prophetic Witness at the Dawn of the Third Reich*. Grand Rapids: Eerdmans, 2013.

Harbinson, Colin. "Restoring the Arts to the Church: The Role of Creativity in the Expression of Truth." http://www.lausanneworldpulse.com/themedarticles-php/409/07-2006.

Harding, Harold Friend. "The Need for a More Creative Trend in American Education." In *A Source Book for Creative Thinking*, edited by Sidney Jay Parnes and Harold Friend Harding, 3–8. New York: Scribner, 1962.

Hayes, John H. *Introduction to the Bible*. Philadelphia: Westminster, 1971.

Heacock, Clint. "Forty Years On: A Critical Reflection of Fred B. Craddock's New Homiletic." https://www.academia.edu/6449917/A_Critical_Analysis_of_Fred_B._Craddocks_New_Homiletic.

Hogue, David. *Remembering the Future, Imagining the Past: Story, Ritual, and the Human Brain*. Eugene, OR: Wipf & Stock, 2009.

Holland, Saba Holland, et al. *A Memoir of the Reverend Sydney Smith*. 2 vols. New York: Harper, 1855.

Hostetler, Michael J. *Introducing the Sermon: The Art of Compelling Beginnings*. The Craft of Preaching Series. Grand Rapids: Zondervan, 1986.

Hume, David. *A Treatise of Human Nature*. Dover Philosophical Classics. Mineola, NY: Dover, 2003.

Inge, William Ralph. *Christian Ethics and Modern Problems*. Westport, CT: Greenwood, 1970.

Johnson, Craig E., and Michael Z. Hackman. *Creative Communication: Principles and Applications*. Prospect Heights, IL: Waveland, 1995.

Kadari, Tamar. "Shiphrah: Midrash and Aggadah." https://jwa.org/encyclopedia/article/shiphrah-midrash-and-aggadah.

Kant, Immanuel. *Critique of Pure Reason*. The Modern Library of the World's Best Books 297. Abridged ed. New York: Modern Library, 1958.

Kay, James F. *Preaching and Theology*. Preaching and Its Partners. Edited by Paul Scott Wilson. St. Louis: Chalice, 2007.

Kim, Eunjoo Mary. *Women Preaching: Theology and Practice Through the Ages*. Cleveland: Pilgrim, 2004.

Kittel, Gerhard, et al. *Theological Dictionary of the New Testament*. 10 vols. Grand Rapids: Eerdmans, 1985.

La Sor, William Sanford, et al. *Old Testament Survey: The Message, Form, and Background of the Old Testament*. Grand Rapids: Eerdmans, 1996.

Lakoff, George, and Mark Johnson. *Metaphors We Live By*. Chicago: University of Chicago Press, 2003.

Lamott, Anne. *Bird by Bird: Some Instructions on Writing and Life*. New York: Anchor, 1995.

Larsen, David L. *The Company of the Preachers: A History of Biblical Preaching from the Old Testament to the Modern Era*. Grand Rapids: Kregel, 1998.

LaRue, Cleophus James. *The Heart of Black Preaching*. 1st ed. Louisville, KY: Westminster John Knox, 2000.

Levine, Lee I. *Judaism and Hellenism in Antiquity: Conflict or Confluence*. The Samuel & Althea Stroum Lectures in Jewish Studies. Seattle: University of Washington Press, 1998.

Lewis, Ralph L., and Gregg Lewis. *Inductive Preaching: Helping People Listen*. Westchester, IL: Crossway, 1983.

Lischer, Richard. *The Company of Preachers: Wisdom on Preaching, Augustine to the Present.* Grand Rapids: Eerdmans, 2002.
———. *The End of Words: The Language of Reconciliation in a Culture of Violence.* The Lyman Beecher Lectures in Preaching. Grand Rapids: Eerdmans, 2005.
———. *A Theology of Preaching: The Dynamics of the Gospel.* Rev. ed. Durham, NC: Labyrinth, 1992.
Livo, Norma J., and Sandra A. Rietz. *Storytelling: Process and Practice.* Littleton, CO: Libraries Unlimited, 1986.
Long, Thomas G. *Preaching from Memory to Hope.* Louisville, KY: Westminster John Knox, 2009.
———. *The Witness of Preaching.* 2nd ed. Louisville, KY: Westminster John Knox, 2005.
Lose, David J. *Confessing Jesus Christ: Preaching in a Postmodern World.* Grand Rapids: Eerdmans, 2003.
Lowry, Eugene L. *Doing Time in the Pulpit: The Relationship between Narrative and Preaching.* Nashville: Abingdon, 1985.
———. *The Homiletical Beat: Why All Sermons Are Narrative.* Nashville: Abingdon, 2012.
———. *The Homiletical Plot: The Sermon as Narrative Art Form.* Atlanta: John Knox, 1980.
———. *How to Preach a Parable: Designs for Narrative Sermons.* Abingdon Preacher's Library. Nashville: Abingdon, 1989.
———. *The Sermon: Dancing on the Edge of Mystery.* Nashville: Abingdon, 1997.
Lucaites, John Louis, et al. *Contemporary Rhetorical Theory: A Reader.* Revisioning Rhetoric. New York: Guilford, 1999.
Ludlam, Kerry. "Hearing Metaphors Activates Sensory Brain Regions." *Emory News Center* (2012).
Lundblad, Barbara K. *Marking Time: Preaching Biblical Stories in Present Tense.* Nashville: Abingdon, 2007.
———. "Narrative Theory." In *The New Interpreter's Handbook of Preaching*, edited by Paul Scott Wilson, 203–4. Nashville: Abingdon, 2008.
Massey, James Earl. *The Burdensome Joy of Preaching.* Nashville: Abingdon, 1998.
———. *Stewards of the Story: The Task of Preaching.* 1st ed. Louisville, KY: Westminster John Knox, 2006.
Massey, James Earl, and William D. Thompson. *Designing the Sermon: Order and Movement in Preaching.* Abingdon Preacher's Library. Nashville: Abingdon, 1980.
McClure, John S. *The Four Codes of Preaching: Rhetorical Strategies.* Grand Rapids: Westminster John Knox, 2003.
———. *Preaching Words: 144 Key Terms in Homiletics.* Louisville: Westminster John Knox, 2007.
McKay, Heather A. *Sabbath and Synagogue: The Question of Sabbath Worship in Ancient Judaism.* Boston: Brill Academic, 2001.
McKenzie, Alyce M. *Novel Preaching: Tips from Top Writers on Crafting Creative Sermons.* 1st ed. Louisville, KY: Westminster John Knox, 2010.
Nieman, James R., and Thomas G. Rogers. *Preaching to Every Pew: Cross Cultural Strategies.* Minneapolis: Augsburg Fortress, 2004.
Old, Hughes Oliphant. *The Reading and Preaching of the Scriptures in the Worship of the Christian Church.* 7 vols. Grand Rapids: Eerdmans, 1998.

Ong, Walter J. *Orality and Literacy: The Technologizing of the Word*. New York: Routledge, 2002.

———. *The Presence of the Word: Some Prolegomena for Cultural and Religious History*. Minneapolis: University of Minnesota Press, 1981.

Pasquarello, Michael. *Christian Preaching: A Trinitarian Theology of Proclamation*. Grand Rapids: Baker Academic, 2006.

———. *Sacred Rhetoric: Preaching as a Theological and Pastoral Practice of the Church*. Grand Rapids: Eerdmans, 2005.

Paul, Annie Murphy. "The Neuroscience of Your Brain on Fiction." *New York Times*, March 18, 2012. https://www.nytimes.com/2012/03/18/opinion/sunday/the-neuroscience-of-your-brain-on-fiction.html.

Peterson, David. *Engaging with God: A Biblical Theology of Worship*. Downers Grove, IL: InterVarsity, 2002.

Peterson, Eugene H. *Eat This Book: A Conversation in the Art of Spiritual Reading*. Grand Rapids: Eerdmans, 2006.

Phelps, Elizabeth A. "Human Emotion and Memory: Interactions of the Amygdala and Hippocampal Complex." *Neurobiology* 14 (2004) 198–202.

Piirto, Jane. *Understanding Creativity*. Scottsdale, AZ: Great Potential, 2004.

Pink, Daniel H. *A Whole New Mind: Moving from the Information Age to the Conceptual Age*. New York: Riverhead, 2005.

Plantinga, Cornelius. *Reading for Preaching: The Preacher in Conversation with Storytellers, Biographers, Poets, and Journalists*. Grand Rapids: Eerdmans, 2013.

Plato, *The Republic of Plato*. Translated by Allan Bloom. New York: Basic, 1991.

Powell, Mark Allan. *What Do They Hear? Bridging the Gap between Pulpit and Pew*. Nashville: Abingdon, 2007.

Ricœur, Paul. *The Rule of Metaphor: Multi-Disciplinary Studies of the Creation of Meaning in Language*. Toronto: University of Toronto Press, 1977.

Rietz, Norma J. and Sandra A. Livo. *Storytelling: Process and Practice*. Littleton, CO: Libraries Unlimited, 1986.

Robinson, Haddon W. *Biblical Preaching: The Development and Delivery of Expository Messages*. 2nd ed. Grand Rapids: Baker Academic, 2001.

Robinson, Haddon W., and Craig Brian Larson. *The Art and Craft of Biblical Preaching: A Comprehensive Resource for Today's Communicators*. 1st ed. Grand Rapids: Zondervan, 2005.

Robinson, Ken. *Out of Our Minds: Learning to Be Creative*. Oxford: Capstone, 2001.

Rosenstein, Leon. "On Aristotle and Thought in the Drama." *Critical Inquiry* 3 (1977) 543–65.

Rush, Brianne Carlon. "Science of Storytelling: Why and How to Use It in Your Marketing." *The Guardian*, August 28, 2014. https://www.theguardian.com/media-network/media-network-blog/2014/aug/28/science-storytelling-digital-marketing.

Russell, Bertrand. *A History of Western Philosophy, and Its Connection with Political and Social Circumstances from the Earliest Times to the Present Day*. New York: Simon & Schuster, 1945.

Sanders, E. P. "Common Judaism and the Synagogue in the First Century." In *Jews, Christians, and Polytheists in the Ancient Synagogue: Cultural Interaction During the Greco-Roman Period*, edited by Steven Fine, 1–17. New York: Routledge, 1999.

Satterlee, Craig A., and Lester Ruth. *Creative Preaching on the Sacraments*. Nashville: Discipleship Resources, 2003.
Schmit, Clayton J. *Public Reading of Scripture: A Handbook*. Nashville: Abingdon, 2002.
———. *Sent and Gathered: A Worship Manual for the Missional Church, Engaging Worship*. Grand Rapids: Baker Academic, 2009.
———. *Too Deep for Words: A Theology of Liturgical Expression*. 1st ed. Louisville, KY: Westminster John Knox, 2002.
Schmit, Clayton J., and Richard J. Mouw. *A Teaching Hymnal: Ecumenical and Evangelical. Art for Faith's Sake*. Eugene, OR: Cascade, 2018.
Schühlein, F. "The Catholic Encyclopedia." https://www.newadvent.org/cathen/14454b.htm.
Silberman, Lou Hackett. "Talmud and Midrash." *Encyclopedia Britannica Online*. https://www.britannica.com/topic/Talmud.
Smith, James K. A. *Desiring the Kingdom: Worship, Worldview, and Cultural Formation*. Cultural Liturgies 1. Grand Rapids: Baker Academic, 2009.
Speiser, E. A. *Genesis*. The Anchor Bible. 1st ed. Garden City, NY: Doubleday, 1964.
Stott, John R. W. *Between Two Worlds: The Art of Preaching in the Twentieth Century*. Grand Rapids: Eerdmans, 1982.
Strege, Merle D. *Bible Backgrounds: Explanatory Notes on the Bible*. Anderson, IN: Warner, 2006.
Strong, Marie. *Basic Teachings from Patmos*. Anderson, IN: Warner, 1980.
Strong, Marie, and Juanita Evans Leonard. *Called to Minister, Empowered to Serve: Women in Ministry and Missions in the Church of God Reformation Movement*. Anderson, IN: Warner, 1989.
Tierno, Michael. *Aristotle's Poetics for Screenwriters*. New York: Hachette, 2002.
Tobias, Ronald B. *20 Master Plots (and How to Build Them)*. 1st ed. Cincinnati: Writer's Digest, 1993.
Troeger, Thomas H. "Imagination/Creativity." In *The New Interpreters Handbook of Preaching*, edited by Paul Scott Wilson, 428–33. Nashville: Abingdon, 2008.
———. *Imagining a Sermon*. Abingdon Preacher's Library. Nashville: Abingdon, 1990.
Truby, John. *The Anatomy of Story: 22 Steps to Becoming a Master Storyteller*. 1st ed. New York: Faber & Faber, 2007.
Turner, Harold W. *From Temple to Meeting House: The Phenomenology and Theology of Places of Worship*. Religion and Society 16. The Hague: De Gruyter Mouton, 1979.
Varughese, Alex, et al. *Numbers: A Commentary in the Wesleyan Tradition*. New Beacon Bible Commentary. Kansas City, MO: Beacon Hill Press of Kansas City, 2021.
Venter, C. "Ordering Ideas or Ordering Experience? E.L. Lowry's Homiletical Plot Structure—an Exploration and Evaluation." *In die Skriflig/In Luce Verbi [Online]* 41 (2007). https://indieskriflig.org.za/index.php/skriflig.
Walsh, John. *The Art of Storytelling: Easy Steps to Presenting an Unforgettable Story*. Chicago: Moody, 2003.
Ward, Richard F. "Performing the Manuscript." In *The New Interpreter's Handbook of Preaching*, edited by Paul Scott Wilson, 356–58. Nashville: Abingdon, 2008.
Ward, Richard F., and David Trobisch. *Bringing the Word to Life: Engaging the New Testament through Performing It*. Grand Rapids: Eerdmans, 2013.
Webb, Stephen H. *The Divine Voice: Christian Proclamation and the Theology of Sound*. Grand Rapids: Brazos, 2004.

Weldon, Michelle. "Your Brain on Story: Why Narratives Win Our Hearts and Minds." *Pacific Standard*, April 22, 2014. https://psmag.com/social-justice/pulitzer-prizes-journalism-reporting-your-brain-on-story-why-narratives-win-our-hearts-and-minds-79824.

Willimon, William H. *Conversations with Barth on Preaching*. Nashville: Abingdon, 2006.

Willimon, William H., and Richard Lischer. *Concise Encyclopedia of Preaching*. 1st ed. Louisville, KY: Westminster John Knox, 1995.

Wilson, Paul Scott. *A Concise History of Preaching*. Nashville: Abingdon, 1992.

———. *The Four Pages of the Sermon: A Guide to Biblical Preaching*. Nashville: Abingdon, 1999.

———. *The New Interpreter's Handbook of Preaching*. Nashville: Abingdon, 2008.

———. *The Practice of Preaching*. Rev. ed. Nashville: Abingdon, 2007.

Wright, N. T. *Paul: A Biography*. San Francisco: Harper One, 2018.

Zak, Paul J. "Why Your Brain Loves Good Storytelling." *Harvard Business Review*, October 28, 2014. https://hbr.org/2014/10/why-your-brain-loves-good-storytelling.

www.ingramcontent.com/pod-product-compliance
Lightning Source LLC
Chambersburg PA
CBHW021726220426
43662CB00008B/722